EVERYDAY THINGS
IN
ANCIENT GREECE

Books by the same Authors

EVERYDAY LIFE IN PREHISTORIC TIMES
EVERYDAY LIFE IN ROMAN AND ANGLO-SAXON TIMES

A HISTORY OF EVERYDAY THINGS IN ENGLAND
    VOLUME I.   FROM 1066 TO 1499
    VOLUME II. FROM 1500 TO 1799
    VOLUME III. FROM 1733 TO 1851
    VOLUME IV. FROM 1851 TO 1914

EVERYDAY THINGS IN ANCIENT GREECE

By
MARJORIE & C. H. B. QUENNELL

Revised by
KATHLEEN FREEMAN

LONDON: B. T. BATSFORD LTD
NEW YORK: G. P. PUTNAM'S SONS

Revised Edition, 1954
Sixth Impression, 1968

MADE AND PRINTED IN GREAT BRITAIN BY JARROLD AND SONS LTD
LONDON AND NORWICH FOR THE PUBLISHERS
B. T. BATSFORD LTD
4 Fitzhardinge Street, Portman Square, London, W.1

G. P. PUTNAM'S SONS
200 Madison Avenue, New York, N.Y. 10016

PREFACE

TODAY there is hardly a science or art whose beginnings cannot be traced back to Greece. Homer laid the foundations of literature in Western Europe, and Plato has guided all the philosophers who have followed him. Herodotus and Thucydides founded schools of history. Wherever we turn, we find that Greece led the way.

Hippocrates, born about 460 B.C., was not only a great doctor, but his oath defined for the first time the obligation of a professional man to regard his work as more important than its monetary reward. The engineers and technicians of today make all their calculations on principles discovered by the mathematicians of Greece, who substituted the Rule of Knowledge for Rule of Thumb.

Since this is true, it seems to us obvious that we all need a classical education. If, as we think, the Greeks have educated the Old and New Worlds, then we must start with Homer, because he was the educator of Greece.

In Part I we have written of the Trojan War and of the heroes who sustained the Greeks in their early struggles. Here Homer is our chief source.

Part II deals with the Archaic period (about 560 to 480 B.C.) ending with the great struggle between Greeks and Persians which culminated in the victory of the Greeks at Salamis, as related in the delightful History of Herodotus. At the same time the arts and sciences were arising and gradually coming to their full strength. In architecture the details of the Doric style were finally fixed, and the Ionic style was being experimented with as at Ephesus; sculpture and pottery were achieving new and graceful forms.

All these activities led the way to the glories of the Classical period, especially at Athens, where the Parthenon and the Erechtheum exhibited the completed Doric and Ionic styles, where tragedy and comedy developed, and where the products of the craftsmen excelled.

Part III begins with the story of how the Greeks went to work after Salamis and built on the well-laid foundations a civilization which ever since has been regarded as Classical; it closes with the account in the History of Thucydides of the struggle between Athens and Sparta and the failure of the Athenian Expedition to Sicily. This struggle, called the Peloponnesian War, arose out of the dissensions and jealousies between the Ionians and Dorians, the two great branches of the Greek race of which Athens and Sparta were the

PREFACE

rival leaders: the envy and fear felt by the other Greek city-States against Athens because of the growth of her power led inevitably to military conflict. Tragic as the tale is, it is redeemed by the fact that though the soldiers and politicians destroyed the Athenian Empire, the work done by the artists was destined to live on and make the Greeks famous throughout the ages.

In this book we have attempted to show some of the beautiful products of these artists, and their use in everyday life. It is our hope that the boys and girls who read it will discover that the Greeks were not a people extremely foreign and remote, who spoke a difficult language, but folk much like themselves, who lived and worked and played in the surroundings and among the objects we have depicted and described. Great works of literature, and great speeches like the Funeral Oration of Pericles, will become more real to us if we can set them in their environment, reconstructed and repeopled by our imaginations.

EDITOR'S NOTE

In revising the three volumes on Greece in the famous EVERYDAY THINGS series for publication in one volume, I have had to be governed by considerations of space; but my excisions have had as their object that of bringing the work within the required compass without destroying the arrangement and, even more, the spirit of the originals which has made them such a valuable aid to the imaginative study of the past.

For this reason also I have thought it best not to add more than an occasional reference to the archæological discoveries of the last twenty years: the original volumes aimed at giving typical examples of objects and processes, not at exhaustive treatment. The list of Recommended Books has been revised and brought up to date, so that those who want to learn about more recent finds will know where to look for information.

I hope that the single-volume edition will bring the Quennell books to all who are setting out on the delectable journey to Ancient Greece and her incomparable civilization.

K. F.

The Publishers wish to thank the following whose photographs are reproduced in this book:

The Trustees of the British Museum, for figs. 49, 50, 105, 174, 175 and 176; the late J. Deakin, for fig. 57; G. Hoyningen-Huene, for fig. 136; Joan Eyres Monsell, for figs. 48, 56 and 137; Dr. C. H. V. Sutherland, for fig. 176.

CONTENTS

	Page
PREFACE	v
LIST OF ILLUSTRATIONS	viii
RECOMMENDED BOOKS	xiii

Part I: HOMERIC GREECE

Chapter
I	THE ARGONAUTS	3
II	THE *Iliad*	14
III	THE *Odyssey*	34
IV	EVERYDAY THINGS	59

Part II: ARCHAIC GREECE

V	HERODOTUS AND HIS HISTORY	87
VI	THE TEMPLE AND THE HOUSE	108
VII	LIFE INSIDE THE HOUSE	125
VIII	LIFE OUTSIDE THE HOUSE	145

Part III: CLASSICAL GREECE

IX	GREEK ARCHITECTURE	165
X	THE TOWN AND ITS PUBLIC BUILDINGS	189
XI	TOWN HOUSES AND EVERYDAY LIFE	207
XII	SEA FIGHTS AND LAND BATTLES	231
	INDEX	249

LIST OF ILLUSTRATIONS

The figures in parentheses in the text refer to the *figure numbers* of the illustrations

Figure		page
1	The victims for the sacrifice passing up through the Propylæa	*Frontispiece*
2	Map of the Greek World	xvi
3	A sacrifice	5
4	Boxers	7
5	Plan of the Palace of Cnossos	11
6	Warriors	17
7	The back-bent bow of Odysseus	18
8	A figure from Dodona	19
9	A reconstruction of a chariot	20
10	Face of Gorgon	21
11	A merchant ship	23
12	Chest and table	25
13	The fight over the body of Patroklos	26
14	Gathering olives	27
15	Wrestling	29
16	A jumper holding lead jumping weights	31
17	Hermes and satyr	35
18	A reconstruction of the raft of Odysseus	39
19	A ball game	41
20	A dancer	43
21	Odysseus under the ram	45
22	Asphodel	46
23	An epinetron or spinning instrument	48
24	Spinning	49
25	Telemachus and Penelope at her loom	50
26	Washing the feet of Odysseus	51
27	Boatbuilding	52
28	Homeric lock	53
29	Odysseus shooting the wooers	54
30	The slaying of the wooers	55
31	A boar hunt	56
32	Draughts	57
33	The Grave Circle at Mycenæ	60
34	Reconstruction of the interior of the Lion Gate	61
35	The "Tomb of Agamemnon"	63
36	A reconstructed bird's-eye view of Tiryns from the north-east	65
37	A reconstruction of the Great Hall at Tiryns	67
38	A reconstructed bird's-eye view of Tiryns from the south-west	69

LIST OF ILLUSTRATIONS

Figure		page
39	A reconstruction of the interior of the Megaron at Tiryns	71
40	Mycenæan arms	73
41	Mycenæan bronze lamp from Cyprus	75
42	A bath from Tiryns	76
43	Tapered terra-cotta drain-pipes from Tiryns	77
44	Mycenæan figures	78
45	Mycenæan pottery	79
46	Ploughing	80

Facing page

47	Tiryns: a gallery in the thickness of the wall	80
48	The Lion Gate at Mycenæ	80
49	Vaphio Cup	81
50	Nestor's Cup	81

page

51	Modern Algerian plough	81
52	An eighth-century B.C. war galley	83
53	Part of a frieze from Xanthos	89

Facing page

54	The warrior's departure	90

page

55	Part of a frieze from the acropolis at Xanthos	92

Facing page

56	Paestum: a close-up view of the Temple of Poseidon	96
57	Acragas, Sicily: the so-called "Temple of Concord"	96
58	Reconstruction of the Archaic Temple at Ephesus	97

page

59	Frieze from the walls of a tomb at Xanthos	99
60	Helmets and crests from black-figure vases	103
61	A device on a shield	106
62	Types of temples	109
63	The timber origin of the Doric style	112
64	Later marble construction of the Doric style	113
65	The west pediment of the Temple at Ægina	116
66	A lion's head, from Doric temple at Himera, Sicily	117
67	A reconstruction of the Ionic Order of the Archaic Temple at Ephesus	118
68	A Minoan house	120
69	A house at Orchomenus, Bœotia, Greece	121
70	A reconstruction based on a hut urn from the island of Melos	122
71	An apsidal house at Korakou, Corinth	123
72	Plan and reconstruction of a house at Dystus, Eubœa, Greece	124
73	The fountain	126
74	A Kamares vase	127
75	A late Minoan vase	127
76	A late Mycenæan vase	128

LIST OF ILLUSTRATIONS

Figure		page
77	Types of Greek vases	129
78	Athenian feeding-bottle	130
79	An oil flask, Athenian black figure	130
80	The Dorian chiton	131
81	The Ionian chiton	131
82	A bronze statuette	132
83	A warrior blowing a trumpet through the mouthpiece	133
84	An archer in Asiatic costume blowing a trumpet through the mouthpiece	133
85	Hermes	134
86	A couch and table	134
87	A baby's cot	135
88	A chair from the Harpies' Tomb	135
89, 90	Chairs from the Harpies' Tomb	136
91	A stool from the Parthenon frieze	136
92	A chair of figures from Branchidæ	136
93	A folding stool	136
94	The music lesson	141
95	The construction of the lyre	142
96	Treading grapes	146
97	A satyr with wineskin	147
98	Dionysus	147
99	The penteconter	149
100	The merchant ship	150
101	A carpenter with an adze	151
102	The loading of silphion at Cyrene, Africa	152

Facing page

103, 104	Bas-reliefs from the Ludovisi Throne, now in Rome	152
105	A Tanagra figure of a lady wearing a sun-hat	153
106	The life-size figure of a charioteer	153

page

107	Iron smelting	153
108	A cart	155
109	Heracles	157
110	The pankration	159
111	A cock-fight	159
112	A huntsman with fox and hare	160
113	Olpe	160
114	The Harpies' Tomb, from Xanthos, Lycia, Asia Minor	161
115	View of the Acropolis, Athens, from the Hill of the Pnyx	166
116	The entrance front of the Propylæa, Athens	168

Facing page

117	Restoration of the Erechtheum, Athens	168
118	Restoration of the Parthenon, Athens	169

page

119	The Propylæa of the Acropolis	169
120	The kithara	170

x

LIST OF ILLUSTRATIONS

Figure		page
121	Plan of the Acropolis	172
122	A bird's-eye view of the Erechtheum	174
123	Greek hair-dressing	176
124	A relief plan of the Parthenon from Penrose's survey	177

Facing page

125	Restoration of the South Peristyle of the Parthenon	184
126	Restoration of the East Front of the Parthenon	185

page

127	Diagrammatic bird's-eye view of Delphi	185
128	The Greek horses at St. Mark's, Venice	187
129	The town of Priene	190–1
130	A Greek surgeon	193
131	The goat-dance	196
132	The bird-dance	197
133	The Choragic Monument of Lysicrates, Athens	199
134	A comic actor seated on an altar	200

Facing page

135	The Temple of Athena Niké at Athens	200
136	The Athenian Treasury at Delphi	200
137	The Theatre and the Temple of Apollo, Delphi	201

page

138	Mask of a negro	201
139	Comic performance	202
140	The ruined walls and towers of Ithome	203
141	Plan of the Theatre at Epidaurus	204
142	A reconstruction of the castle at Euryelus, Epipolæ, Syracuse, Sicily	205
143	Plan of a house at Priene	207
144	A reconstruction of the courtyard to a house at Priene	208
145	Plan of a house at Delos	210
146	The klismos	210
147	Decking the bride	214
148	Marriage ceremony	215
149	The sunshade	216

Facing page

150	Epidaurus: the Theatre	216
151	The monument to Hegesa, at Athens	217
152	A relief from the Temple of Athena Niké at Athens	217

page

153	Toy rabbit	218
154	Baby's rattle	218
155	A terra-cotta toy	219
156	A terra-cotta doll	220
157	An unkind girl plays with a tortoise	221
158	The swing	221
159	The dancing lesson	222
160	The dance	222

LIST OF ILLUSTRATIONS

Figure		page
161	A musician	223
162	The harp	223
163	Hockey	224
164	A boy with a fighting quail	224
165	A hare hunt among the tombs	225
166	A shoemaker	225
167	A woman tumbler	226
168	Base of kottabos stand	226
169	Men playing kottabos	227
170	Horseman wearing riding-cloak	227
171	A fifth- or fourth-century Greek bit	228
172	A Greek trireme	229
173	How the trireme was rowed	230

Facing page

174	A sacrifice, on a vase of the fourth century B.C.	232
175	Theseus killing the Minotaur, on a vase of the fifth century B.C.	232
176	Gold and silver coins	233

page

177	Greek swords and spear	234
178	Arms and armour	235
179	An Attic helmet	236
180	Map of Pylos	237
181	The flame-thrower	238
182	Hermes	239
183	Diagram of the Siege of Syracuse	242

xii

RECOMMENDED BOOKS
I. TRANSLATIONS

An increasing number of good modern translations of Greek literature, besides those mentioned below, is becoming available in cheap editions. The series of Penguin Classics is particularly worth exploring.

HOMER
No translation of Homer is satisfactory: these great poems must be read in the original to be appreciated.

The best translations into prose remain:
Lang, Leaf and Myers. THE ILIAD OF HOMER (Macmillan, 1919)
Butcher and Lang. THE ODYSSEY OF HOMER (Macmillan, 1924)

Also useful:
   A. T. Murray. HOMER, THE ILIAD, *and* THE ODYSSEY (4 vols., Loeb, 1924, 1919)

A prose version in modern idiom is that of:
E. V. Rieu. ILIAD *and* ODYSSEY (2 vols., Penguin Classics, 1950, 1946)

An acceptable verse translation:
S. O. Drew. HOMER'S ODYSSEY (Dent, 1948)

HESIOD
Prose:
H. G. Evelyn-White. HESIOD *with the Homeric Hymns* (Loeb)

HERODOTUS
G. Rawlinson. HERODOTUS (1875; reprinted in Everyman series)
J. E. Powell. HERODOTUS (Oxford University Press, 1949)

PAUSANIAS
W. H. S. Jones and H. A. Omerod. PAUSANIAS (5 vols., Loeb)

THUCYDIDES
C. Foster-Smith. THUCYDIDES, HISTORY OF THE PELOPONNESIAN WAR (4 vols. Loeb)
Richard Crawley. HISTORY OF THE PELOPONNESIAN WAR (Everyman)

XENOPHON
E. C. Marchant. XENOPHON, OECONOMICUS (Loeb)

PLATO
(By various translators) FIVE DIALOGUES (Everyman, 1947)
A. D. Lindsay. PLATO'S REPUBLIC (Everyman, 1948)

PLATO and XENOPHON
(By various translators) SOCRATIC DISCOURSES (Everyman, 1947)

RECOMMENDED BOOKS

APOLLONIUS RHODIUS
E. V. Rieu. THE VOYAGE OF ARGO (Penguin Classics, 1959)
VITRUVIUS
F. Granger. VITRUVIUS (2 vols., Loeb)

II. GENERAL

A COMPANION TO GREEK STUDIES. *Edited by Leonard Whibley* (Cambridge University Press, 1916)

THE OXFORD CLASSICAL DICTIONARY (Oxford University Press, 1949)

SMITH'S SMALLER CLASSICAL DICTIONARY, *revised by E. H. Blakeney and J. Warrington* (Everyman)

HISTORY OF ANCIENT CIVILIZATION, *by Albert E. Trever* (Harrap, 1937)

THE GREEK EXPERIENCE, *by C. M. Bowra* (Weidenfeld and Nicolson)

HISTORY OF GREECE, *by J. B. Bury* (3rd edition, *revised by Russell Meiggs*, Macmillan, 1951)

A HISTORY OF GREECE TO 322 B.C., *by N. G. L. Hammond* (Oxford University Press, 1959)

THE LITERATURE OF ANCIENT GREECE, *by G. Murray* (3rd edition, Phoenix Books, Chicago University Press, 1956)

III. ARCHÆOLOGY AND ART

1. *Minoan and Mycenæn civilisation*

   The original discoveries in Crete were recorded in the lavishly illustrated series:

   Sir Arthur Evans. THE PALACE OF MINOS AT KNOSSOS (4 vols., Macmillan, 1921–35)

   See also:

   J. D. S. Pendlebury. THE ARCHÆOLOGY OF CRETE: AN INTRODUCTION (Methuen, 1939)

   H. R. Hall. THE CIVILIZATION OF GREECE IN THE BRONZE AGE (Methuen, 1928)

   J. Chadwick. THE DECIPHERMENT OF LINEAR B (Cambridge, 1958)

   L. R. Palmer. MYCENÆANS AND MINOANS (Faber and Faber, 1961)

   and the relevant chapters in the works listed above under GENERAL.

2. *Town planning and Architecture*

   R. E. Wycherley. HOW THE GREEKS BUILT CITIES (Macmillan, 1949)
   Ida Thallon Hill. THE ANCIENT CITY OF ATHENS (Methuen, 1953)
   Kathleen Freeman. GREEK CITY-STATES (Macdonald, 1950)
   A. W. Lawrence. GREEK ARCHITECTURE (The Pelican History of Art. Penguin Books, 1957)

RECOMMENDED BOOKS

3. *Art*

G. M. A. Richter. A HANDBOOK OF GREEK ART (Phaidon, 1959)

J. D. Beazley and Bernard Ashmole. GREEK SCULPTURE AND PAINTING (Cambridge University Press, 1932)

R. M. Cook. GREEK PAINTED POTTERY (Methuen, 1960)

M. Robertson. GREEK PAINTING (Skira, 1959)

Charles Seltman. A BOOK OF GREEK COINS (Penguin Books, 1952)

4. *Drama and the Theatre*

P. Arnott. AN INTRODUCTION TO THE GREEK THEATRE (Macmillan, 1959)

D. W. Lucas. THE GREEK TRAGIC POETS (Cohen and West, 2nd edition, 1959)

Gilbert Norwood. GREEK COMEDY (Methuen, 2nd edition, 1950)

IV. WAY OF LIFE

M. Cary. THE GEOGRAPHIC BACKGROUND OF GREEK AND ROMAN HISTORY (Oxford University Press, 1949)

Alfred Zimmern. THE GREEK COMMONWEALTH (*preface by Russell Meiggs*, 5th edition, Oxford Paperbacks, Oxford University Press, 1961)

Kathleen Freeman. THE GREEK WAY: AN ANTHOLOGY (Macdonald, 1947)

Victor Ehrenberg. THE PEOPLE OF ARISTOPHANES (Blackwell, 2nd edition, 1951)

E. Norman Gardiner. ATHLETICS OF THE ANCIENT WORLD (Oxford, 1930)

Kenneth J. Freeman. SCHOOLS OF HELLAS (Macmillan, 1922)

V. ATLASES

ATLAS OF ANCIENT AND CLASSICAL HISTORY, edited by Ramsay Muir and George Philip (George Philip and Son, 1938). This atlas has excellent contour maps.

EVERYMAN'S CLASSICAL ATLAS, edited by J. O. Thomson (Dent, 1961)

ATLAS OF THE CLASSICAL WORLD, edited by A. A. M. van der Heyden and H. H. Scullard (Nelson and Sons, 1959)

VI. LANGUAGE

For those wishing to begin the study of Greek without a teacher, there can be no better aids than:

F. Kinchin Smith and T. W. Melluish. TEACH YOURSELF GREEK (E.U.P. series, Hodder and Stoughton, 1947)

or: (slightly more advanced) KEPOS: GREEK IN TWO YEARS (E.U.P., 1951)

with: J. A. and M. A. Nairn. GREEK THROUGH READING (Ginn, 1952).

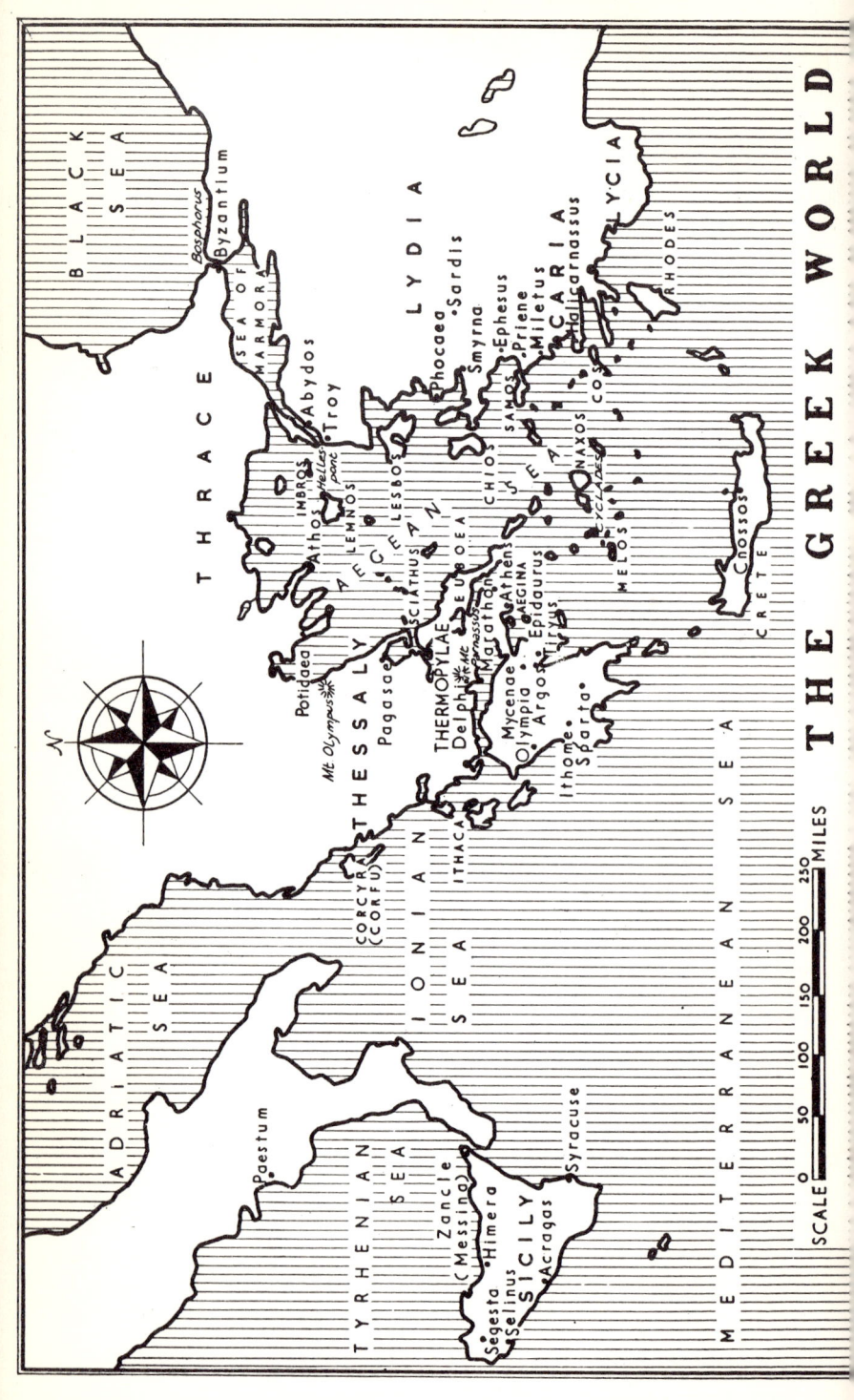

PART I
Homeric Greece

I. PRE-HOMERIC AND HOMERIC PERIOD

DATES (APPROXIMATE)	CRETE, ÆGEAN ISLANDS AND ASIA MINOR	MAINLAND OF GREECE
Earliest times to about 3500 B.C.	Neolithic civilisation	
3500 to about 1200 B.C.	Bronze Age	
About 2000 B.C.	Crete a great maritime power. Several palaces built at Cnossus and sacked by invaders, then rebuilt. Troy and the islands trade with Egypt and Crete	Migrations of Greek-speaking peoples into peninsula from north begin and continue
About 1650–1450	Crete at height of power	Cretan influence powerful. Mycenæ, Tiryns and other cities ruled by Crete
1400–1000	Use of iron gradually replaces bronze	
About 1400	Crete invaded. Cnossus destroyed. Cretan domination ends	Mycenæ, Tiryns and other cities freed from Cretan rule. Civilisation as described by Homer
About 1200	Greek cities of mainland combine to attack Troy. Trojan War (traditional date 1192–1183 B.C.)	
1100–1000 B.C.		Mycenæ and other cities captured by invaders from north (Dorian Migration)
1000–800 B.C.	Ægean islands and coast of Asia Minor occupied by Greeks. *Iliad* and *Odyssey* composed for recitation	Pressure of immigrants drives mainland Greeks overseas
800–700 B.C.	Epic poetry continues to flourish	

Chapter I

THE ARGONAUTS

IN any book which deals with Greece, the first name to be mentioned should be that of Homer. He was the great educator of Ancient Greece. Xenophon makes one of his characters in the *Symposium* say, "My father, anxious that I should become a good man, made me learn all the poems of Homer."

Herodotus, the father of History, who wrote in the fifth century B.C., opens his book with references to the voyage of the Argonauts and the Siege of Troy, and by the far more critical Thucydides, who wrote at the end of the same century, Homer was evidently regarded as a historian to be quoted as an authority. If we follow their example, we shall be in excellent company.

We will begin with the voyage of the Argonauts, because in this tale we find the spirit of adventure and love of the sea, or rather use of the sea, which was to be so characteristic of the Greeks of Classical times. We may be able to capture some of the atmosphere of that Heroic Age, when gods like men, and men like gods, lived, loved, and fought together.

As to our authorities on the adventures of the Argonauts, Homer does not say very much, evidently thinking that his readers would know all about them. This is shown in the twelfth book of the *Odyssey*. "One ship only of all that fare by sea hath passed that way, even *Argo*, that is in all men's minds, on her voyage from Æetes." Fortunately for us, the details which were in all men's minds were gathered together by Apollonius Rhodius, who lived in Alexandria in the third century B.C. The details we give are quoted from his book *Argonautica*.

This opens with a scene at the Court of Pelias, King of Iolcus, in Thessaly, who is disturbed because he has heard from an oracle "that a dreadful doom awaited him—that he should be slain at the bidding of one man whom he saw coming forth from the people with but one sandal". When Jason arrives with only one sandal, having lost the other in the mud, it is not to be wondered at that he found his welcome a little chilly. "Quickly

THE ARGONAUTS

the king spied him and, brooding on it, plotted for him the toil of a troublous voyage, that on the sea or among strangers he might miss his home-coming."

The troublous voyage was to sail to Colchis and find the oak-grove wherein was suspended the Golden Fleece, guarded by a dragon, and having found the Fleece, to bring it back. Here was a task worthy of heroes. Jason gathered together a band. First came Orpheus, the music of whose lyre "bewitched the stubborn rocks on the mountain-side and the rivers in their courses". Then Polyphemus who, in his youth, fought with the Lapithæ against the Centaurs, and Heracles himself came from the market-place of Mycenæ, and many others, sons and grandsons of the immortals.

The goddess Athene "planned the swift ship, and Argus, son of Arestor, fashioned it at her bidding. And thus it proved itself excellent above all other ships that have ventured onto the sea with their oars"—which only means that there was a streak of genius in the design of the *Argo*, because genius is a gift from the gods.

Jason was appointed leader, and preparations were made for launching the *Argo*. "First of all, at the command of Argus, they girded the ship strongly outside with a well-twisted rope, pulling it taut on both sides, that the bolts might hold the planks fast and the planks withstand the battering of the surge." The heroes then dug a trench down to the sea and placed rollers under the keel. Then they reversed the oars, putting the handles outboard, and bound them to the thole-pins, and the heroes, standing on each side of the boat, used the projecting handles of the oars to push the *Argo* down into the sea. Then the mast and sails were fitted, and they drew lots for the benches for rowing, two to each bench.

"Next, heaping shingle near the sea, there on the shore they built an altar to Apollo . . . and quickly spread about it logs of dried olive wood." Two steers were brought, and lustral water, and barley-meal, and Jason prayed to Apollo to guide their ship on its voyage and bring them all back safe and sound to Hellas, "and with his prayer cast the barley-meal". Heracles and Ancæus killed the steers.

Heracles struck one of the steers with his club in the middle of the brow, and dropping in a heap where it stood, it tumbled to the ground;

JASON AND THE HEROES

Ancæus smote on the broad neck of the other with his brazen axe and cut through the mighty sinews; and it fell prone on both its horns. Quickly their comrades slit the victims' throats and flayed the hides; they severed the joints and cut up the flesh, then hacked out the sacred thigh bones,

3 A Sacrifice

and when they had wrapped them about with fat, burnt them upon cloven wood. And Jason poured out pure libations.

This was the general practice. Sacrifices were offered to the gods on all important occasions. The sacred thigh bones were burnt in their honour, and the joints eaten by the people in the festival which followed.

Achilles, the son of Peleus, who was to become a great hero himself, was brought by his mother to see the departure.

After the heroes had feasted and slept, they went on board the *Argo* and sailed away "Eastward Ho", or, rather, rowed away. To the sound of Orpheus' lyre they

smote the swelling brine with their oars, and the surge broke over the oar-blades; and on this side and on that the dark water seethed with spume, foaming terribly under the strokes of the mighty heroes. The ship sped on, their arms glittering like flame in the sunlight, and, like a path seen over a green plain, ever behind them shone their wake.

Presently they raised the tall mast in the mast-box, and fastened it with the forestays, pulling them taut on both sides, and when they had hauled it to the top-mast, they lowered the sail.

We cannot follow the Argonauts through all their travels, but the first part of their voyage was to Colchis, which, in Greek mythology, was situated at the eastern end of the Black Sea. There the Argonauts voyaged, hugging the shores as they went. They did not reach Colchis without adventure—heroes never do. In the Sea of Marmora they encountered insolent and fierce men, "born of the Earth, a marvel to see for those that dwelt about them, each with six mighty hands that he raises, two springing from his sturdy shoulders, and four beneath, fitting closely to his terrible sides". The Argonauts were attacked by these Earth-children, but Heracles "swiftly bent his back-springing bow against the monsters, and one after another brought them to ground".

Then for twelve days and nights fierce tempests arose and kept them from sailing, so they sacrificed to Rhea, the mother of all gods, that the stormy blasts might cease. "At the same time, at Orpheus' bidding, the youths danced a measure, fully armed, clashing with their swords on their bucklers."

At another time "around the burning sacrifice they set up a broad dancing-ring, singing, 'All hail, fair god of healing, all hail!'"

It was in the Cianian land that Heracles and Polyphemus were lost, while searching for Hylas, who had been carried off by a water-nymph, and so the heroes sailed without them. Here it was that the heroes made fire by twirling sticks.

They next arrived at the land of the Bebrycians, where they found that all strangers had to box with King Amycus. Polydeuces stood forth as the Argonauts' champion. A place of battle having been selected, "Lycoreus, the henchman of Amycus, laid at their feet on each side two pairs of gloves made of raw hides, dry and exceeding tough." Just as modern prize-fighters tell the world how they are going to make mince-meat of their opponents, so Amycus warned Polydeuces that he was to learn "how skilled I am in carving the dry oxhides, and in spattering men's faces with blood". The fight was truly heroic, "cheek and jaw bones clattered on both sides, and a mighty rattling of teeth arose, nor did they give over from fisticuffs until a gasping for breath had overcome them both". The fight was brought to an end when Amycus, rising on tiptoe, swung his heavy hand down on Polydeuces, who, sidestepping, struck the king above the ear and so killed him.

Their next adventure was in the Bithynian land, where they came to the assistance of Phineus, who was plagued by the Harpies, who came swooping through the clouds and snatched his food away with their crooked beaks. In return for their help, Phineus tells them of the dangers which still await them on the way to Colchis. So they were able to pass safely through the rocks which clashed together face to face.

It was in the land of the Mariandyni that Idmon, one of the

THE VOYAGE TO COLCHIS

heroes, was killed by a boar, and a barrow raised to his memory. Then they came to the land of the Amazons, but did not stop to fight the war-loving maids.

Next they came to the land of the Chalybes, who

4 Boxers

take no thought for ploughing with oxen nor for planting any honey-sweet fruit; they do not pasture flocks in the dewy meadows. But they burrow the tough iron-bearing soil, and what they earn they barter for their daily food; never a day dawns for them but it finds them hard at work, amid drear sooty flames and smoke they endure heavy labour.

When they came to the island of Ares and its dangerous birds, "on their heads they set helmets of bronze, gleaming terribly, with tossing blood-red crests"; as well, they had to hold their shields roof-wise over the *Argo* to defend themselves from the feathers which the birds there could discharge from their wings like arrows.

On and on they went, until

the precipices of the Caucasian Mountains towered overhead, where, bound on hard rocks by galling fetters of bronze, Prometheus fed with his liver an eagle that ever swooped back upon its prey. High above the ship in the evening they saw it flying close under the clouds, with a loud whir of wings. It set all the sails quivering with the beat of those huge pinions. Its form was not the form of a bird of the air, but it kept poising its long flight-feathers like polished oar-shafts. And soon after they heard the bitter cry Prometheus gave as his liver was torn away; and the air rang with his yells until they sighted the ravening eagle soaring back again from the mountain on the self-same track.

Not long after they came to the mouth of the River Phasis, and "on their left hand was the lofty Caucasus and the Cytæan city of Æa [Colchis], and on the other hand the plain of Ares and Ares' sacred grove, where the serpent kept watch and ward

7

over the Fleece, hanging on the leafy branches of an oak". So the heroes anchored the *Argo* in a shady backwater, and there debated how they should achieve their end. Fortunately for them, Hera and Athene decided to come to their assistance, in a way we will tell later. The heroes' own idea was the extremely simple one of going up to the Court of King Æetes and asking him to give them the Fleece. Jason was sent, and the king, on hearing the request, was filled with rage, and said, "Were it not that you had been guests at my table, verily I would have cut out your tongues and chopped off both hands and sped you forth with your feet alone." The king, being unable to do this, as they had broken bread with him, thought of a tremendous trial:

Two brazen-footed bulls are mine, that pasture on the Plain of Ares, and breathe forth flame from their jaws; them I yoke and drive over the stubborn field of Ares, four plough-gates; quickly I furrow it with the plough-share as far as the headland, casting into the furrows by way of seed, not the corn of Demeter, but the teeth of a dreadful serpent which spring up into the fashion of armed men; them I slay at once, laying them low beneath my spear as they leap against me on every side. In the morning I yoke the oxen, and in the evening I cease from the harvest. And thou, if thou canst accomplish such deeds as these, on that very day thou shalt carry off the Fleece.

Jason was not cheered by the prospect, and "sat where he was, mute and helpless in a sorry plight". The time had come for Hera and Athene to help him. Their plan was to persuade Eros to "let fly his arrow at the daughter of Æetes [Medea] and bewitch her with love for Jason". As some of the most beautiful writing in the poem is concerned with the love-making of Jason and Medea, we will give a few details. Eros had passed into the palace with Jason, and Medea was watching his interview with her father, Æetes. Eros took the opportunity to string his bow quickly and fit an arrow from his quiver, and shoot at Medea.

Deep into the maiden's heart like a flame burnt his shaft; and ever she kept darting bright glances straight up at Æson's son, while inside her breast the heart panted quick in its anguish; all recollection left her, and with the sweet pain her very soul melted.

JASON AND MEDEA

Poor Medea retired to her chamber, after she had heard the judgment of her father Æetes, and

in her soul much she pondered all the cares that the Loves arouse. And before her eyes the vision still remained—the likeness of himself, how he was clad, such words as he spake, how he sat in his chair, how he went out towards the door—and, brooding, she thought there never was such another man; while always in her ears rang his voice and the honey-sweet words which he had uttered. And she feared for him

Was there ever such a dilemma for a poor maiden? Jason did not even know that she loved him, and how was she to tell him? Æetes wanted to kill Jason, and Medea very much wanted to keep him alive. Medea wanted to help Jason with her magic arts, because she was something of a sorceress, and yet that seemed very disloyal to her own father. In the end love won, of course, and a message was sent to Jason to meet her at the holy shrine of Hecate. There Medea waited for him, and when he came and spoke to her, "her soul melted within her, uplifted by his praise, and she gazed upon him face to face; nor did she know what word to utter first, but was eager to pour out everything at once". Jason began to see what was in the wind: we read a little later, "now both were abashed and fixed their eyes upon the ground, and again they glanced up at one another, smiling with the light of love beneath their radiant brows".

So Medea gave a charm to Jason which enabled him to carry out the hard task imposed by Æetes. Then the Golden Fleece was seized by the Argonauts, and carried off, and with them went Medea, because she feared her father's wrath. Of their marriage, which was not happy, or the further travels of the Argonauts before they reached home, we can read in the remainder of the poem *Argonautica*.

Modern scholars think that the *Voyage of the Argonauts* was a poetical description of the travels of men seeking the Land of Gold. The early miners first found gold by its sparkle in the beds of streams. They traced it to the rocks from which it had been washed out. Then they are supposed to have recovered the gold dust, which was being carried downstream, by suspending a fleece in the water so that the grains would be caught in the oily wool. When Jason snatched the Golden Fleece from the

THE ARGONAUTS

oak-grove, "from the shimmering of the flocks of wool there settled on his fair cheeks and brow a red flush like a flame".

Down through all the ages men have desired gold for the sheen of its beauty. A visit to the Prehistoric Room at the British Museum will show you how much it was used here in England for ornaments in the Bronze Age.

The legendary history of the *Argo* will have helped us to understand the love of adventure and movement of the Greek people. The character of the country played a great part in their development. As in Norway, the fertile plains are cut off one from another by mountain ranges in between. This led to the founding of small city-States. When the inhabitants of these small States became too numerous to be supported by the surrounding countryside, like the Norseman later on, they were forced to go to sea as sailors, traders, or pirates. Sailing about, they discovered other desirable places, and so founded colonies. The incomparable beauty of their country turned them into poets. The people lived on the plains, and their gods on the cloud-topped mountains.

A glance at the map of their world will show that Greece was well placed to play a part in classical times as a maritime nation. The Great Powers then were Egypt, Assyria, and Persia, and the trading ports in Asia Minor could easily be reached by Greek boats. Yet they were far enough away not to be a source of danger, unless the enemy understood the use of the sea; and they did not. When Persia did at last attack Greece, their navy was only used as an auxiliary to their army, which had to cross the Hellespont, and make the weary journey by land, through Macedonia and Thessaly. Greece was left to herself, free to grow, until she was strong enough to resist oppression.

Another Great Power had to wax and wane before her time came. The Minoans, a Mediterranean people living in the island of Crete, had developed the wonderful civilisation which was revealed by Sir Arthur Evans in the palace at Cnossus.

Their greatest period seems to have been between 1650 and 1450 B.C., and then catastrophe fell upon them. They were another seafaring people, and built up their kingdom on trade. Their ships sailed to the Nile with oil and wine, wheel-made pottery and sponges, and they were known there as the Keftiu. The Minoans must have had some early connection with Greece.

THE MINOANS

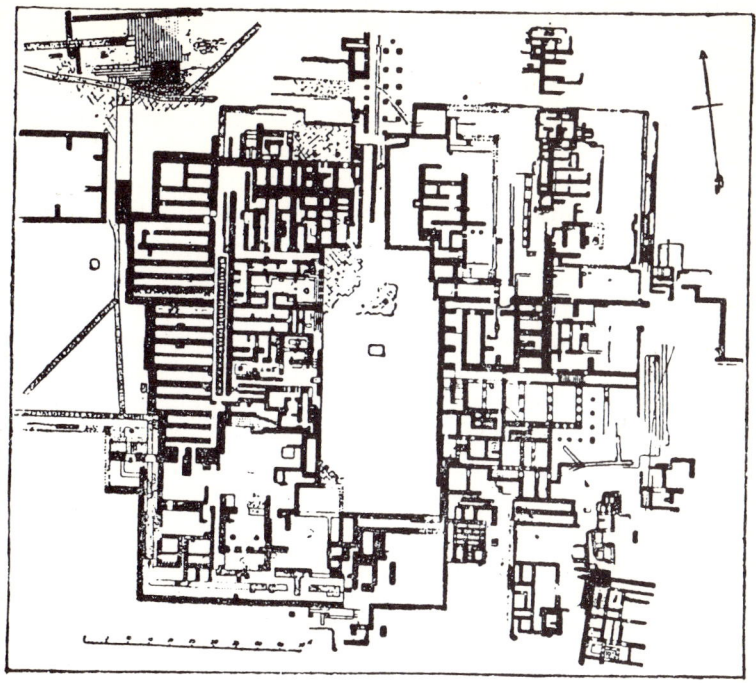

5   Plan of the Palace of Cnossos

The legend of the Minotaur, a huge bull-like monster kept in a labyrinth at Cnossos, and fed on seven youths and seven maidens sent each year by the Athenians, is, in all probability, a poetical rendering of some less bloodthirsty tribute.

Theseus, the great hero of the Greeks, went one year, and Ariadne, the daughter of Minos, the King of Crete, fell in love with him. She provided Theseus with a sword to kill the Minotaur, and a thread to find his way out of the labyrinth. If you go to Cnossos today to see the ruins uncovered by the patient labour of British archæologists, it is easy to see how the legend of the labyrinth may have grown up. The palace had a great central courtyard surrounded by a perfect maze of small chambers and winding passages in which any stranger must have lost his way. Great stairs led down from the courtyard to the king's quarters. The characteristic Minoan columns with shafts tapering downwards supported an upper storey.

THE ARGONAUTS

Of course the palace, which was destroyed about 1450 B.C., was much later than the one of the legend of Theseus, but the legend is proof that in that earlier time Crete was great and powerful, and Greece had to depend on her heroes for protection. Theseus was a friend of the Argonauts. The palace was built in a pleasant valley, some few miles from the sea, and was not defended by any system of fortifications. The ruins today conjure up in one's mind a picture of all that one ever imagined of Eastern palaces, and it is difficult to find any resemblance between the plan of Cnossos and the later fortified acropolis of the Greeks. But many of the Minoan details were transplanted, as we shall see. These details may have been learned from articles which were imported into Greece from Crete. The celebrated gold cups, found at Vaphio in Laconia, are undoubtedly of Minoan manufacture (49). They may have been brought in legitimate trade, but more probably they formed part of the loot of a raid, and for this reason. It is thought that about 1450 B.C., northerners began to filter down into Greece, and to these men the name of Achæans has been given. The closest parallel would be those other Northmen, Norsemen, or Normans, who attacked the Franks and settled down in a part of Gaul, Normandy, in A.D. 912. We know that the Normans when they arrived were much like the people described in *Beowulf*. They were not bent on destruction, but once secure in their new home were content to learn from the Franks how to build stone castles and wonderful cathedrals.

In much the same way it would seem that the Achæans did not destroy the Minoan influence on the mainland of Greece, but instead learned how to build from the work they found there. They used the inverted tapering columns, and other details of decoration, but the planning of the buildings was made to correspond to their particular needs, and, like the Normans, they wanted, not palaces, but fortified castles. Here we might remind our readers that, though we are writing of what happened over 3,500 years ago, that it is only yesterday so far as the history of the Mediterranean is concerned—Sir Arthur Evans found Neolithic, or New Stone Age, remains under the buildings at Cnossos, and it is probable that the Minoans were descended from the same Mediterranean stock that found their way to England in the New Stone Age.

CNOSSOS AND GREECE

We must mention also another name honoured in archæology, that of Dr. Schliemann. As a poor boy, he conceived the idea of excavating Troy. During his youth and middle age, everything was subordinated to this one purpose, and when at last his dream came true, his excavations at Troy, Mycenæ, and Tiryns laid bare the background of a life like that described in the Homeric poems.

Chapter II

THE *ILIAD*

BOOK I

THE first book of the *Iliad* opens when the Greeks have been besieging Ilios or Troy for nine years. There is no dull setting of the scene, but we are at once plunged into the quarrel between Agamemnon and Achilles. Agamemnon had taken the daughter of Chryses, the priest, who prays without avail that she may be restored to him. Then Phœbus Apollo was wroth at heart, and the dread clanging of his bow was heard, and for nine days the god's shafts ranged through the host. Agamemnon is persuaded to send back Chryseis to her father, but takes Briseis from Achilles, who is restrained by the goddess Athene from taking vengeance on Agamemnon.

As so often happened, the heroes had sprung from the immortals, and though the father of Achilles was Peleus, King of the Myrmidons, his mother was Thetis, a goddess of the sea. She, indignant at the slight put on her son, rose up from the waves, and went to the home of the gods on many-ridged Olympus. There she spoke to Zeus, son of Cronos, and father of the gods, and prayed him to grant victory to the Trojans, until the Greeks should honour her son Achilles. Zeus is troubled, being a little afraid what ox-eyed Hera, his wife, will say. She does upbraid him, and lame Hephæstos, their son, tries to make peace, saying, "Verily a sorry business this will be and not endurable, if ye two thus fall out for mortals' sake, and bring dissension among the gods."

This is just what does happen in the *Iliad*. Not only do the mortals fight on earth, but the gods descend from Olympus and take sides, and the whole heavens become full of the thunder of their tremendous combat.

There are many interesting details in this first book. Odysseus of many devices, takes back Chryseis to her father in a ship with twenty oarsmen, and a hecatomb of a hundred animals to be

THE QUARREL

sacrificed to the far-darter Apollo. Arrived at Chryse, "they furled their sails and stowed them in the black ship; the mast they lowered by the forestays and quickly brought it to the crutch, and rowed her with oars to the anchorage. Then they flung out the anchor stones and made fast the hawsers." Then follow details of the sacrifice to Apollo. The animals are set in order round the altar. The men wash their hands and take up the barley-meal. The priest prays to Apollo to stay his affliction of the Greeks, and sprinkles the barley-meal. The animals' heads are drawn back, and they are slaughtered and flayed. Slices are cut from the thighs and wrapped in fat, making a double fold. Raw collops were laid thereon, and the priest "burnt them on billets of wood and poured libation over them of gleaming wine; and at his side the young men held five-pronged forks. Now, when the thighs were consumed and they had tasted of the vitals, then all the rest they carved up and spitted it and roasted it well, and took it off the fire again." Then they feasted, and after worshipped the god with music.

This ceremonial of the sacrifice followed by the feast was to remain until Christian times. Pope Gregory even recommended that the early Christians "no more offer beasts to the devil, but kill cattle to the praise of God in their eating".

It should be noted that we have not yet been told why the Greeks had gone to besiege Troy. There is one reference in the quarrel between Achilles and Agamemnon, where Achilles says: "... But it was thy lead we followed here, thou shameless one, for thy pleasure, to win thee thy due from the Trojans, thee and Menelaos, thou dog-face!"

It was not necessary for Homer to tell his audience that Paris, or Alexandros, the son of the King of Troy, had stolen Helen of Argos, the wife of Menelaos, who was the brother of Agamemnon. The *Iliad*, like our own Anglo-Saxon poem, *Beowulf*, was a tale that had been told, and retold, a thousand times, until it was fixed into its final form by the genius of Homer.

BOOK II—In the second book we find how the Greeks are moved to renew their attack on the Trojans, and then follows a catalogue of the men and their ships. They had come from Athens and Argos, and Tiryns of the great walls, from Corinth, Sparta, and Arcadia. "Odysseus led the great-hearted Cephallenians, them that possessed Ithaca and Neriton with quivering

THE *ILIAD*

leafage." From all parts of Greece they came, and their great opponent was Hector of the glancing helm, the son of Priam, and leader of the Trojans.

BOOK III—In the third book we find the Greeks and Trojans drawn up in battle array against one another.

Then comes the challenge of Paris, who stole Helen, to all the chieftains of the Argives, to fight him man to man in deadly combat, and the challenge is taken up by Menelaos, the injured husband. Then Paris was daunted, and shrank back, until Hector his brother drives him to fight. It was then arranged that the two should fight, and the winner was to have Helen and all her wealth, and the war between the Greeks and the Trojans was to cease. The men in the ranks of the Greeks and Trojans sat down. Lambs were brought for sacrifice, and Priam was sent for that he might pledge the oath. Helen was told that: "Alexandros and Menelaos, dear to the war-god, will contest thee with their long spears; thou shalt be proclaimed dear wife of him who conquers." The sacrifice was offered, then Paris gained the right to cast the first spear.

And upon his back fair Alexandros girt his splendid harness, Alexandros, spouse to Helen of the lovely hair. First of all upon his legs he donned his greaves, which were beautiful to see, and clasped with silver round the ankles. Then upon his breast he put the corselet of his brother Lykaon, settling it to fit him. Across his shoulders he threw his brazen sword, silver studded, taking as well a shield, huge and sturdy. Upon his mighty head he placed a strongly wrought helmet, topped with an awful plume of nodding horsehair, and picked a strong spear, easy to his hand. And thus, too, did warlike Menelaos gird on his harness. . . .

The fight is described: first Alexandros

flung his spear whose shadow flies afar; and it drove against Menelaos' round target, but its bronze point did not pierce the stout target, but turned back. . . .

Then Menelaos

lifted and hurled his spear and struck against the round target of Priam's son. Into the bright shield drove the heavy shaft, and on into the wrought corselet, until it had ripped the jerkin at his flank; but he plunged aside and so shunned black death. Then Menelaos drew his sword and, heaving up his arm brought it down upon

FIGHT BETWEEN PARIS AND MENELAOS

the other's helmet-ridge, but the steel shivered into three and four pieces, and dropped from his hand.

Then comes the typically Greek touch to the tale.

Menelaos leapt upon Paris, and caught him by the horsehair crest of his helmet, and would have killed him, and gained again his wife Helen.

6 Warriors

But this would have been far too like plain sailing. Man would not have been shown as the sport of the gods, struggling along a difficult path, and only winning to his end, or losing all, through tragic happenings. Zeus' daughter, Aphrodite, comes to the assistance of Paris, and carries him through thick darkness to safety in the palace of Priam. The Trojans were quite innocent of any wish to hide him from Menelaos, because "he was hated of all, even as black death".

The fates were against them all; they needs must fight, and from this there was no escape.

BOOK IV—The fourth book opens with a consultation between the gods as to "whether once more we shall arouse ill war and the dread battle-din, or put friendship between the foes".

Father Zeus, who loves the men of holy Ilios (Troy), wishes for peace, but Athene and Hera sit by him, and devise ills for the Trojans. It is Hera who conceives the diabolical plan of making the Trojans break their oath, and do violence to the Greeks. Athene is sent in the likeness of a man, and persuades Pandaros to shoot an arrow at Menelaos. "Forthwith he unsheathed his polished bow of horn of wild ibex." Pandaros had shot the ibex himself, and taken the horns, sixteen palms in length, to a worker in horn, who joined them cunningly together and polished them all well, and set the tip of gold thereon. After the bow had been strung, Pandaros' comrades held their shields before him, and he took a feathered arrow and laid the bitter dart upon the string,

THE *ILIAD*

and vowed to Apollo, the lord of archery, one hundred firstling lambs.

... He drew his bow, holding in the same grasp the arrow-notch and the bow-string of ox's sinew, and stretched back the bow-string as far as his breast, and the iron arrow-head as far as the bow, and, when he had drawn the great bow into a circle, the bow twanged and the string hummed aloud and the sharp arrow sped forth, keen to wing its way into the press. ...

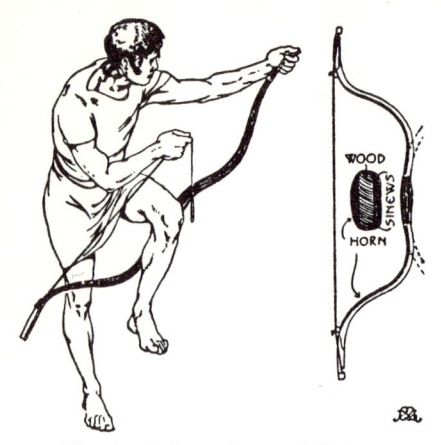

7 The back-bent bow of Odysseus

The daughter of Zeus protected Menelaos, and turned the arrow aside from the flesh, so that

on the clasped belt it struck and drove through the rich belt and through the curious corselet, on through the metal-studded apron which he wore to guard his flesh against darts; and this it was defended him best, but this too did the arrow pierce, grazing his outermost flesh, and straightway the dark blood poured from his wound. ...

The taslet made by the coppersmith was worn beneath the corselet. Menelaos' legs were stained with blood, "just as when a Maionian or Karian woman stains ivory with scarlet to make the cheek-piece that horses wear". These ivory cheek-pieces for horses were used here in England in the Bronze Age.

The Greeks had army doctors, because Machaon, the hero son of Asclepius, the noble leech, is called in. He draws out the arrow from the wound, sucks out the blood, and cunningly spreads thereon soothing drugs.

This treachery, to which the Trojans were forced by the gods, leads to renewed battle between them and the Greeks.

The method of fighting described by Homer is different from that of Classical Greece. Nestor of the Pylians

first drew up the charioteers with their horses and their chariots, and behind them the infantry many and brave, to be a bulwark in fight.

METHOD OF FIGHTING

The cowards he thrust into the middle, that, however backward a man might be, willy-nilly they must all do battle. And to the charioteers first he gave their orders, bidding them hold in their horses, and see to it that they did not become entangled in the press. "Nor do any of you," he said, "because he trusts in his skill with horses and in his valour, hanker after fighting the Trojans alone in front of the rest, nor yet draw back behind his fellows. So will your force be diminished. But, when a man from his own chariot can come at the chariot of a foeman, then let him drive in his spear; thus it is best." Thus, too, did men of olden times lay low cities and ramparts, having such council as this. . . .

8   A figure from Dodona

The men fought with spear and sword, or cast stones at one another, and protected themselves with bucklers. It is difficult to discover any method in the fighting in the pages of Homer, because he lays stress on a series of combats between champions of either side, sometimes on foot and sometimes in their chariots. Only, "Achilles, son of fair-haired Thetis, fights not, but among the ships nurses his bitter rage."

BOOK V—In the fifth book Diomedes is helped by Pallas Athene to distinguish between god and man, but warned that " . . . if any god comes here to try thee, fight thou not face to face with any other immortal, but only Aphrodite, daughter of Zeus—if she should enter the battle, let drive at her with the sharp bronze".

Diomedes attacked the Trojans with fury, and came near to killing Aineias, whose mother was Aphrodite. She came to her son's assistance, only to be wounded herself by Diomedes.

Then started forth the blood of the immortal goddess, ichor, such as flows in the veins of the blessed gods; bread they do not eat, nor

THE *ILIAD*

9   A reconstruction of a chariot

do they drink gleaming wine, wherefore are they bloodless and are called immortals. So, with a loud cry, she let fall her son; and him Phœbus Apollo lifted in his arms and sheltered him in a dark cloud.

Aphrodite escapes to Olympus, and there stirs up Ares, bloodstained bane of mortals, to encourage the Trojans to fresh effort, which meets with such success that Hera comes to the assistance of the Greeks with her daughter Athene.

Then Hera, the goddess queen, daughter of great Cronos, busied herself harnessing the horses with their golden frontlets, and Hebe swiftly put to the car, on either side, its curved brazen wheels, eight-spoked, fitted upon iron axle-trees; of these the felloe is wrought in imperishable gold, and over them are bronze tyres, a marvel to see; the naves are silver, which revolve on this side and on that; the body of the car is woven tight with plait-work of gold and silver thongs, and rimmed about with two rails. From the body stood a silver pole, upon the end of which she fastened the splendid golden yoke, throwing over it the golden breast-straps. And beneath the yoke Hera led the fleet-footed horses; and she longed for the battle and the sound of the war-cry. And Athene, daughter of Zeus who bears the ægis, slipped off, upon the floor of her father's house, her fine, many-coloured robe that her own hands had woven, putting on, instead, the tunic of cloud-gathering Zeus, and donned her armour for woeful strife. About her shoulders she cast the terrible tasselled ægis. Panic is set all about it like a crown, and Discord is therein, and Valour, Onset

THE GODS TAKE PART

too, that makes the blood run cold, and therein is the Gorgon's head [Medusa, killed by Perseus], that dreadful monster, awful and grim, a portent of Zeus who bears the ægis. Upon her head she placed the golden helmet, two-horned and set with bosses four, decked with the men-at-arms of a hundred cities. Into the flaming chariot then she stepped, and grasping her spear, heavy and huge and stout, with which she vanquishes the ranks of men, of heroes, even, against whom she is wroth, Athene, daughter of the awful sire.

10 Face of Gorgon—Corinthian, *c.* 570 B.C.

They go to Olympus, and ask Father Zeus if they may "smite Ares and drive him from the battle in sorry plight". They obtain his permission, and then seek Diomedes on the battlefield. The Greeks have had to give ground to the Trojans, who have been helped by Ares. Athene mounts a chariot by the side of Diomedes, and the goddess drives it against Ares, and Diomedes with her assistance wounds him with a spear. "Then brazen Ares bellowed out aloud as nine thousand warriors, or as ten thousand, shouting in battle, when they mingle in the war-god's strife. And trembling came upon Achæans and Trojans alike; fear took hold of them; so mighty was the bellowing of Ares, the greedy of battle." This is an extraordinary thing, that Homer could have thought of a god as so human that he bellows out loud when he is wounded.

So, in the words of the *Iliad*, the dread fray of Trojans and Greeks swayed oft this way and that across the plain, as they aimed against each other their bronze-shod javelins.

To us, as a work of art, the *Iliad* presents a tremendous picture of war and strife; but to the Greek, and to the Greek child of Classical times, the effect of hearing it spoken with dramatic emphasis must have been terrific. To us the gods of the *Iliad* are the gods of mythology; to the Greeks, Athene was the

THE *ILIAD*

goddess to whom Pericles caused the Parthenon to be built on the Acropolis in Athens.

BOOK VI—In the sixth book Hector goes to Troy, to ask his mother to vow to sacrifice to Athene, if she will have mercy on the city and the Trojans' wives and little children. There he meets Andromache, his wife, and then follows the pathetic scene in which they lament the fate that threatens Troy. She reminds him: ". . . No, Hector, to me thou art father and queenly mother; brother thou art and valiant husband besides. Come now, take pity on me; stay here on the wall, lest thou shouldst make thy child an orphan, and a widow me thy wife."

But Hector cannot shrink from battle, even though as he says: "This I know in my heart and in my soul: the day will come when sacred Ilios will be laid low, and Priam, and his people who wield the good ash spear . . ." and Andromache would be led captive by the Greeks. Then Hector cries: "But dead may I be and the heaped-up earth covering me, before I hear thy cries as they carry thee away into bondage."

BOOK VII—In the seventh book Apollo and Athene stay the general battle, and Apollo suggests: ". . . Let us stir up the valiant spirit of Hector, tamer-of-horses, that perchance he may challenge some one of the Danaans, in single fight, to encounter him man to man in deadly combat."

The warriors are given a rest, "and Athene and Apollo of the silver bow settled upon the tall oak tree of Father Zeus, who bears the ægis, in the shape of twin vultures, rejoicing in the warriors, where they sat together, packed close, bristling with shields and helms and spears".

The Greeks cast lots, and Aias in this way becomes their champion, and goes to meet Hector,

carrying his shield that was like a city-wall, a brazen shield, with sevenfold bull's-hide skilfully wrought him by Tychios—Tychios far best of all the workers in hide, who dwelt at Hyle, and had made him his flashing shield, of seven hides of mighty bulls and over them an eighth layer of bronze.

Then follows a long description of the fight, and as neither is able to kill the other, they exchange gifts instead. This sounds extraordinary, until we remember that much the same thing is written about in the pages of our own fourteenth-century

11 A merchant ship
Reconstructed from a black-figure vase in the British Museum

Froissart. In both periods fighting was regarded as the riskiest of the sports.

As the general fighting was not renewed, the opportunity was taken to

assemble and carry hither the dead bodies on carts, with oxen and with mules; a little way distant from the ships will we burn them, so that every man, whensoever we return to our native land, may bear their bones home to their children; about the pyre let us raise one single barrow, rearing it from the plain for all of them in common; and thereby, with such speed as may be, let us build ourselves a lofty wall, as defence for us and for our ships. And in the midst thereof let us contrive close-shutting gates that they may afford a passage for chariots; and without let us dig a deep ditch close by, which shall intervene and hold off chariots and infantry, if ever we should be hard put to it by the onslaught of the lordly Trojans.

It seems rather late in the day for the Greeks to have fortified their camp. Their usual practice was to pull their ships up, and then protect them on the land side by a palisade. In this chapter we find them importing their supplies. Wine came from Lemnos, "and the long-haired Achæans brought them wine, some for bronze, some for gleaming iron, some for hides, some for whole cattle, and some for bond-slaves".

THE *ILIAD*

Fresh attempts at peace were made, this time by the Trojans, but Paris, who is the villain, refuses to give up Helen.

BOOK VIII—In the eighth book the fight is renewed, but it must be remembered that all this time Achilles had not been fighting because of the wrong done him by Agamemnon. The gods still remember the plea of Thetis, the mother of Achilles, that the Trojans were to be victorious, until the Greeks should do honour to her son. ". . . Then the father lifted his golden balances, setting in the scales twin fates of grievous death, one for the horse-taming Trojans and one for the bronze-mailed Achæans; and, taking the scale-yard by the midst, he raised it, and the Achæans' day of doom sank down."

At the end of the book the Greeks are driven back within the walls of their camp by the ships.

BOOK IX—The ninth book finds the Greeks dispirited, and Agamemnon tries to make friends with Achilles. He offers him ". . . seven tripods that fire has never touched, and ten talents of gold, and twenty shining cauldrons, and twelve strong horses, whose swiftness has won prizes in the race". He even offers to return the daughter of Briseus. Odysseus, of many wiles, is sent to make the offer to Achilles, who rejects it, saying: "His gifts are hateful to me, and himself I hold not worth a straw."

BOOK X—The tenth book recounts the adventures of Odysseus and Diomedes, who go at night as spies to the camp of the Trojans.

BOOK XI—In the eleventh book Agamemnon, Diomedes, and Odysseus are all wounded. Now we begin to hear more of Patroklos, the friend of Achilles. He is sent to inquire how it is that Nestor was borne out of the fight. Arrived at the hut, he finds that Hekamede has mixed for them a restorative.

. . . First she drew before the two of them a fair, well-polished table with feet of cyanus, setting on it a vessel of bronze, with onion, as a relish to their drink, and pale honey and meal of sacred barley; and at their side a splendid cup that the old man had brought with him from home; embossed with golden studs it was, and there were four handles, and about each pair of handles were doves feeding, and below the cup stood upon two feet. Another man would scarce have found the strength to raise that cup from the table, when it was full, but old Nestor could lift it easily enough. In this cup the woman, like to the goddesses, mixed a potion for them with Pramnian wine,

DEATH OF PATROKLOS

grating into it, with a brazen grater, goat's milk cheese, and sprinkling in white barley meal; and when she had prepared the potion she bade them drink (50).

BOOK XII—In the twelfth book the Trojans besiege the Greeks in their camp, and in the end break down the walls and drive them to their ships.

BOOK XIII—In the thirteenth book Poseidon, the god of the seas, goes to the assistance of the Greeks, and the fight continues among the ships.

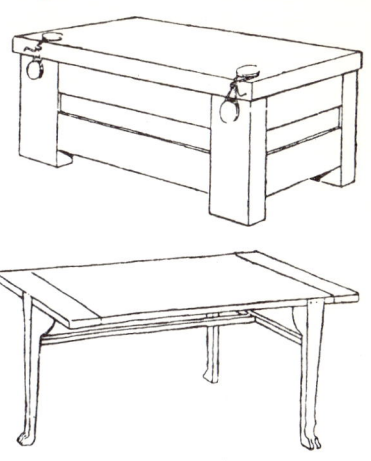

12 Chest and table

BOOK XIV—In the fourteenth book things continue to go so badly with the Greeks that Agamemnon suggests launching the first line of ships, and mooring them with stones so as to be able to escape. He is strongly rebuked by Odysseus. Poseidon again stirs up the Greeks to the attack, and Zeus is beguiled to sleep by Hera. The Greeks drive the Trojans from the camp, and Hector is wounded.

BOOK XV—In the fifteenth book Zeus awakes from his sleep, and is angry to find that Hector has been wounded. He sends Iris as messenger to Poseidon, that he must cease helping the Greeks, and return to the sea. Apollo is sent to encourage Hector, and the Trojans carry the fight back to the ships, and throw fire at that belonging to Protesilaos.

BOOK XVI—In the sixteenth book Patroklos beseeches Achilles to come to the assistance of the Greeks, and when he refuses, asks to be allowed to lead the Myrmidons himself. He borrows the armour of Achilles, and fights so well that he pushes the Trojans back to the walls of Troy. In the end Patroklos is killed by Hector. This, as we shall see, is the turning-point of the story.

BOOK XVII—In the seventeenth book the fight rages round the body of Patroklos, whose armour, borrowed from Achilles, is stripped off by Hector.

THE *ILIAD*

BOOK XVIII—In the eighteenth book Achilles hears of the death of his comrade:

... and in both his hands he scooped up black dust, and poured it on his head and fouled his comely face; and down on his sweet-scented jerkin rained the dark ashes. And there, in his mightiness, he lay outstretched in the dust, and, with his own hands, he tore and despoiled his hair. ...

His mother Thetis comes to comfort him, and promises to bring him new armour in the morning. Meanwhile, without armour, he encourages the Greeks, and helps them to bring back the body of Patroklos. The body is washed.

... Noble Achilles bade his comrades set a great cauldron on the fire that, as soon as might be, they should wash from Patroklos' body the bloody gore. And on the blazing fire they put the cauldron for filling the bath, pouring in water and taking wood and kindling it beneath. Then round the belly of the cauldron played the flames, and the water grew hot. And when the water was boiling within the bright bronze, then did they wash his body, anointing him richly with oil, salving his wounds with rare ointment; and they laid him on his bed, and from head to foot swathed him in a soft linen cloth and, above that, in a white robe. Then, all night long, round swift-footed Achilles, the Myrmidons bewailed and lamented Patroklos.

Thetis goes to Hephæstos, the lame god, to ask him to make new armour for Achilles, and Hephæstos

... went to his bellows and, turning them towards the fire, bade them work. Then the bellows, that numbered twenty in all, blew upon the

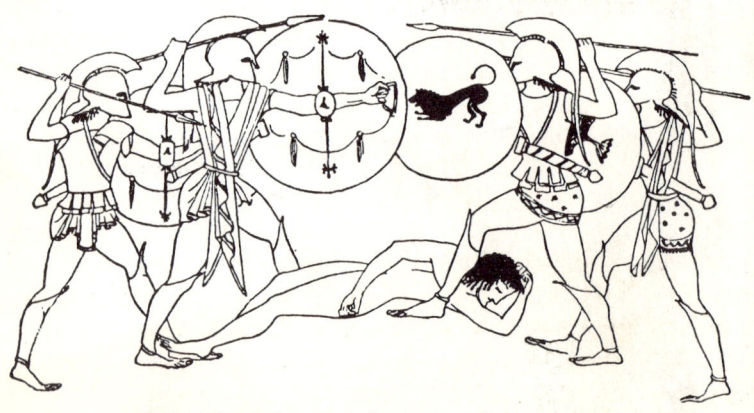

13 The fight over the body of Patroklos

NEW ARMOUR FOR ACHILLES

melting-vats, or pots, sending forth deft blasts of variable strength, now to further his labour, and now again however Hephæstos might will it, according as his work went on. And on to the fire he threw tough bronze and tin and precious gold and silver.

Bronze was smelted here in England in the Bronze Age in just the same way.

Hephæstos first fashioned

14   Gathering olives

a shield huge and strong, adorning it cunningly all over, circling it with a shining rim, threefold and glittering, and hung from it a baldric of silver. With five layers was covered the shield itself; and into it he put much cunning workmanship, with his curious skill.

It was decorated with emblems of the earth, the heavens, the sun, moon, and stars, and fair cities of mortal men, and beautiful pictures of country life. Homer is evidently telling of scenes with which he was familiar. You read of the hinds reaping with sharp sickles, and the sheaf binders following with twisted bands of straw, while others beneath an oak made ready a feast. Then we hear of the vintage, and a boy making pleasant music while the grapes are gathered. Again of a dancing place, and a great company standing around the lovely dance in joy. Hephæstos was right when he promised Thetis that, though he could not ward off dolorous death from Achilles, his armour should be the marvel of all men.

BOOK XIX—The nineteenth book opens with the reconciliation between Agamemnon and Achilles. Only a day has passed since Odysseus first went to the hut of Achilles with the offer of peace, and now the gifts are accepted, and Briseis goes back. Achilles puts on his armour—greaves for his legs, with silver ankle-pieces, and a cuirass round his breast. A silver-studded bronze sword hung from his shoulder, and the great shield to ward off blows. A stout helmet with a horsehair crest covered his head, and in his hand he carried his father's spear. So armed, Achilles joins in the fight, and plays havoc with the Trojans, and this is told in the twentieth book.

BOOK XX—Zeus calls the gods to council. He determines to remain within the fold of Olympus himself, where he can gladden his heart with gazing at the battle, but gives the other gods permission to help whom they will.

... So spake the son of Cronos and roused implacable war. And the gods went forth to the battle, some on this side and some on that: to the ships went Hera, and in her company Pallas Athene, and Earth-shaking Poseidon, and Hermes the Helper, who excelled them all in his subtlety; with them too went Hephaistos, in the pride of his great strength, limping, but under him his spindle legs moved nimbly. To the Trojans went Ares of the glancing helmet, and with him Phœbus the unshorn, and Artemis the Archer, and Leto and Xanthos and Aphrodite the laughter-loving.

Thus we have the amazing spectacle of not only men, but the actual gods warring between themselves.

BOOK XXI—In the twenty-first book Achilles captures twelve young men alive, and binding them with thongs, sends them back to the Greek ships. In this chapter Achilles fights with the River Xanthos. We must remember that to the Greeks a river could be a god, to be propitiated by sacrifice.

Nor shall the river avail you anything, fair-flowing with its silver eddies, though long time have you made him sacrifice of many bulls, and thrown down single-hooved horses, still living, into his eddies.

This river in the *Iliad* is something so alive that it can call on Apollo to help it against Achilles.

Just as when a man from its dark spring leads forth a stream of water along a channel amid his crops and garden, and, a mattock in his hand, clears all hindrances from its path; and, as it flows, it sweeps the pebbles before it, and, murmuring, swiftly on it slides, down a sloping place, and outstrips even him who leads it; so did the river-flood overtake Achilles, make what speed he could; for the gods are mightier than men.

And the river comes near to drowning Achilles, until Hephæstos comes to his assistance, with a great fire that parches the plain and stays the water. After, the Greeks, with the assistance of Achilles, drive the Trojans in flight within the walls of Troy.

ACHILLES AND HECTOR

BOOK XXII—In the twenty-second book Hector is shown outside the walls awaiting the onslaught of Achilles. He reproaches himself because he did not take the advice of Polydamas, who had suggested that they retire within the walls of Troy when they first heard that Achilles was to take the field again. Hector flees from Achilles: "And so, with flying feet, did these two thrice make the circle of Priam's city; and all the gods gazed down on them." And always Achilles headed him off towards the plain, and prevented Hector from running under the walls to gain the help of the archers on the battlements.

15 Wrestling

... But when a fourth time they had reached the springs, then the father lifted up his golden balances, and in them set two fates of gloomy death, one for Achilles and one for horse-taming Hector, grasping the balance at the midpoint and poising it. Then down sank Hector's dooms-day and descended into the house of Hades; and Phœbus Apollo deserted him.

Athene, by a base trick, urges Hector to the fight, and he is killed by Achilles, who

... contrived a shameful treatment for goodly Hector, slitting behind the tendons of both his feet from the heel up to the ankle, threading through ox-hide thongs binding them to the chariot and leaving the head to trail. Then he mounted his chariot and, after he had lifted in with him the famous armour, he lashed up his horses and they sprang forward with a will. And about Hector, as they dragged him along, rose the dust, his dark locks streaming loose on either side; and now in the dust lay that head once so fair, for Zeus had given him over to his enemies, to suffer shameful treatment in his own native land.

Andromache

gained the wall and the throng of men who stood there, and, standing still, she looked and saw him where he was being dragged before the city; ruthlessly were the swift horses dragging him away towards the hollow ships of the Achæans. Then the darkness of night settled down over her eyes and wrapped her about, and she reeled backwards and panted forth her spirit.

THE *ILIAD*

BOOK XXIII—In the twenty-third book the funeral feast of Patroklos is described. Oxen, sheep, goats, and boars were sacrificed. At night the spirit of Patroklos appears to his friend.

Thou sleepest and has forgotten me, Achilles. While I lived never didst thou forget me, and only now that I am dead. Bury me with all despatch, so I may pass the gate of Hades. Far do the spirits keep me off, the spirits of men out-worn; they suffer not that I should join their company beyond the River; and vain are my wanderings through the wide-gated house of Hades. Pitifully I beg that thou shouldst give me thy hand; never again shall I come back from Hades, once you have granted me my due of fire.

In the morning " . . . Lord Agamemnon despatched men from all the huts with mules, to gather firewood". This was brought down to the shore and laid in great piles. The Myrmidons then armed themselves, the men in chariots going first and the foot-men following, and in the midst was the body of Patroklos, borne by his comrades, who had cut off their hair and heaped it on the body. A great pyre was made of wood. Then sheep and oxen were sacrificed, and the corpse of Patroklos was wrapped from head to foot in the fat taken from their bodies, and then placed on the pyre, the flayed bodies of the animals around it. Two-handled jars of honey and oil were added, and four strong-necked horses and two house-dogs. Then the twelve unfortunate Trojan youths captured alive by Achilles were killed, and their bodies went to swell the pile. All night long the pyre burned, and in the morning Achilles called on the chiefs of the Greeks to

quench first the burning of the pyre with wine, even so far as the might of the flames has reached; then let us gather up the bones of Patroklos, Menoitios' son, taking good care to single them out from the rest; easy they are to discern, since he lay in the middle of the pyre and the others upon its verge, apart, huddled together, horses and men. His bones let us place in a golden urn, and wrap them in a double fold of fat, till I too be hidden in Hades. No monstrous barrow do I ask that you should labour to raise—a decent barrow, no more; afterwards, you may raise it broad and high, such of you as may remain among the benched ships when I am gone.

Then follows an account of the funeral games:

Achilles checked the people where they stood; he made them sit down in a wide company, from his ships bringing out prizes—cauldrons and tripods, horses and mules and strong oxen, and

FUNERAL OF PATROKLOS

fair-girdled women and grey iron.

For swift chariot-racers first he awarded a splendid prize—a woman skilful at fair handiwork for the winner to lead home, as well as an eared tripod that would hold twenty-two measures; so much for the first; for the second he awarded a six-year-old mare, unbroken; for the third a splendid cauldron untouched by fire, bright even as when it was first made; for the fourth two talents of gold; and for the fifth a two-handled urn that the fire had never scathed.

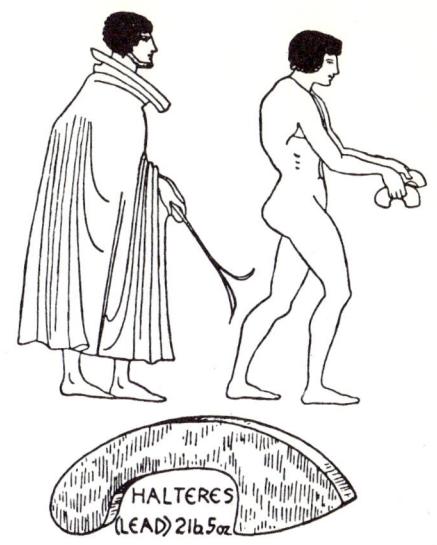

16 A jumper holding lead jumping weights

The winner of the boxing match obtained a sturdy mule, and the loser a two-handled cup. For wrestling, the first prize was a great tripod for standing on the fire, but curiously enough for the loser, Achilles "... led a woman into the midst, one skilled in many crafts, and whose worth they valued at four oxen". The wrestlers were Aias, son of Telamon, and Odysseus, and as neither could obtain the advantage, they were told to take equal prizes, and we do not know who got the woman valued at four oxen.

For the running races a mixing bowl of silver from Sidon, an ox, great and very fat, and a half talent of gold.

BOOK XXIV—In the last book Priam comes to Achilles, and ransoms the body of Hector. Achilles promises to hold back the battle for twelve days, whilst the funeral ceremonies of Hector are being carried on.

Priam, helped by Hermes, brings back Hector's body to Troy, and the people make lamentations.

Helen's tribute is:

Thou wouldst allay their anger with thy words, and restrain them by the gentleness of thy spirit and by thy gentle speech.

THE *ILIAD*

Then the body of Hector was burned as was that of Patroklos.

But when the young dawn shone forth, rosy-fingered Morning, then gathered the people round glorious Hector's pyre. Assembling, they first of all quenched the flames of the pyre with wine, even as far as the might of the flames had reached, and thereupon his brethren and friends gathered his white bones, mourning him with big tears coursing down their cheeks. The bones they took and laid away in a golden urn, wrapping them up in soft purple robes, and quickly set the urn in a hollow grave, and heaped above great stones, closely placed. Then hastily they piled a barrow, while everywhere about watchers were posted, through fear that the well-greaved Achæans might make an onslaught before the time. And, when the barrow was piled, they went back and, assembling, duly feasted and well in the palace of Priam, that king fostered by Zeus. Thus did they hold funeral for Hector, tamer-of-horses.

And that is the end of the *Iliad*, and the Trojan, like all other wars, had a very sad end. We shall be quite wrong if we think of Homer as glorifying war. He showed men fighting, because they needs must fight against fate. The gods cast the lots, and the men had to fight, and fighting, behaved as heroes. Consider what the Trojan War meant to the Greeks. For long weary years they were exiled from home, and few returned. Agamemnon their king was one, but he took the virgin priestess Cassandra with him as a slave, and went to his death at the hands of Ægisthus, the lover of his own wife Clytemnestra. Odysseus, perhaps because of his share in urging the death of the babe Astyanax, was condemned to wander for yet another ten years before he saw his wife Penelope again, and his mother died of a broken heart while he was away.

On the Trojan side the men were slaughtered and the women taken into slavery by the Greeks. Euripides' tragedy, *The Trojan Women*, is a terrible picture of the aftermath of war. Andromache, Hector's wife, has been allotted to Pyrrhus, Achilles' son, and Hecuba, Hector's mother, tries to console her. She points out that Andromache is sweet and gentle, and if she tries to please Pyrrhus, perhaps he in turn will be kind to her son Astyanax. The Greeks, however, had no idea of leaving Astyanax to grow up and avenge his father Hector, and a herald is sent to take the boy away and cast him from the walls. The scene which follows is described by Professor

THE END OF TROY

Gilbert Murray as "perhaps the most absolutely heart-rending in all the tragic literature of the world".

> *Quick! take him; drag him; cast him from the wall,*
> *If cast ye will! Tear him, ye beasts, be swift!*
> *God hath undone me, and I cannot lift*
> *One hand, one hand, to save my child from death . . .*
> *O, hide my head for shame: fling me beneath*
> *Your galley's benches!*
>
> Gilbert Murray's translation

Andromache is led away captive, and the dead boy is brought back to his grandmother Hecuba, who places him in Hector's shield and mourns over him.

Euripides may have been affected by the happenings of his own time. Another disgraceful massacre had taken place when the Athenians killed all the men of Melos and enslaved the women. This was in 416 B.C. In 415 the disastrous expedition to Syracuse set sail. Athens was in the hands of a war party bent on creating an empire. *The Trojan Women* was produced just before the expedition sailed, and must have been meant to sound a note of warning.

Chapter III
THE *ODYSSEY*

BOOK I

IF we wish to find out what happened after the Siege of Troy we must turn to the *Odyssey* of Homer, which is concerned with the travels of Odysseus. It is interesting to note that, just as in the *Iliad* our attention was at once riveted by an account of the quarrel between Achilles and Agamemnon, so in the *Odyssey* the first book gives an outline of the good things which are in store for us. We hear that Odysseus is held captive by the nymph Calypso in her hollow caves; that all the gods pity him, except Poseidon, who is angered with Odysseus because he blinded his son Polyphemus, one of the Cyclopes and a cannibal giant. The whole story really hinges on this quarrel.

The goddess Athene intercedes with Father Zeus on behalf of Odysseus, and Hermes is dispatched to Calypso, to tell her that Odysseus is to be released and sped on his way. Athene herself goes to Ithaca, the home of Odysseus, and "in the semblance of a stranger", introduces herself to Telemachus, the son of Odysseus. From him the goddess learns how the wealth of Odysseus is being wasted by many princes who, thinking that Odysseus is dead, are wooing his wife Penelope. These wooers are the villains of the piece.

Athene recommends that Telemachus should fit out a ship and go to make inquiries of Nestor and Menelaos, who were at the Siege of Troy with Odysseus, to see if by chance they have news of him. The goddess plants courage in the heart of Telemachus: he tells the wooer that they must leave his halls.

BOOK II—In book two Telemachus calls an assembly of the Achæans (the first since the departure of Odysseus), and the staff being placed in his hand, tells them of the misdeeds of the wooers. But Antinous, who was one of them, made answer that the fault was Penelope's, who gave hope to all, that now Odysseus was dead she would wed one of them when she had woven a shroud for Laërtes, his father. "And this craft she

TELEMACHUS AND THE WOOERS

planned in her heart, too; she set up in her halls a great web, fine-threaded and very broad, whereat she wove...." Then at night Penelope unravelled her day's work, "and so for three whole years she hid from the Achæans by her craft, and thus beguiled them".

The wooers tell the assembly that until Penelope makes up her mind, they will remain in the house of Telemachus,

17 Hermes and satyr

and they continue to waste his substance in riotous feastings.

Telemachus makes ready for his voyage to Sparta and sandy Pylos. He goes to the treasure chamber

... where lay heaps of gold and bronze, and raiment in chests, and a good stock of fragrant olive-oil. And there stood jars of wine, old and sweet, which held a divine, unmixed drink.

He tells the guardian to

... draw me wine in jars, sweet wine and the choicest after that which thou art keeping against the return of the hapless one, if ever he come home again I know not whence, even Zeus-born Odysseus, having shunned death and the fates. Twelve jars fill and close them all with lids, and pour me barley-meal into well-sewn skins; let there be twenty measures of ground barley-meal.

Telemachus and the crew carry all on board, and Athene sends them a favourable wind.

And when they had reared the fir-wood mast, they set it in its socket-hole and made it fast with the forestays, and with thongs of oxhide hoisted the white sail. So the wind filled the belly of the sail, and the dark wave surged loudly about the stem of the flying ship.

BOOK III—Athene, in the guise of Mentor, and Telemachus arrive at Pylos, where the American archæologist Professor Blegen has in recent years excavated Nestor's actual palace. Athene and Telemachus find Nestor on the seashore sacrificing

THE *ODYSSEY*

to Poseidon. Telemachus appeals to Nestor for news of his father Odysseus, but Nestor can only tell him how the return of the Achæans, after the sack of Troy, was spoiled by dissensions. He tells the tale how Agamemnon returned to find that his wife had a lover, Ægisthus, by whom he was slain, and who reigned in Mycenæ for seven years until he in turn was killed by Orestes, the son of Agamemnon. The tale of Nestor shows how much the Greeks were at the mercy of the sea in their ships. With their one square sail they could only sail with the wind, and had to wait until that wind was favourable. If the wind became an unfavourable gale, they toiled at their oars, and when their strength failed were blown out of their course. This is what happened to the Achæans returning from Troy.

BOOK IV—In the fourth book Telemachus and Peisistratus arrive by chariot in Sparta at the house of Menelaos. This is how they were received:

And the sweating horses they loosed from under the yoke, and, tethering them at the horses' stalls, they threw before them spelt, mixing in with it white barley. The chariot they tilted up against the shining walls of the entry, and led the men away into the divine palace hall.

After they had seen the palace,

they went to the polished baths and bathed them. [Then] . . . they sat down on chairs, beside Menelaos, Atreus' son. Then a maid-servant brought water for their hands in a golden pitcher and poured it over a silver basin, so they might wash, drawing up at their side a polished table. And a sober housewife brought and set by them bread, and dainties too in abundance, giving them freely of her store. And a carver lifted and put by them platters of all kinds of meat, and near them he set two golden bowls.

Menelaos, as a sign of honour, gave them some of his own dish of fat ox-chine roasted. All this time they are entertained as strangers by Menelaos, who, however, has been struck by the resemblance of Telemachus to his friend Odysseus.

Then Helen, for whom the Achæans fought at Troy, comes in, and she too marks the likeness.

She tells Telemachus tales of his father, of how, at the Siege of Troy, he disguised himself as a beggar and passed into the Trojan city as a spy. Menelaos tells her:

TELEMACHUS SEEKS NEWS OF ODYSSEUS

Never yet have mine eyes beheld such another man as was steadfast-hearted Odysseus, no such another deed as he planned and dared, in the carven horse, wherein sat all we chiefs of the Argives, carrying to the Trojans death and doom.

And how Helen came and

three times didst thou circle round the hollow ambush and try it with thy hands, calling aloud by name on the chiefs of the Argives, and with thy voice mimicking the voices of the wives of all the Danaans. Now I and Tydeus' son and goodly Odysseus were sitting in the midst; we heard thee call, and the two of us were anxious to rise and come forth, or straightway answer thee from within. Yet, for all our eagerness, Odysseus held us back and kept us there. Then, likewise, did the other sons of the Achæans keep silence; only Anticlus would have answered; but Odysseus shut his mouth with his strong hands and so saved all the Achæans, holding him thus till Pallas Athene led thee away again.

Telemachus then asks that he may be allowed to sleep,

... and Argive Helen ordered her maids that they should set bedsteads beneath the gallery of the entrance, and should lay on them fair purple blankets and above these spread coverlets, and thereover fleecy cloaks as a topmost covering of all. So, torch in hand, the maids went out of the hall and laid the bedding, and a serving-man led forth the guests. So there they slept in the forehall of the house, noble Telemachus and Nestor's glorious son; but the son of Atreus slept in the inmost chamber of the high-roofed house, and at his side lay Helen of the long robes, that goddess among women.

In the morning, Menelaos tells Telemachus of how, in his own eight years' wandering, he heard from Proteus, the thrall of Poseidon, how Odysseus was held captive by Calypso. Beyond that he cannot tell Telemachus anything.

Meantime the wooers " ... in front of the palace of Odysseus took their pleasure in throwing the discus and the javelin, upon a levelled place, as was their custom, in the insolence of their pride".

They also laid plans to kill Telemachus on his return from Pylos, and dispatched a ship to wait in the strait between Ithaca and Samos (Cephallenia). The details of the return journey are given in the fifteenth book.

BOOK V—In the fifth book Athene goes to the gods, who are in council, and asks Zeus that Calypso should free Odysseus. Hermes is sent to her with a message that she is to do so. Calypso

THE *ODYSSEY*

must needs obey Zeus, but bewails the hard lot of goddesses who fall in love with mortals: "Harsh are ye gods and jealous above all others, who grudge that goddesses should openly mate themselves to mortal men." She points out how she had saved Odysseus from shipwreck when he "all alone was riding the keel of his ship".

Now it is that we first meet Odysseus in the *Odyssey*. The first four books have served to whet our curiosity, and have provided as well a sequel to the *Iliad*.

Calypso finds Odysseus sitting on the seashore bewailing his fate. Without ship or men, how can he hope to reach Ithaca again? This is what Calypso said to him:

Luckless man, sorrow here no longer I beg thee, nor pine away. Ready and willing I am even now to speed thee hence. So come rise, and with an axe hew long beams and build a broad raft, fastening upon it cross-planks to make a raised deck, that it may carry thee over the misty deep. Therein will I stow bread and water and red wine such as will satisfy thy heart, to ward off hunger. . . .

And right well Calypso helped him.

She gave him a great axe such as was well suited to his grasp; a brazen axe it was, double-edged, and in it securely fastened a good handle of olive. She gave him too a polished adze, and presently led the way to the furthest part of the island, where grew tall trees, the alder and the poplar and the fir, which reaches unto the skies, seasoned and dry that would float buoyantly for him. So, once she had shown him where the tall trees grew, the fair goddess Calypso set off homewards, and he set to cutting him timber, and busily his work went forward. Twenty trees he felled and trimmed with the axe; then cleverly he smoothed them, straightening them by the line. Meanwhile, Calypso brought him augers, with which he bored every piece, jointing them together and securing them with pegs and morticings. Wide as the hull of a broad-beamed freight-ship, traced by some skilful carpenter, so wide was the raft Odysseus made. And, labouring, he set up deck-beams and bolted them to the close-set ribs and finished off his work with long gunwales. And in the raft he put a mast and a yard-arm fitted to it, a rudder as well to help him steer a course. From the stem to the stern he fenced it about with wattled osiers, as a bulwark against the waves, and strewed in much brush.

Then Calypso brought him cloth for sail-making. These, too,

ODYSSEUS BUILDS A RAFT

18 A reconstruction of the raft of Odysseus

did he contrive in his skill. And braces and halyards and sheets he made fast in his raft, and then with rollers pushed it down to the fair salt sea.

It took Odysseus four days to build his raft, and on the fifth he sailed away, and Calypso sent a gentle favouring wind, and for seventeen days he sailed, and on the eighteenth day he came within sight of the land of the Phæacians (Corfu), and all would have been well had not Poseidon seen him from afar off. The sea-god knew that Zeus must have come to the assistance of Odysseus, but notwithstanding this, determines to gather the clouds, and trouble the waters, and rouse the winds. As a result, Odysseus narrowly escapes with his life, and is cast ashore more dead than alive.

BOOK VI—The sixth book opens with a beautiful description of how Athene contrives that Nausicaa, the daughter of Alcinous, King of the Phæacians, should take the family washing down to a little stream, near where Odysseus is sleeping. She asks her father for a wagon, and he replies: "Neither the mules nor aught else do I grudge thee, my dear child. Go now, and the slaves shall make ready for thee the wagon that is tall and strong of wheel and fitted with a frame above."

And so saying, he called up his men, and outside the palace they made ready the easy-running mule cart and led the mules under the yoke and harnessed them, while from her room the maiden brought out the bright raiment and stowed it in the polished car. In a basket her mother put all kinds of food, such as satisfy the heart, and set therein, too, dainties, and filled a goatskin bottle with wine. Then Nausicaa mounted the cart, and her mother gave her smooth olive-oil in a golden flask that, after they had bathed, she and her maidens might anoint themselves. So Nausicaa took the whip and the bright reins, and touching the mules, she started them. Then, with a clatter of hooves, forward they strained, never flagging, with the load of raiment and the maidens behind. She did not go alone, but her attendants bore her company.

When they got to the river they took the garments and trod them in the washing trenches, and then spread them out to dry. Then they bathed and anointed themselves with olive-oil, and took their midday meal on the river's bank. After, they fell to playing ball, and Nausicaa began to sing. The ball fell into the river and they all raised a piercing cry, and then, of course, Odysseus woke up and the maidens fled, all except Nausicaa of the white arms, and to her Odysseus came as a suppliant. She provided him with a mantle and doublet, one supposes, from the washing which was now dry, and soft olive-oil in a golden cruse. Then Odysseus washed and anointed himself with oil and put on the fine raiment, and then Athene ". . . caused him to seem taller and more mighty, and from his head made the locks curl down in tresses like a hyacinth flower".

She shed so much grace on him that it went hardly with Nausicaa when she saw him again, and her heart went pit-a-pat. She gives Odysseus instructions how he may find his way to the palace of Alcinous.

BOOK VII—In the seventh book Odysseus finds his way to the high-roofed hall of Alcinous:

Brazen were the walls which from the threshold to the inmost chamber ran this way and that, and round them a frieze of blue. Golden were the doors which enclosed the well-built house, and silver door-posts stood upon the brazen threshold. Silver was the lintel above them, and of gold the hook of the door.

There were seats around the walls with finely woven coverings. Fifty handmaids did the spinning and weaving, and ground corn in the millstones. There were gardens of pear trees and

NAUSICAA AND ODYSSEUS

pomegranates, and apple trees and sweet figs, and olives, and a vineyard. There were all manner of garden beds, and two fountains of water.

Odysseus stood and gazed, and passed quickly into the hall and fell at the knees of Arete, the wife of Alcinous, and implored her protection and asked to be sped on his way. He was raised up by the king and set in a chair, and Odysseus tells the king of his adventures since he left the isle of Calypso on his raft. Odysseus goes to sleep beneath the gallery. This seems to have been the place for strangers.

19 A ball game

BOOK VIII—In the eighth book the Phæacians are called to assembly, and Alcinous tells them of the stranger that has come amongst them, and orders that a black ship be drawn to the sea, and fifty-two noble youths chosen for her crew, and then after this is done, all are to come to the palace to help entertain the stranger. At the palace twelve sheep were sacrificed, and eight boars and two oxen, and here it is that we are given an indication of how the *Odyssey* itself may have come into its final shape as a tale told and retold until its form was perfect, and not written as it would be now. At the palace a henchman brings in the beloved minstrel, who is blind, and sets him on a chair close by a pillar on which hangs his lyre.

The minstrel is stirred by the tune to sing the songs of famous men, and Odysseus is moved to tears.

After the feast they go to the place of assembly, and have games of running, wrestling, and boxing. Odysseus distinguishes himself by casting a great stone. Then they

levelled a place for dancing and drew out a fair wide ring. Then the herald approached bearing to Demodocus the clear-toned lyre. So he went into the midst, and round him stood boys in the first bloom of their youth, such as were skilled at the dance. And they struck the good dancing floor with their feet. And Odysseus watched the twinkling movement of their feet and marvelled in his spirit.

Then Alcinous bade Halius and Laodamas dance alone, for none could equal their skill. So they took into their hands the beautiful purple ball, which clever Polybus had made them, and, the one leaning back and tossing it up towards the shadowy clouds, the other would spring from the ground and catch it again before ever his feet touched the earth. And when they had tried their skill at flinging the ball straight up, then they began to dance upon the bounteous earth and pass the ball from hand to hand, and the other youths stood by in the lists and kept time, and a great clamour arose.

Then the kindly Alcinous suggested that the twelve princes who ruled under him should join in giving a stranger's gift to Odysseus, so that he might go to supper with a glad heart. At supper Odysseus ". . . carved off a helping of the chine of a white-toothed boar, of which yet more was left over, rich with fat on either side". This he sent by a henchman to the minstrel Demodocus, and asked that he would tell them of the wooden horse. In this way we get fuller details than were given by Menelaos in the fourth book. The minstrel tells how that Odysseus had fashioned the horse and filled it with the bravest Greeks. To lull Trojan suspicion, other Greeks set fire to the huts of their camp, and went aboard their ships, and sailed away. The Trojans dragged the horse into Troy itself, and sat around wondering and debating what to do with it, and then the sons of the Achæans poured forth from the horse and sacked the city. It must be remembered that all this time the Phæacians do not know that they are entertaining Odysseus.

At the end of the eighth book Alcinous calls on him to tell them of his adventures, and in the ninth book he does so, and begins:

BOOK IX—"I am Odysseus, Laërtes' son, who am known among all men for my wiles."

This is the tale that Odysseus told the Phæacians: when he and his men left Troy, the wind carried their ships to Ismarus in Thrace, where they sacked the city and slew many of the inhabitants, until the neighbours coming to their assistance, the Achæans were driven back to their ships.

For nine whole days they were driven by storms until they came to ". . . the country of the lotus-eaters, who eat a flowery food". This was tasted by certain of the company who were sent out to reconnoitre.

ODYSSEUS BEGINS HIS STORY

Now such of them as ate the honey-sweet fruit of the lotus had no longer any wish to bring tidings nor to return, but there he was minded to stay among the lotus-eating men, feeding on the lotus and forgetful of the homeward way. But them weeping did I hale back to the ships, unwilling as they were, and binding them thrust them beneath the benches of the hollow ships.

Again they set sail, and this time they came to the land of the Cyclopes in Sicily. Here Odysseus and twelve of his men went prospecting, and came to the cave of a giant. They waited, expecting to be charitably entertained, but when the giant returned, and threw down a great log for the fire, Odysseus and his men fled into the back of the cavern, while the giant blocked the door with a great stone, and then made preparations for his supper. Soon he saw the Achæans and, notwithstanding the explanations of Odysseus,

20 A dancer

he answered not at all; but, springing up, he laid hands upon my comrades, and grasping two of them at once, dashed them against the earth as they might have been puppies, so their brains ran out upon the ground and the earth was wet with them. Then he carved them limb from limb, and made ready his supper. Like a mountain-bred lion he ate, and stinted not; for the entrails he ate as well as the flesh and also the bones with their marrow.

Then the giant slept. In the morning two more of the men were devoured, and the giant went out, putting the door stone in position to keep them prisoners.

Odysseus planned their escape. The Cyclops had left a great club in the cave, and we can form some idea of what a giant he was, when we hear that it was equal in size ". . . to the mast of a black ship, twenty-oared".

Odysseus cut a fathom's length off this (six feet), and fined it down, and made it even, and sharpened it to a point, and hardened it in the fire.

In the evening the giant returned, and drove his sheep into the cave, and two more men were eaten. Now, Odysseus had brought wine with him, which he had in the cave, and first one cup and then another was given to the giant until he at last became drunk. Before this Odysseus tells the giant that his name is No-man. Now was the time for action, and

> they took the sharp-pointed stake of olive-wood and plunged it into his eye, while, bearing upon it from my place above, I turned it about, as when a man bores a ship's timber with a drill and below his fellows spin it with a thong which they hold at either end and the drill runs round unceasingly; so in his eye we took and whirled about the fiery-pointed stake, and blood flowed round the heated bar and the flame singed his eyelids and his brows on every side, as the eyeball consumed and its roots crackled in the fire. Just as when a smith dips some great axe or an adze hissing into cold water that it may be tempered—for thence proceeds the strength of the iron— even so did his eye hiss round the olive-wood stake. Terrible then was the bellow he raised, till the rocks rang round about; in terror we fled, and he plucked forth the stake all blood-bedabbled from his eye.

The giant in his agony calls so loudly that his neighbours come to his assistance and ask him from outside the cave what is the matter, to which he replies that "no man is killing him". And they quite properly reply that if no man is killing him, what is all the to-do about?

The giant then groped his way to the door, and lifted away the great stone and sat in the entry, so that the Achæans might not escape. However, Odysseus contrives this by lashing the sheep together in threes with withies. The middle sheep of each set of three supported one man, who suspended himself below the sheep. Odysseus himself used the ram in this way. The blinded giant felt along the backs of the sheep and did not discover them.

Now the giant Polyphemus was a son of Poseidon, the god of the seas, and he prayed to him that Odysseus and his men might never come to their home in Ithaca, or, if they did, only after much tribulation. This was the beginning of the troubles of Odysseus.

BOOK X—In the tenth book they reach the island home of Æolus, which floated on the sea, and had cliffs which ran up from the seas with walls of unbroken bronze. There Odysseus was kindly entertained, and sped on his way. All might have been well because Æolus was the keeper of the winds, and he

THE CYCLOPS. CIRCE

provided a good west wind which was what Odysseus needed, and bound all the others in an oxhide wallet. The west wind carried them to within sight of Ithaca, but while Odysseus was asleep his men opened the wallet to find what treasure it contained; then out burst all the noisy winds and carried them back to the Æolian isle. Here they were badly received, and driven away as being ". . . hated by the immortal gods".

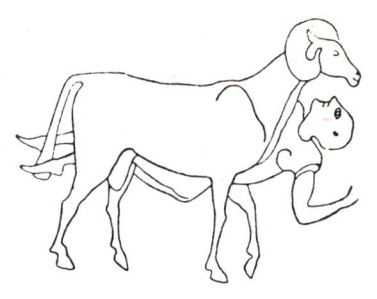

21 Odysseus under the ram

For six days they sailed, and on the seventh came to Lamos. Here they were attacked by the people, who were giants, and of the twelve ships, only the one of Odysseus and his men escaped. Now the one ship sailed on alone, and came to the Ææan isle, where dwelt Circe of the braided tresses.

Eurylochus was sent forward with some of the men and came to the halls of Circe.

And round the palace roamed mountain-bred wolves and lions, whom Circe herself had bewitched by the evil drugs that she gave them. These did not set upon my men, but ramped round fawning upon them and wagging their long tails.

When they came to the palace the men went in, and Circe offered them wine, but Eurylochus tarried behind, and saw with horror that when his companions had

drunk it off, presently she struck them with a wand and penned them in the sties. The head and the voice they had, and the bristles and the shape of swine, but their minds remained as before. So penned, they were weeping, and Circe flung them to eat, acorns and mast and the berries of the cornel tree, such provender as wallowing swine are wont to batten on.

Hermes came to the assistance of Odysseus, and gave him a herb of virtue to resist the charms of Circe, and being able to resist, he makes a bargain that his men should be restored to human shape, and this being done, they remained there a year "feasting on abundant flesh and on sweet wine".

THE *ODYSSEY*

BOOK XI—In the eleventh book Odysseus takes leave of Circe, and sails to the limits of the world and the dwelling of Hades and dread Persephone. There he sacrifices, and the spirits of the dead come to him. One, Teiresias, warns him that his own death will come from the sea, and recommends that on his return to Ithaca, Odysseus should take with him

... a shapen oar, till thou shalt reach men who know not the sea, nor eat salt mixed with their food, nor know anything of purple-cheeked ships nor of shapen oars that are the wings of ships. I will tell thee a sign so plain that it cannot escape thee; whenever another traveller encountering thee shall say that it is a winnowing-fan thou art carrying on thy strong shoulder, then do thou drive thy shapen oar into the ground and make goodly sacrifice to Lord Poseidon. ...

Odysseus sees the spirit of his own mother, and she tells him: "... No, it was my longing for thee, great Odysseus, and for thy counsels and for thy loving kindness that robbed me of sweet life."

Many other phantoms of men outworn came to Odysseus across the mead of asphodel—Agamemnon, Achilles, and Patroklos who had fought with him at Troy. Tantalus was there in torment, standing in water up to his chin, which always fell away as he stooped to drink, and under tall trees which tossed their fruit away as he clutched at them. And there was Sisyphus, who continually rolled a great stone uphill.

22 Asphodel

HADES. SCYLLA AND CHARYBDIS

BOOK XII—In the twelfth book Odysseus has left the land of Hades, and his next adventure is the passage of the island of the Sirens, who bewitched men by their songs, and lured them to destruction. Odysseus was bound to the mast of his ship, and the ears of his men stopped with wax so that they might not hear the music.

Then came the adventure of Scylla and Charybdis. Scylla was a dreadful monster, with twelve feet and six necks with a head on each and therein three rows of teeth. Living in a cave, she swooped down and caught up out of the ship six of Odysseus' men. Charybdis was a whirlpool that sucked down the water and spouted it up again. When they have passed these perils, disaster overtakes them, because the men kill the cattle of Helios, on the isle of Thrinacia. Because of this, the ship and the men are destroyed in a great storm, and only Odysseus is rescued by Calypso, to live with her on the isle of Ogygia, and this is where we first meet Odysseus in the *Odyssey*.

Henceforward the tale becomes a straightforward recital of Odysseus' return to Ithaca, but our interest is sustained because we know that there must be dramatic happenings when the wooers are discovered.

BOOK XIII—In the thirteenth book Odysseus is sent back to Ithaca by Alcinous, and, going to sleep in the ship, is put on shore without being awakened, and then the kindly Phæacians sailed back. It is sad to relate that Poseidon had his revenge, because as the ship neared home, "then near her drew the shaker of the earth, and he struck and changed her into a stone and rooted her fast to the ocean bed with a blow of the flat of his hand".

Today, in Corfu, the people show you an island which, they say, is Odysseus' ship turned into stone.

When Odysseus awakened, he found his constant friend Athene by him, and she contrived that: "I will wrinkle the fair skin on thy supple limbs, and from off thy head I will make to fall thy yellow hair, and wrap thee in a foul garment, such that one would shudder to see a man clothed therein."

It is in this guise that he goes to the house of Eumæus, the swineherd, while Athene hastes to Sparta to bring back Telemachus. This brings us back to the doings recounted in the fourth book.

THE *ODYSSEY*

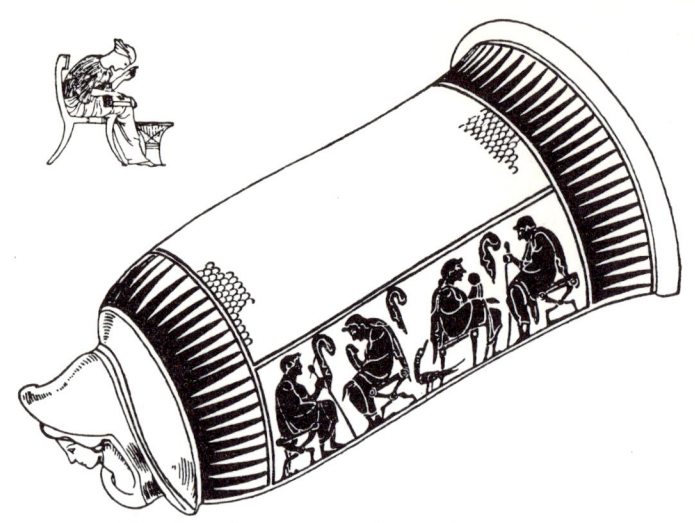

23 An epinetron or spinning instrument

BOOK XIV—In the fourteenth book Odysseus arrives at the house of the swineherd, and

found him sitting in the forehall of his house, where his courtyard was builded high, in a place overlooking a wide prospect; a great court it was, and goodly, with an open space all around. This the swineherd himself had built for his master's swine, his master who was far away, and his mistress and the old man Laërtes knew nothing of it. With huge stones he had built it, and fenced it in with a hedge of white thorn. Outside, splitting oak to the dark core, he had driven in stakes the whole length of it on either side, set thick and close; and within the courtyard he made twelve sties, near by one another, as beds for the swine, and in each sty fifty were penned, fifty wallowing swine sows for breeding; but the boars slept without.

Odysseus is kindly entertained by the swineherd, and given roasted pork sprinkled with white barley-meal to eat; he hears of the misdeeds of the wooers.

BOOK XV—In the fifteenth book Telemachus is brought back by Athene, and, escaping the wooers who lay in wait for him, goes to the house of the swineherd.

BOOK XVI—In the sixteenth book Eumæus is sent to the town, and Odysseus makes himself known to his son. To assist him in this, "Athene touched him with her golden wand. A fresh

ODYSSEUS REACHES ITHACA

cloak and a tunic she first of all cast about his chest, and she heightened his stature and the bloom of his manhood. Warm once more grew his colour; his cheeks plumpened, and thickly round his chin sprang the black beard."

When the swineherd returns, Odysseus becomes an old beggar-man again.

BOOK XVII—In the seventeenth book Telemachus goes to tell his mother Penelope of his journey, and in the evening Odysseus and the swineherd go to "... the fair house of Odysseus: easily a man would know it, though he saw it among many others. There is building beyond building, and the courtyard of the house is closed in with a wall and battlements, and well-fenced are the folding doors".

24 Spinning

They meet Melanthius, the goatherd, who reviles them. Here no one knows him except his old hound, Argos, who lay "upon the deep dung of mules and kine, that lay heaped up before the doors, till the slaves of Odysseus should carry it away to manure his wide lands". Yet the hound recognised the voice of his master, and "wagging his tail dropped both ears, but nearer to his master he had no longer strength to come. And Odysseus glanced away, wiping a tear that he easily hid from Eumæus. . . . But as for Argos, black death descended on him in that same hour that he saw Odysseus again, in the twentieth year of his age."

Then Odysseus entered the house, sat down within the doorway, and watched the feast and listened to the minstrel; and Telemachus was there and sent him food by the swineherd, and told him to beg of the wooers as well. Athene urged him in the same way to make test of them. All gave him somewhat, except Antinous, who caught up a footstool and struck him with it on the back. Penelope hears of this, and is ashamed that a stranger should have been treated in this way, and sends for Odysseus.

BOOK XVIII—In the eighteenth book a real beggar, Arnæus by name, comes up to the house, and thinking of Odysseus as a rival would have driven him away. The wooers encourage the quarrel and promise the winner a present: "Here are goats'

25 Telemachus and Penelope at her loom

bellies lying by the fire, which we laid by at supper-time and filled with fat and blood. Now, whichever of the two wins, and shows himself the better man, let him stand up and take his choice of these puddings."

In the boxing match which followed, Odysseus is easily the winner, and wins the pudding.

Then Penelope, attended by her maidens, came down from her upper chamber to the hall, and Athene steeped her with beauty imperishable. "Standing by the pillar of the well-built roof", she chided Telemachus for allowing the stranger to be ill-used. Penelope's great beauty moved the wooers to renewed efforts to win her, and

each man sent a henchman to bring his gifts. For Antinous his henchman bare a broidered robe, great and very fair, wherein were golden brooches, twelve in all, fitted with well-bent clasps. And the henchman straightway bare for Eurymachus a golden chain of curious work, strung with amber beads, shining like the sun. And his squires bare for Eurydamas a pair of ear-rings with three drops well wrought, and much grace shone from them. And out of the house of Peisander, the prince, the son of Polyctor, the squire brought a necklet, a very

PENELOPE

lovely jewel. And likewise the Achæans brought each one some other beautiful gift.

Odysseus rejoiced that Penelope had tricked the wooers in this way.

When Penelope retired with the gifts, the wooers turned to dancing.

Presently they set up three braziers in the hall to light them, and on these they piled firewood all around, faggots long seasoned and dry, new split with the axe. And midway by the braziers they placed torches, and the maids of brave-hearted Odysseus held up the lights in turn.

Odysseus tells the maidens to go to their quarters and twist yarn, or card wool, but they only laugh, and the wooers fall to taunting Odysseus and then go home.

BOOK XIX—In the nineteenth book Odysseus arranges with Telemachus to remove the arms out of the hall, and tells him how he is to explain to the wooers that this has been done in case they quarrel between themselves and wound one another, "for iron draws a man unto it of itself".

This is the first reference to iron weapons—hitherto we have only heard of bronze. The good nurse Euryclea was called in to assist, and the arms are taken to the armoury, and Pallas Athene carried a light, and its radiance caused Telemachus to wonder.

Truly, father, a great marvel is this which mine eyes behold; surely the walls of the house and the fair roof-beams and the cross-beams of pine, and the pillars that reach aloft glow as it were with the light of a blazing fire. No doubt some god is within doors, one of those that hold the wide heaven.

Telemachus retires to rest, and Penelope comes down to the hall,

and they placed a chair for her close by before the fire, where she used to sit; a well-wrought chair it was, inlaid with ivory and silver, that once the craftsman Icmalius had fashioned, joining a footstool, that was part of the chair, whereover they were wont to spread a great fleece.

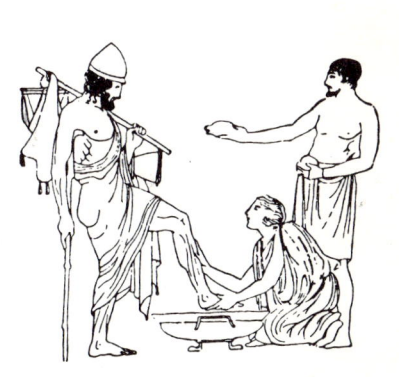

26 Washing the feet of Odysseus

THE *ODYSSEY*

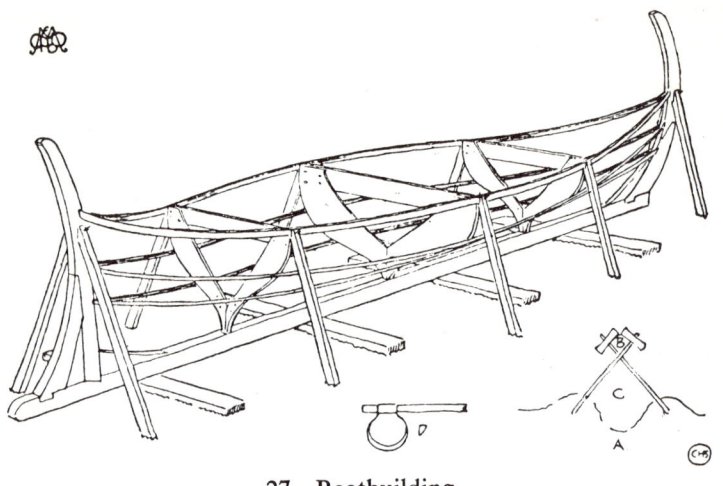

27   Boatbuilding

Penelope talks to Odysseus, and tells him how she is plagued by the wooers, and how she tricked them for three years by weaving a shroud for Laërtes by day, and then unravelling it by night, but that now she could not put off the wooers much longer: "But longing for Odysseus, I waste my heart away."

Odysseus dare not make himself known to his wife, so tells her "many a false tale in the seeming of the truth", but warns her that her husband is at hand. Penelope can hardly hope that this is true, and sends for the old nurse Euryclea to wash his feet, and the nurse recognises Odysseus by a scar on his leg, left from an old hunting wound. Penelope does not notice the recognition. She tells Odysseus how she will make trial of the wooers in the morning.

I am about to order that a contest shall be held with those axes that he was wont to set up in a row in his halls, like oaken props in shipbuilding, twelve of them in all; he would stand far off and shoot his arrow through them every one. This contest I will now appoint for the wooers: him who shall most easily string the bow in his hands, and shoot through all twelve axes, him will I follow and forsake this house, this house of my wedding; so far it is and filled with livelihood, that methinks I shall still remember, aye, even though it be in a dream.

Penelope then goes to her upper chamber.

CONTEST OF THE AXES

BOOK XX—In the twentieth book Odysseus sleeps in the vestibule of the house, and in the morning the wooers come to resume their feastings, and Athene stirs them to wrath against Odysseus.

BOOK XXI—In the twenty-first book Penelope descends

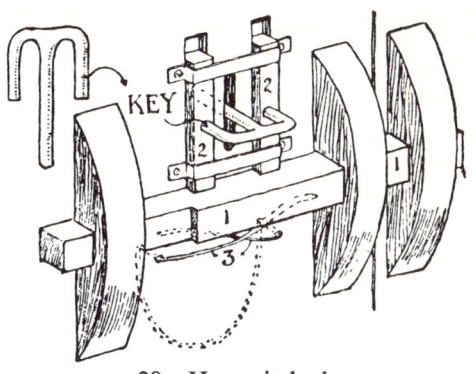

28 Homeric lock

the tall staircase of her chamber, takes the well-bent key of bronze with an ivory handle, and goes to the treasure chamber. "Then quickly she loosed the strap from the handle of the door and in she thrust the key, and with a sure aim shot back the bolts." There she finds the back-bent bow of Odysseus, with its quiver and arrows. These she takes to the wooers in the hall, and arranges a contest for them with herself as the prize, saying: "Whoso shall most readily string the bow in his hands and shoot through every one of the twelve axes, him will I follow and with him forsake this house."

Telemachus sets up the axes. "First he dug a trench, and in it set up the axes, one long trench for them all, making it straight to the line, and round them stamping down the earth."

He then tries to string the bow, but fails, and after him Leodes, with the same result. Antinous, another of the wooers, then commands the goatherd: "Come now, Melanthius, light us a fire in the hall, and put a great settle by the fire and a fleece covering it, and bring forth from within a great ball of lard, that we young men may warm the bow and grease it with the fat, and so make trial of it and bring an end to the contest." But the fire and the lard do not help, and the wooers fail one by one to bend the bow. While this is going on, Odysseus draws the neatherd and the swineherd from the hall, and after testing them makes himself known to them. He arranges their return to the hall separately, and tells Eumæus, the swineherd, to contrive that the bow is handed to him and "bid the women bar the well-fitting doors of their hall. If any of them hear the sound of groaning or the din of men within our walls, let them not run forth, but stay where they are in silence at their work."

Philœtius, the neatherd, is told "to bolt and bar the outer gate of the courtyard, and quickly tie the knot".

The wooers by this time have all made trial and failed to string the bow, so Odysseus asks that he may be allowed to try, but this enrages the wooers. Telemachus sends his mother from the hall to her upper chamber, and the bow is given to Odysseus, and the swineherd warns the nurse Euryclea to bar the doors of the women's chambers, and the neatherd hastes silently and closes the gates of the court. The stage is now set for the last act, and Odysseus takes up the great bow, and "even as when a man is skilled at playing the lyre and in song easily stretches a string about a new peg, tying the twisted sheep-gut at either end, even so did Odysseus straightway bend the great bow without effort, and taking it in his right hand he tested the bow-string, which hummed sweetly at his touch, in tone like a swallow". And great grief comes upon the wooers. Odysseus then takes one of the arrows, and "with straight aim let fly the arrow; not one of the axes did he miss; but starting from the first axe-handle, the bronze weighted shaft passed clean through and out at the last".

Then "Telemachus, the dear son of divine Odysseus, girt about him his sharp sword and took the spear in his grasp, and stood by the chair at his father's side armed with the gleaming bronze".

BOOK XXII—In the twenty-second book Odysseus strips off his rags and leaps to the great threshold with his bow and quiver full of arrows. With his first shot he kills Antinous, and the wooers searching for shields, or spears, find that these have been removed from the hall. Then Odysseus makes himself

29 Odysseus shooting the wooers

THE SLAYING OF THE WOOERS

known to them, and the killing proceeds apace. The wooers draw their swords and "pick up the tables to ward off the arrows of swift death".

Amphinomus now attacks Odysseus by the door, but Telemachus casts his spear and, killing him from behind, runs to his father.... Odysseus then sends

30 The slaying of the wooers

Telemachus for arms, and he goes "forth to the chamber where his famous weapons lay stored". There he takes four helmets and shields and eight spears. That is, a helmet and shield and two spears each for Odysseus, Telemachus, the swineherd, and the neatherd, who fight on their side.

Now, in the well-built wall there was a certain postern raised above the floor, and there, by the topmost level of the threshold of the stablished hall, was a way into a passage, shut by well-fitted folding doors. So Odysseus bade the goodly swineherd stand near by and watch this postern, for thither was there but one approach.

One of the wooers then asks if anyone can climb up to the postern, the ordinary approach being guarded, and raise a cry for assistance. Melanthius, the goatherd, who fights on the side of the wooers, thinks this is impossible, but volunteers to climb "by the clerestory of the hall to the inner chambers of Odysseus". There he finds twelve helmets, shields, and spears, and brings them back to the wooers. How he manages to get back we are not told. It was the same chamber, because Telemachus remembers that he left the door open. The door must have been visible from the hall, because Telemachus says that one of the wooers must have been quick enough to spy it. Melanthius makes another trip, and Eumæus and the neatherd are sent to catch him, which they do, and, after binding, pull him up and leave him dangling from the roof-beams.

Then Athene comes to the assistance of Odysseus, and "darted up into the roof timbers of the murky hall, like a swallow in

THE *ODYSSEY*

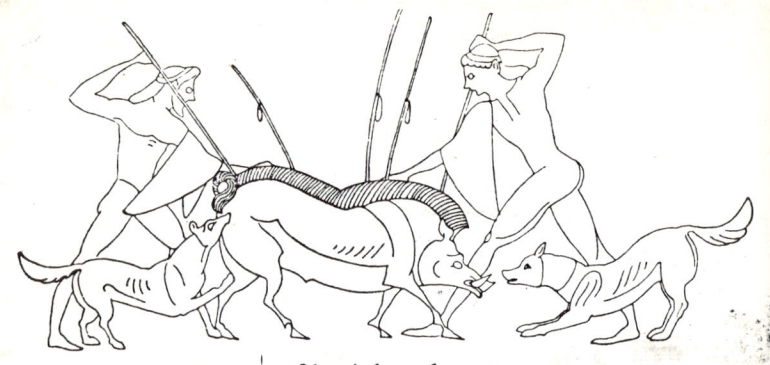

31 A boar hunt

its flight, and there sat down". And the wooers cast their spears in vain. Then the company of Odysseus "set upon the wooers, and right and left they smote them through the hall, and there a hideous moaning arose as their heads were smitten, and all the floor ran with blood".

Only the minstrel Phemius and the henchman Medon are spared, and go out and sit by the altar. Telemachus is sent to call the old nurse, Euryclea, and Odysseus tells her to send women to clean the hall, and as well demands the names of the maids who have dishonoured themselves with the wooers. Then Odysseus tells Telemachus to slay the maidens, and they were led forth from the stablished hall to a "narrow space between the vaulted chamber and the stout fence of the courtyard". A ship's cable was tied to a great pillar, and around the vaulted room, and nooses were placed around the necks of the women and they were hanged on the cable, and "for a little while they writhed with their feet, but not for long".

Then they washed and purified the house with burning sulphur, and "the adventure was over".

BOOK XXIII—In the twenty-third book the old nurse goes up to Penelope's chamber to tell her the good news of Odysseus' return, but Penelope thinks the nurse is distraught, and refuses to believe her. However, she goes down from her upper chamber and enters the hall by the threshold of stone, and sits down over against Odysseus in the light of the fire, and still finds it difficult to believe that this stranger in vile raiment can be her noble husband who left her twenty years before. Telemachus

ODYSSEUS REVEALED

32 Draughts

rebukes her for her doubt, and Odysseus waits for her to speak to him. Athene comes to his assistance, because, after he had bathed and taken new clothes, she sheds great beauty on him and restores his youth—so in the end Penelope knows that verily it is her own husband who has come back.

BOOK XXIV—In the morning Odysseus rouses Telemachus, the neatherd, and the swineherd, and goes to see his old father, Laërtes, who lives in a farm outside the city. "He was clothed in a filthy tunic, patched and unseemly, with cobbled leggings of oxhide bound about his shanks to guard against the scratches of the thorns, and long sleeves over his hands because of the brambles, and on his head he wore a goatskin cap." There they find him digging about a plant, and Odysseus makes himself known. Laërtes asks for a manifest token that he might be assured, and Odysseus shows him the scar from the boar's tusk, and the trees in the garden that were given to him when a child for his own. Then Laërtes knows that his son has come back, and they all go into his house and feast.

Meanwhile news of the slaughter of the wooers has got abroad, and their friends arm themselves to take vengeance on Odysseus. Here Homer must have been at some pains to round off his tale. It is quite obvious that there could be no more killing after the slaughter of the wooers; yet the vengeance of their friends must be satisfied. So the poet makes Athene speak to Father Zeus, who proposes that Odysseus shall be king all his days, and oblivion descend on the avengers so that they forget the slaying of their children and brethren. This would be a characteristically modern happy ending; but it would not have suited Homer's listeners. He makes the avengers start out against Odysseus, and they come to the house of Laërtes while the feast is in progress, and Odysseus and his son rise up and put on their harness, and the old man is happy and says: "What a day is this for me, ye kind gods; yea, a happy man am I! My son and my son's son are vying with one another in bravery."

And the grey-eyed goddess Athene takes compassion on Laërtes; she breathes into him great strength, and his age falls away from him. He is young once again, and catching up a spear hurls it at Eupeithes and kills him, and then, and not till then, is oblivion allowed to fall on all the people, so that they can live happily ever after.

Chapter IV
EVERYDAY THINGS

WE hope our outlines will be sufficient to give such of our readers as do not know the poems a general idea of the *Voyage of the Argonauts*, the *Iliad*, and the *Odyssey*. Just as the voyage was in all probability a poetical account of the search of early Bronze Age men for gold, so the *Iliad* may have been the history of a war waged for the purpose of trade.

If our map (Fig. 2) is consulted, it will be seen what an important position Troy occupied. It commanded the entrance to the Black Sea, and it may be that Greece imported corn from there in Homeric times, as she did later in the Peloponnesian War. Agamemnon perhaps was forced to attack Troy, because the Trojans were interfering with his food supplies. If, like the Greeks, we accept Homer as a historian, we must as well remember that he was a great poet, and his telling of a trade dispute had to be glorified by the radiance of Helen and her beauty. In the same way Odysseus could not sail straight back after the war. Poems were not written that way in olden days. Heroes went, willy-nilly, in search of adventure, and the poet had to give good measure and running over.

The date of the Trojan War is placed about 1200 B.C., that is, just before Greece was overrun by the Dorians from the north. These Dorians were fierce and warlike, and overthrew the civilisation which had been built up on the mainland of Greece after the fall of Cnossos. It was, in fact, a very close parallel to what happened to Romanised Britain, when we were invaded by the Angles, Saxons, and Jutes. Both the Dorians and the Saxons were unable to maintain the essential services of a highly organised State, so both periods were followed by Dark Ages, of which we know nothing at all.

We do not know when Homer lived or wrote, but in all probability it was about the ninth or tenth century B.C., when the Dark Age in Greece was coming to an end. His part was to gather all the legends together and form them into a glorious whole. He sang of a Golden and Heroic Age, and his poems,

EVERYDAY THINGS

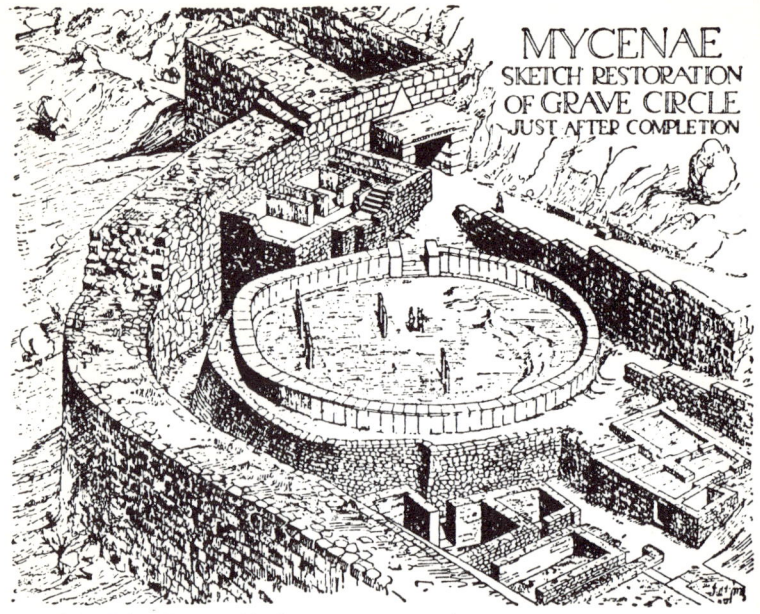

MYCENAE
SKETCH RESTORATION
OF GRAVE CIRCLE
JUST AFTER COMPLETION

33 The Grave Circle at Mycenæ. (Restored by De Jong.)

which became the Bible of the Greeks, must have played a great part in the wonderful renaissance of Classical times.

We have so far illustrated the incidents of the *Iliad* and *Odyssey* by drawings made from Greek vases. These have been drawn mostly from black-figure vases which date from the sixth century B.C. Our illustrations do not give our ideas, but show what the sixth-century Greek accepted as being right.

Now we propose to try to gather the details of everyday life together, and fit them against a background. We shall begin with those early buildings in Greece which, in architecture, are described as of the Mycenæan period.

If we enter Greece at the head of the Argolic Gulf, we come to a remarkable group of places. First, there is Tiryns, a fortified acropolis, then comes Argos, and at the head of the Argive Plain, Mycenæ, the home of Agamemnon. Here we shall find the celebrated Lion Gate, the shaft graves where Schliemann made his discoveries, and the so-called "Tomb of Agamemnon".

About the middle of the fifteenth century B.C. the Mycenæans built the Lion Gate and the circular wall on the left of Fig. 33.

MYCENÆ

This goes round the Grave Circle, in the middle of the picture, which enclosed the shaft graves where Schliemann made his great discovery. The date coincides with the fall of Cnossos and the end of the Cretan supremacy. It seems as if the Mycenæans were moved to protect graves that were already there, or which they constructed hastily to take bodies brought from the tombs outside the walls, like the "Tomb of Agamemnon" (35).

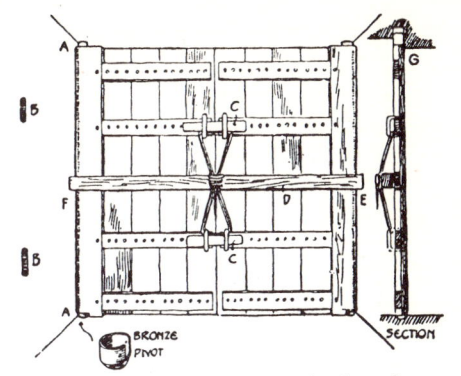

34 Reconstruction of the interior of the Lion Gate

Seventeen bodies were found in the Grave Circle at Mycenæ —eleven men and six women; they had been buried wearing much jewellery and their faces covered with golden masks.

The Lion Gateway is a wonderful architectural composition, expressing strength and dignity, and the lions, or rather, lionesses, are notable as being the first example of Greek sculpture. These have never been buried, and stand up as proudly today as they did when first put up. Originally the heads were probably of bronze, and fixed to the dowel holes which can be seen on the neck of the right-hand lion. The builders seem to have left a triangular void to keep the weight of the wall from the lintel under, and then have filled in the space with the lions as a decorative feature; but they need not have been alarmed, as the lintel is 16 ft. 6 in. long and 3 ft. 6 in. high and 8 ft. deep. The walling is called Cyclopean, because it seems as if it could only have been built by a race of gigantic Cyclopes like Polyphemus. It should be noted that between the lions a small column of Minoan character has been carved by the sculptor.

Fig. 34 is a reconstruction of the gateway inside. The wooden doors are not there now, but the pivot holes in which they turned are, and the bolt holes at E and F, and two other holes into which some form of staples closed when the doors were opened. There are references in the *Odyssey* which explain

EVERYDAY THINGS

the details. In the twenty-first book, when Odysseus is making his preparations for the slaying of the wooers, he sends the neatherd to bolt and bar the outer gate and tie the knot. The doors opened inwards into the gateway and, when shut, could not be pulled open the other way from the outside, because the lintel at G was dropped down and formed a stop to prevent this. The neatherd would have shut the doors against this stop and prevented them from blowing open again by putting the bolts at C through the staples. The bar D, which, when the door was open, was kept pushed back in a long hole in the wall at E, was then drawn out and fitted into a short hole on the other side at F, and then the knot was tied. The doors were made with projecting pins on them at AA. These were not very long, or it would not have been possible to get the door into place. If the top one were rounded, it could be persuaded to go into the top pivot hole, and then the whole door being lifted up, the bottom pin could be dropped into the bronze pivot. One like the sketch was found at Tiryns. Doors like this used to be made in England, and were called Harr-hung, and castle doors were always fastened with bars in the early Middle Ages.

The largest of the "beehive" tombs at Mycenæ, formerly called either the "Tomb of Agamemnon", or the Treasury of Atreus (his father), is really of much earlier date. The form of construction was borrowed from Crete. A long entrance passage was cut into the hill-side, with walls at the side, and the door into the tomb at the end. We have shown this in Fig. 35, with the columns which once flanked it; their intricate ornament of spirals and chevrons gives one some idea of the splendour of the tomb's entrance when first it was finished. Probably the triangular space was once filled with sculpture, as in the Lion Gate. It may give some idea of the scale of the entrance when we say that one of the lintel stones is 29 ft. 6 in. long by 16 ft. 6 in. wide by 3 ft. 4 in. high, and cannot weigh much less than 100 tons. There are pivot holes in the threshold and lintel, as at the Lion Gate, and the wooden doors were probably sheathed with bronze.

The entrance leads directly into a vault of about 48 ft. 6 in. diameter by 45 ft. 6 in. high, which, when you are inside, gives you an impression of much greater size. The dome is formed, not by arched stones whose joints radiate to the centre, but by

MYCENÆ AND TIRYNS

courses laid flat and corbelled over, until at last one stone covers the whole. The internal face was then cut down to the shape it now has, and as there are many dowel holes on this face, it is thought that bronze ornaments were applied originally. The stones, too, are not wedge-shaped on plan, so behind all the vertical joints there are spaces, and these have been taken by bees for their homes. On the right is a small doorway leading into a rectangular burial-chamber cut in the solid rock.

Now we come to one of the most interesting places in Greece—

35 The "Tomb of Agamemnon"

Tiryns. This, like Mycenæ, was excavated by Schliemann assisted by Dr. W. Dörpfeld in 1884 and 1885. Their work laid bare a splendid example of the fortified acropolis. This needs explanation, because it was a new type of building, and quite different from the palace of Cnossos built in a valley without fortifications. Because of the famous Acropolis at Athens, which seems to have been built to enshrine the Parthenon, we have come to think of an acropolis as being a sacred place, whereas the word only means a city on high. This is what the Acropolis at Athens was at first, and because of Schliemann and Dörpfeld's work at Tiryns, we are able to find out what these early fortified cities were like. It is quite obvious that if some of the details of Tiryns are Minoan in character, its general plan is conceived on entirely different lines, and that a different type of people lived there. If Cnossos is Southern, then Tiryns is Northern.

EVERYDAY THINGS

Again, though Ithaca on the west coast of Greece is supposed to have been the home of Odysseus, it is always Tiryns which is used to illustrate the *Odyssey*. It almost seems as if Homer had a somewhat simplified Tiryns in mind when he described Ithaca in his poems. He knew the place; in the second book of the *Iliad* he refers to "Tiryns of the great walls".

Schliemann's plans are generally used to illustrate the place, but as plans are not convincing to many people, we have built up a series of reconstructions based on this plan and our own survey of the site.

Fig. 36 gives a bird's-eye view. The ascending ramp is shown at 1, with a tower commanding the entrance at 2. This ramp is so planned that if besiegers used it to attack the city, their right side, which was not protected by their shields, would have been exposed to archers on the walls above. It must be remembered that Tiryns was a city, forming the headquarters of many hundreds of people. In the *Odyssey* the swineherd raised his swine, and Laërtes farmed outside the city. In times of stress they would have retired to it for protection, and driven their cattle into the outer bailey at 3. Here like a medieval castle, there would have been workshops and sheds and chambers in the walls, which are over 20 ft. thick. There is another strong gate at 4, which turned on pivots, and was fastened with a bar as the Lion Gate (34, 48). This led into a long, narrow court, with a colonnade at the top on the left-hand side, and opposite it, at 6, another gateway, or propylon; this had a central door with a porch on either side.

This gateway is of the greatest interest, because it is the type from which the great Greek gateways, like the Propylæa at Athens, were developed. Architects describe the plan of this gateway as being distyle in antis, meaning two columns standing between antæ. Antæ are pilasters on the side walls. From the inner porch of this gate a passage led to the women's quarters.

This gateway at Tiryns led to another court with colonnades or galleries at 5 around it. These apparently were used for tethering cattle in. In the twentieth book of the *Odyssey* the neatherd brings cattle for the feast, which are tethered carefully beneath the echoing gallery. If the swineherd brought some of his swine as well, one understands the echoing. In any case they would need to be kept close at hand, because they were

TIRYNS

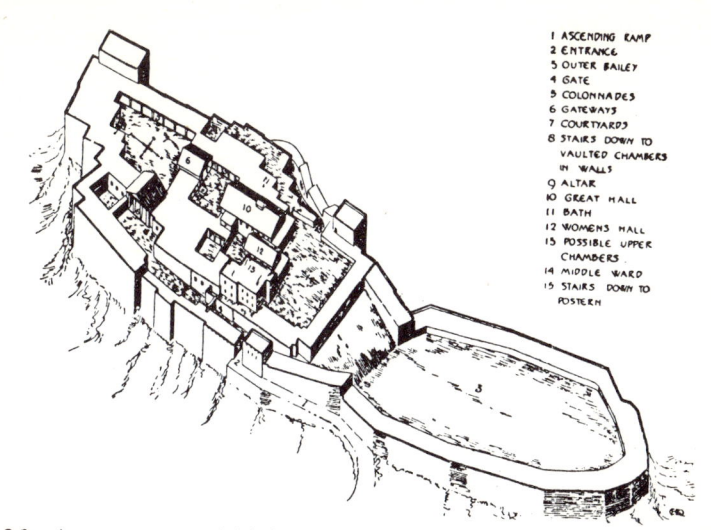

36 A reconstructed bird's-eye view of Tiryns from the north-east

Key:
1 ASCENDING RAMP
2 ENTRANCE
3 OUTER BAILEY
4 GATE
5 COLONNADES
6 GATEWAYS
7 COURTYARDS
8 STAIRS DOWN TO VAULTED CHAMBERS IN WALLS
9 ALTAR
10 GREAT HALL
11 BATH
12 WOMENS HALL
13 POSSIBLE UPPER CHAMBERS
14 MIDDLE WARD
15 STAIRS DOWN TO POSTERN

sacrificed just before the feast. Our readers must not be misled by our neat architectural drawings: Tiryns was probably a very untidy place in its prime. Geese lived in the court and pecked their wheat out of troughs, and the old hound Argos, who was the very first to recognise Odysseus, was found by his master lying on the dung of mules and kine. The light chariots would have been driven right up into the court. When Telemachus arrived at Sparta, they loosed the horses from under the yoke and fastened them in the stalls for the horses, giving them spelt and barley, and tilted the chariot against the gateway.

It was from this outer court that access was gained to the extraordinary vaulted corridors built under in the thickness of the walls. These were constructed, on the same principle as the "Tomb of Agamemnon" at Mycenæ, by the corbelling out of horizontal courses, and not on an arched principle (47).

We can now leave the outer court by another propylon on its north side, which led into the central court of the city. This had the Megaron, or Men's Hall, on its north side, with colonnades on the remaining sides. On the south of the court, on the axial line of the Megaron, was the altar. Here the animals were sacrificed, and their bodies, after due offerings had been made to the gods, taken into the hall to be cooked.

EVERYDAY THINGS

Fig. 37 shows the Megaron, which was the centre of the city, in more detail. The plan shows that the Megaron had three parts. First a porch, or portico, then a vestibule, and then the actual hall. Here there was a central fire; the chief sat on a seat at the side of the hall. We think it is probable that the vestibule had a gallery over it.

The position of the bath-house, on the west side of the hall, should be noted, and how it could be reached from the court, or the vestibule of the hall. Practically adjoining the men's hall, on the east side, came the women's hall, with its own court, and then on the east of this again the private chambers of the chief. There must have been a door at E, Fig. 37, with a guardroom at F, or Penelope would not have been able to make her frequent appearances in the hall at all conveniently. She could hardly have approached the hall by the line GH, though this would have been her way to the bath-house, or the stairs to the garden on the north, or the postern gate.

The retainers slept in the hall with their arms at hand, but Penelope sleeps in an upper chamber which may have been reached by stairs.

Fig. 38 shows the city from the south-west side. At 14 was a middle ward, or garden, which seems to have been for the private use of the chief. Access could only be gained to it by stairs from behind the men's hall, and a passage led to them from the women's quarters. Here Penelope may have walked, and Odysseus, if he so desired, could have left the city to go on a hunting expedition by the stairs to the postern gate at 15.

Having arrived ourselves outside the city again, we can pause to look at the walls. These were celebrated even in early times. Pausanias, who lived in the time of Marcus Aurelius, and wrote one of the earliest guide-books, complained that people in his time wrote of the Pyramids, and "Bestow not a word on the walls of Tiryns, which nevertheless are fully as deserving of admiration." The stones of these are of great size, many of them 6 to 9 ft. long by 3 ft. high and 3 ft. deep. They were roughly dressed and bedded in clay mortar. The rock on which Tiryns is built rises about 60 ft. above the plain. In the seventh book of the *Odyssey* we are told that the long, high walls of the town of the Phæacians were crowned with palisades.

We will now return to the Megaron. This appears to have

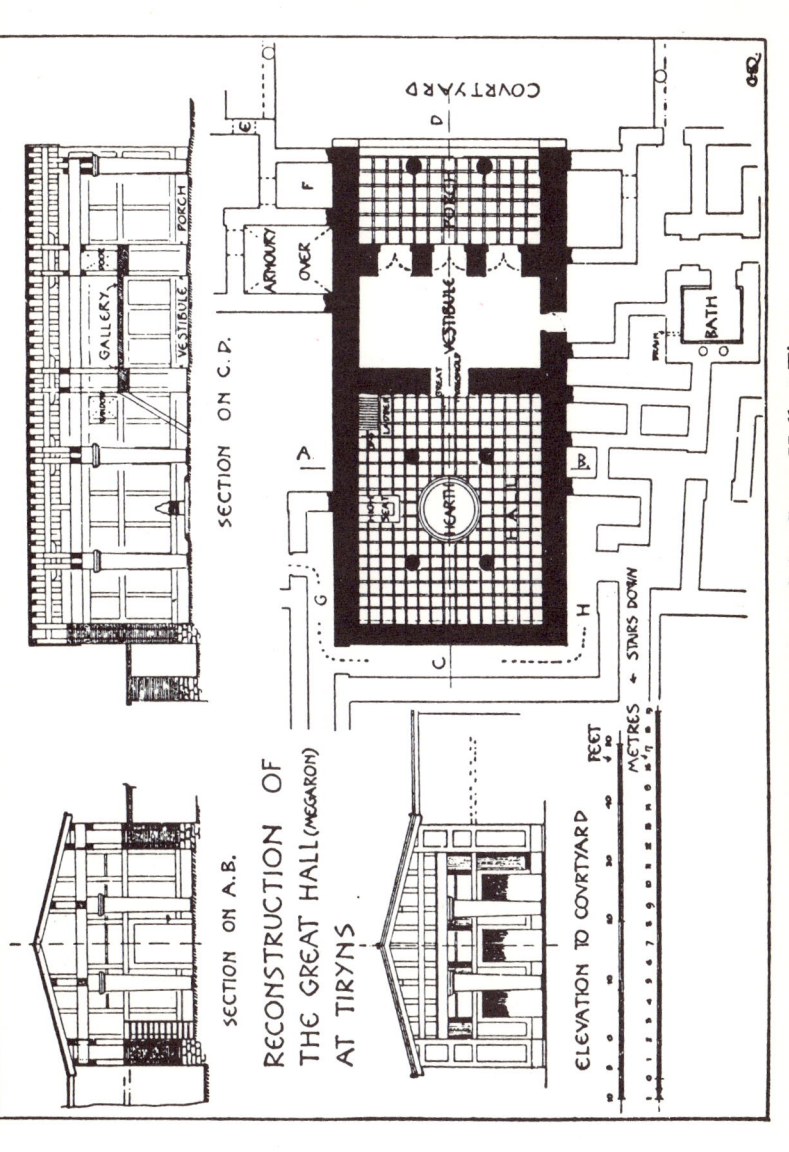

37 A reconstruction of the Great Hall at Tiryns

EVERYDAY THINGS

been framed in timber, built on the top of low masonry walls (see the sections of Fig. 37). In between the timber frames, bricks were filled in, and then the walls were plastered and decorated with wall-paintings. Fragments of these have been found. The roof over the hall and portico was supported on wooden columns, of which the bases remain. The floors were cast in concrete, divided up into squares by lines, and coloured blue and red. There were three doors from the portico to the vestibule, pivot hung, but the opening from the vestibule to the hall was apparently only screened by a curtain. Some say that the roof was flat, others that it was gabled. We incline to the latter view.

Fig. 39 gives our idea of what the interior of the Megaron looked like. It would, however, have been cluttered up with many more things than we have shown. The tall pillars would have had polished spear-stands against them, and other arms hanging on the walls. We know that Odysseus removed these before he started the slaying of the wooers. Around the walls were beds and seats with skin coverlets and three-legged tables set in front of them. Chests were used for storing clothes.

Visitors slept in bedsteads placed in the vestibule, under the echoing gallery. When Telemachus went to Sparta he slept in this way (*Odyssey*, IV). From here they could easily reach the bath-house in which a bath, as Fig. 42, stood. The bath water was heated in a great cauldron. Telemachus' chamber was described in the first book of the *Odyssey* as built high up in a fair court. He went to bed by the light of torches, and hung his tunic on a pin, and slept wrapped in a fleece of wool on a jointed bedstead. The old nurse Euryclea looks after him, and when she leaves closes the door, and then shuts it by pulling the thong outside. In the twenty-first book, when Penelope goes to find the bow of Odysseus, she takes the key, looses the strap, and, inserting the key, shoots the bolts. Fig. 28 explains this.

Fig. 43 shows the ingenious tapered drain-pipes which were used at Tiryns. They are not quite so modern as the circular-jointed and socketed pipes found at Cnossos.

Passing to food and feasting, we know that the sacrifice was an essential part of the ceremony, and much the same as our saying grace. The altar was in the court, immediately opposite the portico. Here the animals were killed with appropriate

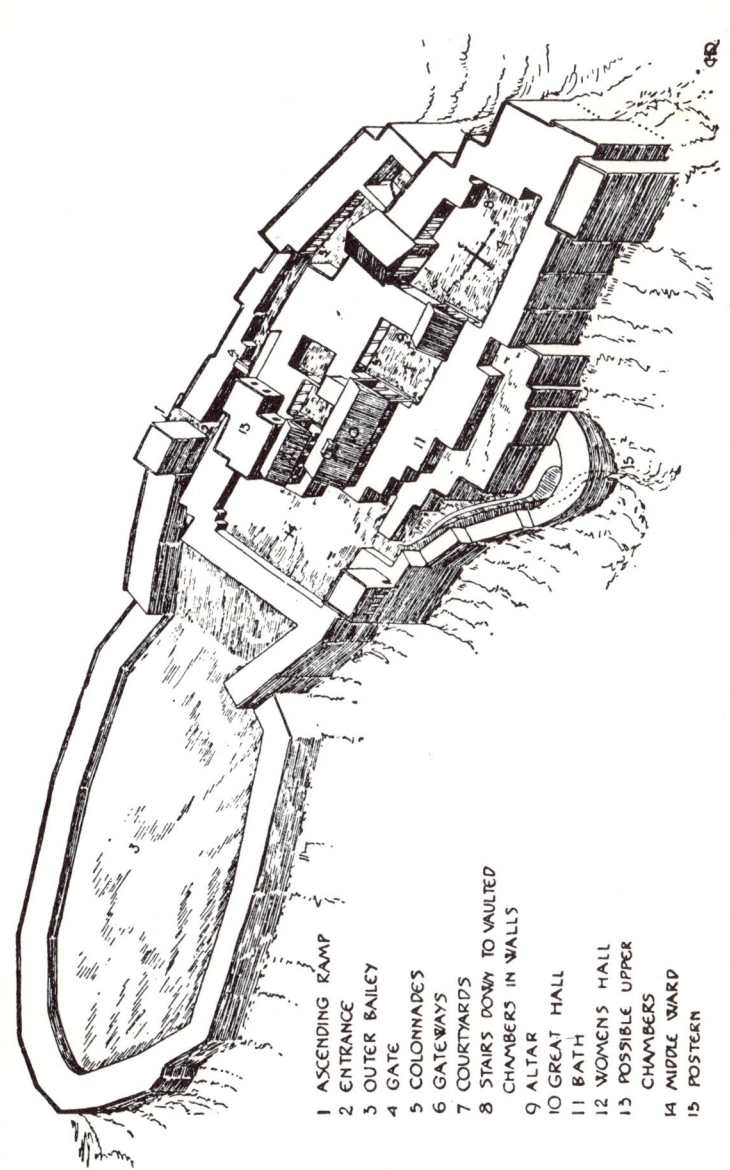

1 ASCENDING RAMP
2 ENTRANCE
3 OUTER BAILEY
4 GATE
5 COLONNADES
6 GATEWAYS
7 COURTYARDS
8 STAIRS DOWN TO VAULTED CHAMBERS IN WALLS
9 ALTAR
10 GREAT HALL
11 BATH
12 WOMENS HALL
13 POSSIBLE UPPER CHAMBERS
14 MIDDLE WARD
15 POSTERN

38 A reconstructed bird's-eye view of Tiryns from the south-west

EVERYDAY THINGS

ceremony, and offerings made to the gods. Portions of flesh were then brought into the hall and roasted on spits in front of the large central fire of cedar and sandalwood. Here they cooked their black puddings made of blood and fat put into the paunch of an animal. These were roasted, not boiled. The women ground barley and wheat in hand-mills to make the meal which was the marrow of men. When Telemachus sailed to Pylos, he took as food olive-oil, wine, and barley-meal. In the fourth book are details of the meal he received when he arrived at Sparta.

In the twentieth book it is interesting to read how they sprinkled the hall and swept it, and wiped the tables clean with sponges, and cleaned the bowls.

Homer gives us many details of the household duties of women. It was Nausicaa who took the family washing down to the stream, and it was cleansed there by being vigorously trodden in trenches. In the twenty-second book of the *Iliad* we are told that the women of Troy did their washing in troughs of stone beside the stream. They would not have had soap, and probably used something like fuller's earth to assist in the cleansing.

Again, women had to make the clothes. The first operation was to cleanse the fleece and then dye it. The wool was then teased or pulled into fluff. Carding came after, and this was like combing it, so that the fibre of the fluff was arranged as lengthways as possible. Fig. 23 is of a curious, but very beautiful, piece of pottery thought to have been used in connection with spinning. It was made so that it could be fitted over the knee. The original is in the British Museum. The little sketch, from a vase drawing, shows it in use, with a basket at the side. Then came the spinning, which was the occupation of the spinsters. Fig. 24, from a black-figure vase, shows how this was done. The spindle was a piece of polished wood, about 12 in. long and $\frac{1}{2}$ in. diameter, and a little from the bottom came the whorl, which helped to spin it. The distaff was held in the left hand, or more usually under the left arm, and had some of the carded wool placed on it. A little of this was drawn out and twisted by hand until it was long enough to fix in a nick at the top of the spindle. This was then spun round by the wool, and as it spun more wool was paid out, and so twisted into yarn. This was then wound on to the spindle, and the operation of spinning continued. In

WOMEN'S WORK

39 A reconstruction of the interior of the Megaron at Tiryns

the fourth book of the *Odyssey* we find that Helen had a golden distaff with violet-blue wool, and a silver basket that ran on wheels was filled with dressed yarns. In the sixth book Nausicaa's mother sits by the hearth with her maids, spinning yarn of sea-purple stain.

There are many references to weaving in Homer. The weavers stood in front of the loom and moved to and fro before it, using a weaving rod at breast height and passing the spool along the warp threads. Penelope seems to have used a warp-weighted loom (Fig. 25 shows a reconstruction of this type from a Greek vase drawing). The vertical threads are the warp, and the horizontal ones—which go over and under the warp threads—are the woof. How this was done is shown on the sections at the side of Fig. 25. The warp threads hang down from a roller, on to which the work is wound as it is finished. The warp threads are divided by what is called a shed-stick at A. This gives a space through which the shuttle carrying the woof threads can be passed, but these latter have to be alternated between each passing of the shuttle. This was done by the heddle-stick C, which was attached by loops to alternate warp strings, and was pulled out for one passing of the shuttle, and then allowed to fall back for the next.

EVERYDAY THINGS

The material which was woven on the looms was made up into clothes without very much cutting. There are not very many references to clothes in Homer. When Odysseus is telling the swineherd of his adventures, he mentions how, on a night expedition, the men wore mantles and tunics, and slept with their shields buckled to their shoulders, and they had leathern aprons in addition. Again, when Odysseus first meets Penelope, after his return, and before he has made himself known to her, he pretends that he has met Odysseus on his travels. Penelope, to test him, asks what Odysseus was wearing, and is told that he had a mantle which was twofold and fastened with a gold brooch, with two sheaths for the pins. The brooch had a device on it of a hound holding in its paws a dappled fawn. Under the mantle a doublet or tunic was worn.

The women's dress would have been much the same as shown on the later Archaic Greek statues. The under-tunic was known as the chiton. This was simply a plain piece of woven material, about the height of the woman, and twice the span of her arms. The top third was folded over, and then the material, being doubled, was slipped over the shoulders and fastened with brooches.

If Homer says little about clothes, he makes up for this by giving very full descriptions of armour. These correspond well with the unique bronze armour of 1450–1400 B.C. found at Dendra in the Peloponnese. In the third book of the *Iliad* details are given of the armour worn by Paris for his fight with Menelaos. Paris put on his greaves first. These were thin sheets of bronze, hammered to the shape of the leg, but open at the back so that they could be slipped on. The elasticity of the metal held them in place. The cuirass, or corselet, was formed of two sheets of bronze fastened together at the sides.

Homer's descriptions agree very closely with the armour shown on the figure from Dodona (8). This shows the early form of Corinthian helmet, with a nasal guard and cheek-pieces. The shield of Homer's time was made of bull's hide. The Dodona figure is carrying what is known as the Bœotian shield, the shape of which is thought to have been formed by stretching a hide on to a frame made with rounded cross-bars at top and bottom fixed to a central bar. The leather at the sides, not having the support of any frame, shrunk, and gave the shield its typical shape.

CLOTHES. ARMOUR

Fig. 40 illustrates some bronze arms from the British Museum of the Mycenæan period, that is, the civilisation which was developed on the mainland of Greece after the fall of Crete. The sword is very beautiful. The spearheads are very like those used in England during our own Bronze Age. Both in the *Iliad* and *Odyssey* the arms are described as being made of bronze, and iron is referred to as if it was rare and costly. In Homer's own time it must have been in common use. It first began to be used in Greece about 1200 B.C., or 750 years before it was introduced into Britain.

The method of fighting described in Homer is quite different from that of Classical times, of which we read in the pages of Thucydides. In the fourth book of the *Iliad* Nestor put the charioteers in the front rank, and behind them came the infantry. The cowards were thrust into the middle. The charioteers appear to have whirled about, and the battle speedily resolved itself into a series of combats between champions. It was only by happy accident that such a method of fighting could lead to any decision; perhaps that is why the Trojan War lasted for so many years.

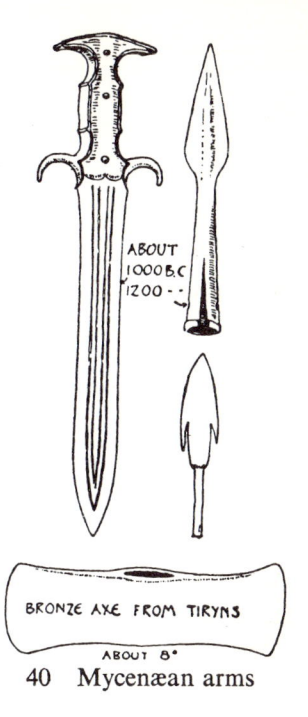

This had been realised by the time of Thucydides, and in the battle he describes, the opponents formed up into line and trusted to sheer weight and fighting power. The danger of this method was that the right wing of each line tended to edge away, because the shield, being carried on the left arm, left the right side exposed, and the tendency was to move to the right; so each left wing ran the danger of being outflanked.

Bowmen were used in Homeric times. In the fourth book of the *Iliad* we hear of Pandaros and his bow, made from ibex horns, sixteen palms in length, cunningly joined together. This does not mean that the bow was made by joining the two horns'

40   Mycenæan arms

ends together in bow form. Obviously a bow so formed could not have been bent. It is thought that the Homeric bow was a composite type, of Cupid's bow form, used in a wide area of Asia from China to Turkey. It was made as Fig. 7. The core was of wood, and on this strips of horn were built up on the inside of the bow. On the outside were layers of sinew protected by a sheathing of bark or leather. When the bow was not strung, it curved out as the dotted lines on the drawing at the side. That is why Penelope refers to the back-bent bow of Odysseus. The horn was strong to resist compression, and the sinew stood tension well. Odysseus left his bow at home; the damp of the sea air would have destroyed it. When the wooers tried to string the bow, Antinous told the goatherd to light a fire and bring a ball of lard, because he thought that the heat and the grease would soften the bow. The figure in the drawing shows how Odysseus did at last string it.

The bow of Odysseus was produced so that Penelope might make trial of the suitors. Telemachus arranges the trial. First he dug a trench and then set up the twelve axes, like the oaken props used in shipbuilding, and made straight the line and stamped down the earth. The suitors cannot even string the bow, and then Odysseus takes and both strings it and shoots the arrow through the axes. This had been a favourite feat of his before he went to the war, and Penelope institutes the trial to find if any of the wooers was as good a man as her husband.

How were the axes arranged? The answer lies in the words, "like props in shipbuilding".

Fig. 27 shows how these props must incline together. The ship of Homeric times was probably built on a slipway in the open. The keel would have been laid down first, and then the stem and stern posts fitted. The next step was to place moulds on the keel and strut these into position. Some few of the planks were fixed to the moulds, and then the ribs were fitted and the moulds could be removed. Homer must have had some such picture as this in his mind, and if this were so, the axes could have been set as A, Fig. 27, and the arrow shot between the space B or C. The axe-head shown in A, Fig. 27, is of the type shown in Fig. 40, which was found at Tiryns.

We can now discuss the chariot which was used both in war and in times of peace. Nestor placed the charioteers in the

BOWS. CHARIOTS

front rank of battle, and Telemachus travelled by chariot to Sparta. Perhaps the best description of it is given in the fifth book of the *Iliad*. When Hera went to the assistance of the Greeks, she harnessed the horses with their golden frontlets.

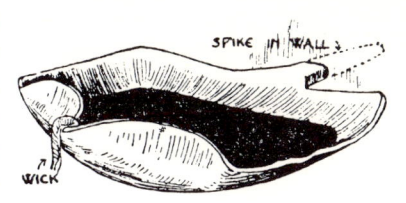

41 Mycenæan bronze lamp from Cyprus

The chariot had eight-spoked brazen wheels, with golden felloes (rims), bronze tyres, and silver naves (hubs), with iron axle-trees. The body of the car was woven plaitwork to lessen the jolting, and had two rails about it. A silver pole stood out from the car, and the first step seems to have been to fasten the golden yoke on top at the end of the pole and put the breast-straps over it. Then the horses were led under the yoke.

In the twenty-fourth book of the *Iliad* details are given of the mule chariot which carried the ransom of Hector to Achilles. In this the body of the chariot was detachable and had to be bound to the frame. The yoke had a knob and was well fitted with guiding rings. There was a yoke-band, 9 cubits long (about 13 ft.). The yoke was set up on the rest at the end of the pole, and a ring slipped over the upright pin, which was part of the pole. Three turns of the yoke-band bound the upright pin on the pole to the knob on the yoke, and then it was belayed round the pole; but the whole 9 cubits would not have been used in this way, and it seems to us that the remainder may have been used as a stay from the head of the pole back to the chariot. On the vase drawings there is always a line in the position shown by A on Fig. 9. In the seventeenth book, yoke cushions are mentioned to keep the yoke from chafing the shoulders of the horses. Usually there were two horses to the chariot. Telemachus had a pair on his journey to Sparta, as did the charioteers in the funeral games of Patroklos, which are described in the twenty-third book of the *Iliad*. By the time of the sixth-century black-figure vases, four horses are generally shown, as the diagram B, Fig. 9. Here it seems as if only the inner pair of horses were yoked, and the question arises, how were the outside pair harnessed? Modern sculptors generally get over the difficulty by using traces with collars, swingle trees, and cross-bars, as C,

EVERYDAY THINGS

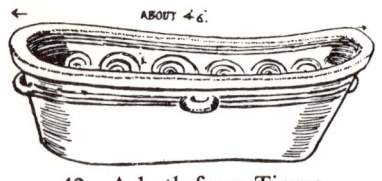

42 A bath from Tiryns

Fig. 9; but there is no evidence for such an arrangement on the black-figure vases, and it would be too heavy and clumsy to be connected to the slight frame of the chariot.

The black-figure vases, when they show four-horsed chariots from the front, give details of the reins, and what seems to be a trace marked by a cross on B, Fig. 9. This appears on the side views as coming between the first and second, and the third and fourth horses, and is then attached to the front of the chariot, as at D, Fig. 9. A short strap from the top of the breast-strap of the trace-horse to the end of the yoke would have prevented it from parting company with its fellows.

Trace-horses are mentioned in the sixteenth book of the *Iliad*, but, curiously enough, only single ones. Patroklos bids Automedon to yoke the horses, Xanthos and Balios, and put Pedasos in the side traces. Pedasos was killed in the battle, and fell shrieking in the dust, and the other two reared up and the yoke creaked. This seems to bear out the suggestion we have made. It should be noted that the chariot had a very wide wheel base to prevent it overturning when being driven at speed.

There are many references in the poems to games. The wooers of Penelope played draughts sitting on oxhides. Another of their diversions was casting weights and spears. When Telemachus visited Menelaos at Sparta, he found a feast in progress in the hall, and part of the entertainment was two tumblers, who whirled to the accompaniment of a minstrel singing to the lyre.

We have already written on p. 40 of Nausicaa playing ball, and on p. 41 of how games of running, wrestling, and boxing were arranged as part of the entertainment of Odysseus by the Phæacians. Here it was that Odysseus distinguished himself by casting a great stone.

We hear of fishermen who, sitting on jutting rocks, cast their lines into the sea, using rods with bent hooks of horn or bronze, and lead weights to carry them down.

Having by now obtained an idea of the kind of life which was lived in the cities—and by cities we mean such places as Tiryns,

GAMES. COUNTRY LIFE

Mycenæ, or Athens as it was at first—we can turn to country life. This was to remain as a healthy feature of life in Greece. A man civilised himself by living in a city and rubbing shoulders with his fellows, but he continually recreated himself by farming in the country.

In the twenty-fourth book of the *Odyssey*, Odysseus goes to make himself known to his father, Laërtes, at his farm, where he had built himself a house with huts for his thralls round about it. This had a great garden and a terraced vineyard. Odysseus reminds his father of the trees which were his own when he was a little child; of how he had thirteen pear trees, ten apple trees, forty figs, and forty rows of vines.

There is an excellent description in the fourteenth book of the *Odyssey* of the house the swineherd built for himself. This was built high, in a place with a wide prospect, and had a porch before it, and was set in a great courtyard fenced with white thorn set on a stone base. Outside was another fence, and inside the courtyard were twelve sties, with fifty wallowing swine in each.

This sounds as if the swineherd's house was like the small terra-cotta model of a house found in an eighth-century B.C. burial at Argos. We have attempted to reconstruct it in words. Its date, the eighth century B.C., places it between the fourteenth-century Megaron at Tiryns and the fifth-century Parthenon at Athens, and there is a more intimate connection between the three buildings than is at first apparent. The Megaron at Tiryns was once the home of living men: the Argos Hut was the home of a dead man, and the Parthenon the home of a god, not a church in which a congregation gathered. The three buildings all have the same central hall, with its portico, or porch, outside, and they belong to the same building tradition, and all had sloping roofs. This method of building, which was started by the Achæan builders at Tiryns, survived in the Greek temple and can be traced under the architectural forms of the

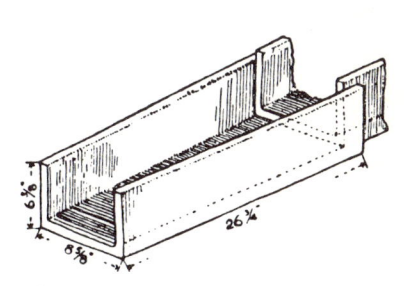

43 Tapered terra-cotta drain-pipes from Tiryns

EVERYDAY THINGS

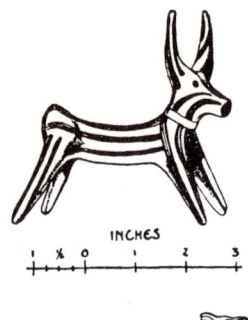

early Roman Basilican churches. It did not survive in the Roman house, but was introduced into England in all its original simplicity by the Saxons. From their time on we became dwellers in halls, like the men at Tiryns, until the Renaissance in the sixteenth century A.D.

There is another description in the twenty-fourth book of the *Iliad* of the lofty hut which the Myrmidons built for Achilles. This was constructed of pine and thatched with rush cut in the meadows. It was set in a great palisaded court with a gateway. The door in the gate was closed with a bar so large that it took three men to draw it.

44 Mycenæan figures

Hesiod is very useful in helping us to understand the references to agriculture in the *Iliad* and *Odyssey*. His poems date from about 750 to 700 B.C., and his great work was *The Works and Days*, addressed to his younger brother, Perses. Hesiod wrote also a *Theogony*, which, together with Homer's poems, seem to have fixed the popular idea of the gods and their life and work. First came Zeus who was the supreme god; he was the son of Cronos and Rhea, and Hera was his wife. He concerned himself with the affairs of men, and his sign is a thunderbolt. Hera was the women's goddess, and is generally drawn wearing a high decorated crown.

Poseidon, Hades, Hestia, and Demeter were the brothers and sisters of Zeus. Poseidon was the god of the sea. He married Amphitrite, and is shown standing with trident and tunny. Hades was the god of the dead, and married Persephone. Hestia was the goddess of the hearth. Demeter was the corn spirit. Athene was born from the head of Zeus, and her birth was a favourite subject with the vase painters. She is shown bearing the ægis (see p. 20). She was the genius of the arts. Apollo was the god of light, and is usually shown with a bow and lyre. Artemis was his feminine counterpart, and carries a bow and

HESIOD

quiver. Hermes was the messenger of the gods and has the herald's staff; Dionysus, the god of the vine and vegetation. Aphrodite was the goddess of love, with Eros as her attendant. Hephæstos was the god of fire and smiths, and Ares of war. It was not necessary to have a priest to intercede with the gods. Anyone could pray to them, though in the house it was the head of the family who officiated at the sacrifice, and the hearth was the place where prayers were offered. The hearth was a sacred place, and the cities had their common hearths.

45 Mycenæan pottery

The Romans inherited their gods from the Greeks: Zeus became their Jupiter, and Hera, Juno; Poseidon, Neptune; Hades, Pluto; Hestia, Vesta; Demeter, Ceres; Athene, Minerva; Artemis, Diana; Hermes, Mercury; Dionysus, Bacchus; Persephone, Proserpina; Aphrodite, Venus; Hephæstos, Vulcan; and Ares, Mars.

Returning to Hesiod's *The Works and Days* for practical information, we find that when the sailor-farmer had laid up his boat for the winter, he started his ploughing in November. Perses was told that, if he wished to be successful, he must plough stripped, sow stripped, and reap stripped. The ground was ploughed again in the spring, and tilled again in the summer. This, of course, applied to the land which was left fallow, and explains the reference in the fifth book of the *Odyssey* to the thrice-ploughed fallow field.

Hesiod describes two ploughs. In one the plough-tail, or handle, was in one piece with the share-beam. In the other the share-beam of oak, and the plough-tail of ilex, and the pole of bay, or elm, were all jointed together. Homer talks of the jointed plough. The pole had an oaken peg driven through the end of it, and the yoke was attached to this by a leather strap. Mules are recommended as being better than oxen, and forty as being the ideal age for a ploughman; his food, a loaf four-square divided into eight parts. Seed was sown by a man

46 Ploughing

following the plough and covered up by a boy with a mattock. The mattock is still used in Italy and Greece, and is rather like a big hoe; another type resembles a garden-fork set on its handle like a hoe. A mattock today in England is like a pick-axe in form, only the points of the pick are chisel shaped, one on the same line as the handle and the other at right angles to it. In the eighth book of the *Odyssey* the length of the furrow that mules could plough in a fallow field without a pause—a furlong—is used as a measurement. There is another reference in the twelfth book of the *Iliad* to men using measuring-rods in a field; the rod, pole, or perch was to become a very common unit.

The harvest was gathered at the beginning of May, and the reaping done, not with a scythe but a sickle.

Corn, beans, and peas were threshed by being trodden out by oxen on a threshing-floor. A windy day was selected for winnowing, and this was done by throwing up husks and grain with a broad shovel. The husks were carried to one side by the wind, while the grain fell down on to the floor.

The farm servants were to be encouraged to build their cabins during the summer. It was only after the harvest that the farmer, according to Hesiod, could allow himself any leisure, and then he suggests a picnic in the shade of the rocks, with a light, well-baked cake, goats' milk, and the flesh of a heifer or kid. Biblian wine is recommended, but one cup of wine had three cups of water added to it. The vines were pruned in early spring, and

47 (*left*) Tiryns: a gallery in the thickness of the wall

48 (*right*) The Lion Gate at Mycenæ

49 Vaphio Cup (see p. 12)

50 Nestor's Cup (see p. 24)
From the reproductions in the British Museum

FARMING

hay and litter for bedding gathered between the harvest and the vintage in September. The grapes were exposed to the sun for ten days, then shaded for five, then trodden in the winepress, and drawn off into vats.

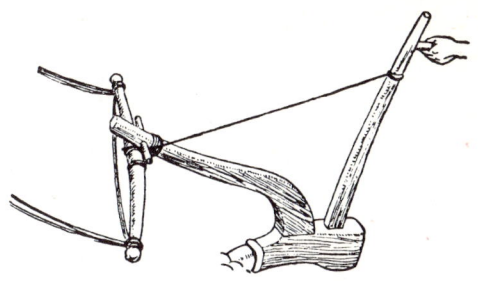

51 Modern Algerian plough, resembling a Homeric one

In the autumn timber was felled, and wooden mortars and pestles made, and axle-trees for wagons, and wooden mallets and wheels for the plough-carriages. Curved pieces of ilex were sought for plough-tails. The axe, the adze, and auger are the tools mentioned as given by Calypso to Odysseus for the building of his raft (p. 38). They would have been made of bronze, as were the tools used by the builders of Mycenæ and Tiryns. The axe was the carpenter's tool right up to the sixteenth century in England. The first plane we know of was the Roman one found at our own Silchester. There is another interesting tool mentioned in the *Odyssey*—the drill which Odysseus used to bore out the eye of Polyphemus. This was turned by a strap, so the rotary movement was on the same principle as the bow-drill used as early as the Old Stone Age, from which the pole-lathe developed, which was used in the Early Iron Age.

Ploughing started again in November.

It is difficult to find out how people clothed themselves in Homeric times, because there are not any illustrations. The black-figure vases, to take one example, show the figures in the costume of the sixth century. Hesiod describes the winter dress of an eighth-century farmer. A frock reaching to the ground and a soft cloak over, woven with a scant warp (the longitudinal threads) and an abundant woof (the cross threads). Sandals were made of oxhide and lined with felt. During wet weather outer cloaks were worn, made of the skins of first-born kids, stitched together with ox-sinew, and on the head a well-wrought felt hat.

Homer tells us how leather was cured. The hide of a great

EVERYDAY THINGS

bull was soaked in fat, the farm people then all stood round in a circle, and, taking the hide up, pulled it out as much as they could. This opened up all the pores of the skin and allowed the moisture to drip out and the fat to sink in.

Hesiod thought that the farmer should not marry before he is thirty, and gives nineteen as a good age for the wife; and he would have to purchase her. Iphidamas, killed by Agamemnon in the Trojan War, gave 100 sheep and promised 1,000 goats and sheep for his wife. The farmer is advised not to cross rivers until he has prayed and washed his hands in its waters. When building a house, you must not leave it unfinished, lest the cawing crow should perch on it and croak. Then various jobs were much better done on certain days in the month. The first, fourth, and seventh days were holy days. The eleventh day was good for shearing sheep, the twelfth for reaping corn; this day, too, a woman could set up her loom. You had to avoid sowing on the thirteenth day, but you could set plants. You could thresh on the well-rounded threshing-floor on the seventeenth, and this day was good as well for making furniture and ships, and so on.

Hesiod tells us that ships were not only used for war and expeditions, but for trade as well. The harvest was finished by the beginning of May, and then came the sailing season, when the farmer could take his corn by sea to the market; a much better way than by land, if the rough roads went over mountain ranges. The farmer had to be back by September for the vintage. Hesiod recommended that when ploughing began in November the ships should be drawn up on land, the keel-plug drawn out, and then covered up with stones to keep off the wind and rain. The rudder was taken indoors and hung up in the smoke of the fire.

The ship was of so much importance to Greece that we must give it some consideration. The Homeric ship probably resembled the one shown on a late Geometric style vase in the British Museum, which dates from about 800 B.C. We have attempted a reconstruction of this in Fig. 52. The vase shows a forty-oared galley, rather larger than the one in which Telemachus went to Pylos, which had only twenty oarsmen. Another interesting detail is that on the bowl the captain is shown clasping the wrist of a wasp-waisted lady who holds a wreath.

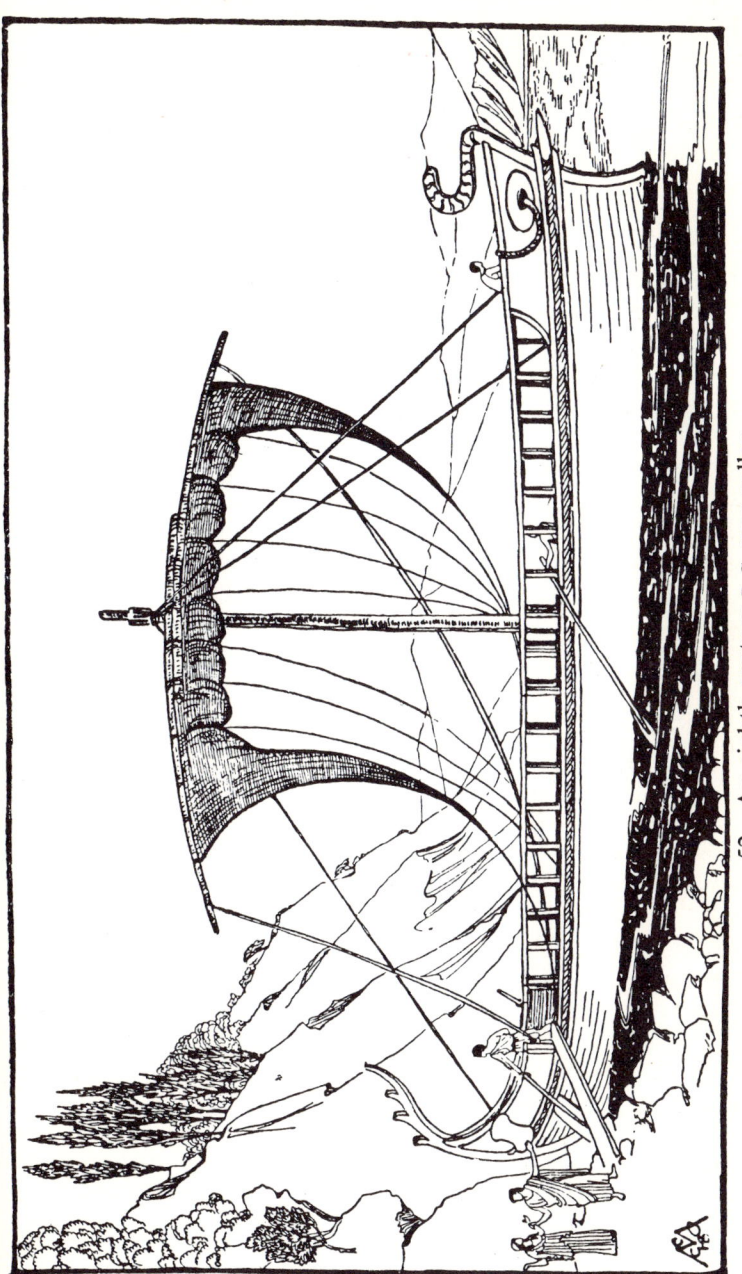

52 An eighth-century B.C. war galley
Reconstructed from a drawing on a vase in the British Museum

EVERYDAY THINGS

Penelope says in the eighteenth book of the *Odyssey*: "Ah, well do I remember when he [Odysseus] set forth and left his own country, how he took me by the right hand at the wrist and spake. . . ."

Many details of the Homeric ship are given in the poems. The mast was made of pine, and it was raised and set in a hole in a cross-plank and had two forestays and backstays, the ropes were made of twisted oxhide, and there was one square sail. The oars, which were used when the winds were contrary, were fixed in leather loops. Sails were shortened by brailing. Thucydides says that the boats of the Trojan expeditions had no decks, and were like pirate ships. He probably meant no raised decks. There must have been something in the nature of a floor under the benches. The space under the rowing benches was used too; Odysseus put the gifts of the Phæacians there. (See p. 74 for details of shipbuilding.) The Homeric Greeks had a system of lighthouses or beacon fires. In the eighteenth book of the *Iliad* a simile is used of a line of beacon fires to warn the dwellers around that their help is needed.

PART II
Archaic Greece

II. ARCHAIC PERIOD

	Current Events	Literature	Science	Art
		Solon, 639–559		c. 620, Heræum-Olym
			624–546. Thales of Miletus	590. Temple of Apollo-Syrac
				580. Olympieum-Syrac
560	Crœsus, King of Lydia		566. Glaucus of Chios invents iron welding	570. Selinus
	Ionian Greek cities reduced to dependence by Crœsus			550. Selinus
553	Cyrus revolts against Astyages			
550	Cyrus overthrows the Medes	Æsopus (Fables) at Court of Crœsus	551. Anaximander of Miletus, geographer	Harpies' Tomb fr Xanthos, Lycia Asia Minor
547	Cyrus conquers Lydia			
545	Cyrus conquers Ionian cities		540. Anaximenes of Miletus	
				c. 540. Temple at Seli
544	Phocæans leave Ionia			c. 540. Temple at Pæst
538	Cyrus takes Babylon		572–496. Pythagoras of Samos	c. 540. Temple at Cori
529	Cambyses succeeds Cyrus on Persian throne			c. 530. Temple at Selir
525	Persians conquer Egypt	Æschylus born		c. 527. Temple at Ath
522	Death of Cambyses			520. Temple at Pæst
521	Dareius becomes King of Persia			
520	Cleomenes, King of Sparta			
517	Persians conquer Barca	518. Birth of Pindar		515. Athenian T sury, Del
514	Scythian expedition of Dareius			510. Acragas-Herac
507	Cleomenes at Athens			
499	Failure of Naxian expedition			
498	Sardis burnt	496. Birth of Sophocles		
493	Persians take Chios, Lesbos, Tenedos	Phrynichus fined		
	Themistocles fortifies the Peiræus			
	Expedition of Mardonius			
491	Persians defeated at Marathon			489. Ægina-Aphæ
487	Egypt revolts			485. Syracuse-Athe
485	Death of Dareius	484. Birth of Herodotus		
480	Salamis	Birth of Euripides		
479	Battle of Platæa			

Chapter V

HERODOTUS AND HIS HISTORY

THE date of the Golden Age of the Trojan War was about 1192–1183 B.C. We wish now to trace what happened between this time and the Battle of Salamis in 480 B.C., when the Greeks defeated the Persians. This battle was very important, because it marked the beginning of the great Classical period in Greece.

After the Trojan War, Agamemnon and his men returned to Mycenæ, and Odysseus to Penelope in Ithaca. About 1100 B.C. there appear to have been disturbances in Thessaly and the regions to the north of Greece. Perhaps news reached the people there of the wealth of Mycenæ. These new-comers were the Dorians, and they descended on Mycenæan Greece from the north, in much the same way as our own Anglo-Saxons did on Roman Britain, and being rough and rude people were quite unable to maintain the Mycenæan civilisation.

So a dark age descended on Greece, and the original inhabitants fled across the Ægean Sea to Asia Minor, where they settled in Æolia and Ionia.

They went as fugitives, and Herodotus tells us that those who came from Athens, and considered themselves the purest Ionians, did not, or could not, take their wives with them, but married and carried off Carian girls, after having killed their fathers. For this reason, the wives bound themselves by oath "that none should ever sit at meat with her husband, or call him by his name".

The next important date is about the tenth or ninth century B.C., when Homer was writing his poems, and not only laying the foundations of literature in Western Europe, but inspiring the scattered Greeks to rise again. It is probable that Homer was himself an Ionian, and wrote for his fellow-countrymen of the glorious life led by their forefathers in the homeland of Greece before their flight.

Without this knowledge of a glorious past, and the feeling that they were descended from heroes, they could not have

HERODOTUS AND HIS HISTORY

emerged from the darkness of the age which followed the overthrow of the Mycenæan civilisation, or have steeled themselves to meet the Persians at Salamis and defeat them, nor would they have been able to build once more another and yet more glorious civilisation in the age of Pericles.

By the eighth century B.C. the Greek colonies in Asia Minor were so well established that Ephesus, Miletus, Smyrna, and Phocæa were great cities.

After a while the Dorians who had settled in Greece began to send out emigrants. The small Greek city-State was rather like a beehive. When its population increased, and food supplies began to fail, a swarm was sent out to find a new home. They were a seafaring people, like our own Vikings, so they took their ships and sailed away to the islands and coast lands of the Mediterranean and the Black Sea, and settled down and founded colonies in the Cyclades, Corcyra (Corfu), and Crete, in Sicily and South Italy, and many other places. In their travels they learned much from the older civilisations of the Near East.

Then some of them returned to Greece. The father of Hesiod, the poet who was thought worthy to rank with Homer, came from Æolia in Asia Minor and settled in Bœotia.

By 776 the Greeks of the homeland and the colonies had so far come together that they were able to hold a great festival at Olympia, and of what this meant we shall write later.

The stage is now set for the introduction of one of the first great characters in Greek history, Herodotus of Halicarnassus, in Caria, Asia Minor, born about 484 B.C., the father and first of all the historians. Like many Greeks, he was forced to fly from his own city, and set out on travels which led him to the island of Samos, to Egypt, and then, in the time of Pericles, to Athens. He was writing his history as late as 428, and died about 425 B.C. As an Ionian he was well qualified to write of the Greek colonies. He explains an Ionian as one who came from Athens and kept the Apaturia (an annual meeting of the Phratries for registering the birth of children entitled to citizenship).

He tells how, when the emigrants left Greece, they took fire from the sacred hearth to the new settlement, where it was kept always alight in the Prytaneum or Government House; it symbolised the life of the State.

So Herodotus tells us of these city-States, and contrasts them

THE GREEK CITY-STATES

with the powers of Egypt, Assyria, and Persia, which waxed and waned as neighbours.

The unity and dramatic quality of his work comes from this conflict between the puny Greek States and the might of Persia. We are interested in the tale because, if the Greeks had not defeated the Persians at Salamis, we in Western Europe would not be leading the lives we are today; Classical Greece would not have come into being, nor our opportunity to inherit, through Rome, some part of her knowledge.

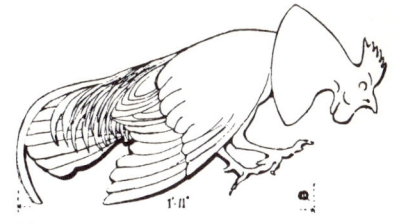

53 Part of a frieze from Xanthos

Herodotus painted his picture on a big canvas, and used many colours. He gives us everything—gossip, legend, and history. He tells us quite frankly that he cannot be sure that all is true, but even with this qualification we feel that it is good to know what was the current gossip of the time, and his book is as alive as a newspaper of today.

Herodotus opens with a reference to the Trojan War, and cites this as the cause of the enmity between the Greeks and Persians.

He divided his history into nine books, or chapters.

In the FIRST BOOK we read how Crœsus, King of Lydia, first conquered the Æolians, Ionians, and Dorians of Asia Minor in 560 B.C. Before his time they had been free, probably because their settlements were not considered to be of much importance. This was the beginning of the long fight which was to terminate at Salamis, after eighty years of crowded history. Ephesus was the first city attacked by Crœsus, and he finally conquered nearly all Asia Minor.

Then, hearing that the Persians under Cyrus were becoming very powerful, he determined to consult various oracles, including the one at Delphi. This is very extraordinary—that Crœsus, who was not a Greek, should have sent to the great shrine in Greece, situated in Phocis, to the north of the Gulf of Corinth. The advice of the Delphic oracle, or Crœsus' interpretation of it, was so disastrous that it would have been better for him if he had refrained. Their first answer was to a test question devised by Crœsus, and was so satisfactory that he sacrificed to the

HERODOTUS AND HIS HISTORY

Delphic gods, and gathered together a great store of golden ingots, the statue of a lion in gold, and another of a woman, bowls of gold and silver, four silver casks, lustral vases, and the necklaces and girdles of his wife. Gold was found in Lydia. All this treasure was sent to Delphi, and the oracles again consulted as to his chance of success if he went to war against the Persians. The oracles replied to this, that if Crœsus attacked the Persians he would destroy a mighty empire, but that he must make alliance with the most powerful of the Greeks. Another answer seemed just as satisfactory, so Crœsus proposed an alliance with the Spartans. They replied that they were willing to help, and sent him a bronze vase, which unfortunately went astray. Meanwhile Crœsus invaded Cappadocia, hoping to defeat Cyrus.

A Lydian wise man warned him against warring with men who wore leathern clothes and trousers; whose country was sterile; who drank water, not wine; who had no figs, nor anything good to eat; and who, if they once realised how pleasant life was in Lydia, would never be content until they conquered the country. At this time the Persians had not been enervated by the luxury which surprised the Greeks after the Battle of Platæa (p. 105).

No decision was reached in the first encounter. The Lydians were a brave and warlike people, who fought on horseback, and carried long lances. Cyrus thought of a clever stratagem, and opposed his camels to the Lydian horses, because horses hate camels, and cannot bear either the sight or smell of them. When the battle began, the Lydian war-horses, seeing and smelling the camels, turned round and galloped off, and Crœsus was defeated. He sent to the Spartans for help; but they were engaged in a private quarrel with the Argives. So no help was sent to Crœsus, and the walled city of Sardis was taken after a fourteen days' siege. He fulfilled the Delphic oracle by destroying not the Persian but his own empire (547 B.C.).

After a while, Crœsus was treated kindly by Cyrus, and when his fetters were struck off, he sent these to Delphi. The Pythoness replied that he should have sent to Delphi again, to find out which empire would be destroyed, so he had only himself to blame. The Pythoness was the medium between the god and the priests.

Herodotus then tells us of all that the Lydians had done, how the tomb of Alyattes, the father of Crœsus, was formed with a

54 The warrior's departure

LYDIANS, MEDES AND PERSIANS

base of immense blocks of stone (the sepulchral chamber), the rest being a vast mound of earth with five stone pillars at the top. It was Alyattes who sent, as an offering to Delphi, a curiously inlaid steel salver made by Glaucus the Chian, who first invented the inlaying of steel.

He tells us as well how the Lydians were the first people to use gold and silver coins, and to sell goods by retail. They claimed also the invention of certain games: there was once a famine through the whole of Lydia, which they bore patiently, but finding that it did not pass away, they set to work to devise remedies for the evil. Various persons invented games of dice, knucklebones, and ball, but not draughts. Then they all played games one day so vigorously that they did not feel hungry, and the next day they ate what was going, but did not play. In this way eighteen years passed.

Herodotus next considers the rise of the Medes and Persians. Deioces, who formed the Medes into a nation, built the city of Agbatana, with walls of great size and strength, which rose in circles one within the other. There were seven of these circular walls, each of which was higher than the one outside it. The outer walls were white, then black, scarlet, blue, orange, silver, and gold for the innermost sanctuary.

Here we see the beginnings of that military achitecture which was to surprise the Crusaders when they went to the Holy Land, and which led to our own concentric castles, like Harlech and Beaumaris in North Wales.

The Medes then conquered the Persians, and together they overthrew the Assyrians in 606.

The Assyrians were fine military engineers; a sculpture in the British Museum of 884–860 B.C. shows a walled city being taken by means of a battering-ram and siege-tower of quite medieval appearance.

We hear how the Medes and Persians were the first to give organisation to an Asiatic army, by dividing the troops into companies, with distinct bodies of spearmen, archers, and cavalry.

Also, they had no images of the gods, or temples, or altars. Herodotus explains that the Persians did not think of the gods as having the same nature as men, as the Greeks did (see p. 108).

Cyrus himself, King of Persia, had a romantic upbringing,

HERODOTUS AND HIS HISTORY

55 Part of a frieze from the acropolis at Xanthos

which came about in this way: Astyages, a Mede, the son of Cyaxares, had a daughter Mandane, who married Cambyses the Persian. In due course she had a baby, and at the same time her father, Astyages, had a dream of a vine which grew so lustily that it overshadowed all Persia. This was interpreted as meaning that his grandson would reign in his stead, so it was arranged when the infant was born that it should be taken by Harpagus, a Mede, and slain, but he, not liking the job, sent for a herdsman, and told him to take the child into the mountains, and there leave him to die. But the herdsman took the infant home to his wife, whose own baby had just died, and this dead baby it was which was exposed, and the live Cyrus lived to grow up and overthrow Astyages, 553 B.C., and found the Persian Empire. The defeat of Crœsus, 547 B.C., made Cyrus master of Asia, and he then moved against the Greeks of Asia Minor. They had offered to become his lieges, but he intended their complete subjugation. They sent to Sparta for assistance, which was not given. Then they consulted the oracle at Branchidæ (p. 135).

Harpagus, a general of Cyrus, besieged the Ionian cities, using mounds. These were heaped against the walls, and so enabled the besiegers to get over them. This explains the reference in 2 Kings, chapter xix, verse 32: "Therefore thus saith the Lord concerning the king of Assyria, He shall not come into this city, nor shoot an arrow there, nor come before it with shield, nor cast a bank against it."

Herodotus tells us that Phocæa was the first city against which Harpagus directed his attack, and as well that the Phocæans of Asia Minor were the first Greeks who performed long voyages, and explored the shores of the Mediterranean as far as the city of Tartessus (near Cadiz). They used in their voyages the long penteconter (Fig. 99), and not the round-built merchant ship, and used it to good effect, for, having obtained a truce from Harpagus, they put their wives and children on board, and loaded up with their treasures, and departed for Chios; but not being allowed to settle there, some

CONQUESTS OF CYRUS

went into Corsica. In a subsequent fight with the Carthaginians many of the Phocæans were killed, and a curse descended on the slayers. On the advice of the Delphic Pythoness the sin was expiated by honouring the dead Phocæans with magnificent funeral rites, and solemn games, both gymnic and equestrian.

Others followed the Phocæan example, but the inhabitants of the other Ionian cities who remained fell into servitude under Cyrus, in 545 B.C. Though the Spartans did not come to the assistance of the Ionians, they sent to Cyrus to warn him against molesting the Greeks. Cyrus' reply is interesting; he told them, "I have never yet been afraid of any men who have a set place in the middle of their city where they come together to cheat each other and forswear themselves." This was as good as telling the Spartans that they were vulgar tradesmen. The Persians apparently did not have markets. The remainder of the first book tells how Cyrus consolidated his power and took Babylon in 538. With the political history we are given many details of everyday life; for example, the Carians invented the use of crests on helmets, and handles and devices on their shields; these the Greeks copied. We hear of early town planning when we are told that Babylon stood on a broad plain, and was an exact square.

The Babylonians had no doctors, but when a man was ill they took him to the public square, so that the passers-by might give him the benefit of their advice, if by any chance they had had a complaint themselves which appeared to resemble his. This chapter finishes with the death of Cyrus, 529 B.C., when Cambyses succeeded to the throne.

The SECOND BOOK deals with the expedition of Cambyses against Egypt, when the Ionian and Æolian Greeks were forced to accompany him as his vassals. This chapter is packed with descriptions of everyday life; we can give only one or two details which bear on Greece. Herodotus tells us that the land in Egypt was divided up into square plots of equal size, and let to the holders for a yearly rent. If the river carried away any portion of a man's lot, surveyors were sent to determine by measurement the exact extent of the loss, so that the rent could be adjusted. From this practice, geometry first came to be known in Egypt, whence it passed into Greece. The sundial, however, and the gnomon, with the division of the day into twelve parts,

HERODOTUS AND HIS HISTORY

came to the Greeks from Babylon. Another interesting detail is that Herodotus, while he was travelling in Egypt, was told by the priests another version of the Trojan War. After the rape of Helen, an army of Greeks sailed to Troy, and demanded the restoration of Helen and the treasures taken with her. The Trojans replied that they could not do this, as both had been taken to Egypt. The Greeks did not believe them, and laid siege to the town, but when they took it, could not find Helen. Menelaos, Helen's husband, was then sent to Egypt, where he found his wife at the Court of Proteus. Herodotus adds that he thinks this was what really did happen, and not the version Homer told.

Herodotus gives us an example of Persian justice. Cambyses, hearing that one of his judges had been bribed, killed and flayed him, and cutting his skin into strips, used it for the seat of the justice throne. The judge's son was appointed in his stead, and told to remember always how his seat was cushioned.

The THIRD BOOK deals with the conquest of Egypt by Cambyses (525 B.C.), the son of Cyrus, and of his madness and death, and how he was succeeded by Dareius.

The FOURTH BOOK opens with the words, "After the taking of Babylon, an expedition was led by Dareius into Scythia", but we are not given any details of this for some time. Herodotus evidently thought that his readers, who would know the positions of Persia and Egypt, might yet be doubtful about Scythia, so the chapter is very interesting, because it gives an idea of early geography. Herodotus thought of Greece as the centre of the world. India was the limit of the inhabited world on the east—Arabia and Libya (Africa) towards the south. Of the north and west, Herodotus did not seem to know anything, and could never obtain any assurance from an eyewitness that there was sea "on the farther side of Europe". He had heard of the Cassiterides, or Tin Islands (it is thought that these may have been the British Isles), and knew that tin and amber came to the Mediterranean, apparently from the ends of the earth.

Herodotus knew that Africa was surrounded by the sea, except for the neck where the Suez Canal is, and even this latter had been attempted before his time. Seti I, in the fourteenth century B.C., cut a canal and joined the Nile and the Red Sea. This was enlarged by Necho, 612 B.C., and after this he sent

THE SCYTHIANS

ships down the Red Sea to sail round Africa. The crew sailed south all along the east coast and, doubling the Cape, came up by the west coast. When they ran out of food they landed and sowed corn, and, waiting for it to grow and ripen, sailed on again after their harvest. In the third year they came to the Pillars of Hercules (the Straits of Gibraltar), and so to their own Mediterranean Sea.

Herodotus by this time had sketched in the outlines of his picture. In the foreground are the tiny Greek city-States of Ionia, surrounded by powerful neighbours like Assyria, Persia, and Egypt. All of them were in a measure civilised, and dwelt within a small compass. We need a reminder of how small a world the Greek world was, and how on the outskirts were barbarians. So Herodotus next traces the journey of Dareius by way of the Bosphorus, up the west coast of the Black Sea, to the Scythian lands where people lived who were prepared to swoop down, like the later Huns, and blot out civilisation. He tells us that they had neither cities nor forts, but were nomads living in their travelling wagons. They could all shoot from horseback, and lived, not by husbandry, but on their cattle.

The Scythian drank the blood of the first man he killed in battle, and cut off all the heads of the remainder and carried them to his king, who was entitled to share the booty, unless he failed to produce at least one head himself. The head was scalped by making a cut round it above the ears, and shaking out the skull. The scalp was used as a napkin, and was hung from the bridle-rein. If the Scythian had good hunting, the scalps were sewn together to make cloaks. Another amiable habit was to flay the right arms of their dead enemies, and tan the skin, with the nails hanging to it, and use it as a covering for their quivers. It is interesting to know that the skin of a man is thick and glossy, and whiter than the other hides. They treated the skulls of those whom they most detested as follows: the portion below the eyebrows having been sawn off, the inside was cleaned out, and the outside covered with leather and used as a drinking-cup. If they wanted to make a good job of it, the inside was lined with gold.

When they took an oath, the parties to it took a large earthen bowl and filled it with wine, and then, wounding themselves, they allowed some of their blood to drop into the wine; then a scimitar, some arrows, a battle-axe, and a javelin were plunged in it: meanwhile prayers were said; then the two drank each a draught of the mixture.

In the funerals of their kings the body was laid in the grave, stretched upon a mattress; spears were fixed in the ground on either side of the corpse, and supported beams stretched across above to form a roof, which was covered with thatch. Around the body of the king they buried one of his concubines, first killed by strangulation, and also his cup-bearer, cook, groom, lackey, messenger, some of his horses, firstlings of all his other possessions, and some golden cups; and then a great mound was raised above the grave.

The Scythian women had an amusing way of cleansing themselves. Cypress, cedar, and frankincense wood was pounded into a paste, with a little water, to a thick consistency. This substance they plastered over their whole bodies. And when on the following day they took off the plaster, their skin was clean and glossy, and a sweet odour had been imparted to them.

The Sauromatæ, neighbours of the Scythians, allowed none of the girls to marry until she had first killed a man in battle.

The Scythians, not having any cities, moved about their country in wagons, and could not be brought to battle by the Persians, so the campaign was indecisive, 514 B.C.

There followed the Persian expeditions to Libya, which again is outside our subject, except that Herodotus gives interesting details of the Greek settlements at Cyrene, on the north coast of Africa. We must bear in mind that emigrants from the homeland went not only to Ionia but to nearly all the Mediterranean coast lands.

The Persians besieged Barca, another Greek city, for nine months, and drove several mines from their own lines to the walls. Their mines were discovered by a brass worker inside the city, who went round with a brazen shield and laid it on the ground. Where the ground was undermined the brass of the shield rang, but in the other places the shield, when he laid it down, was quite dumb. The Barceans counter-mined, and slew the Persian diggers.

Herodotus tells one tale which shows how primitive trade was carried on by the Carthaginians, relating that they used to visit a people in Libya, beyond the Pillars of Hercules (that

56 (*left*) Paestum: a close-up view of the Temple of Poseidon (about 450 B.C.)

57 (*below*) Acragas, Sicily: the so-called "Temple of Concord" (about 440 B.C.)

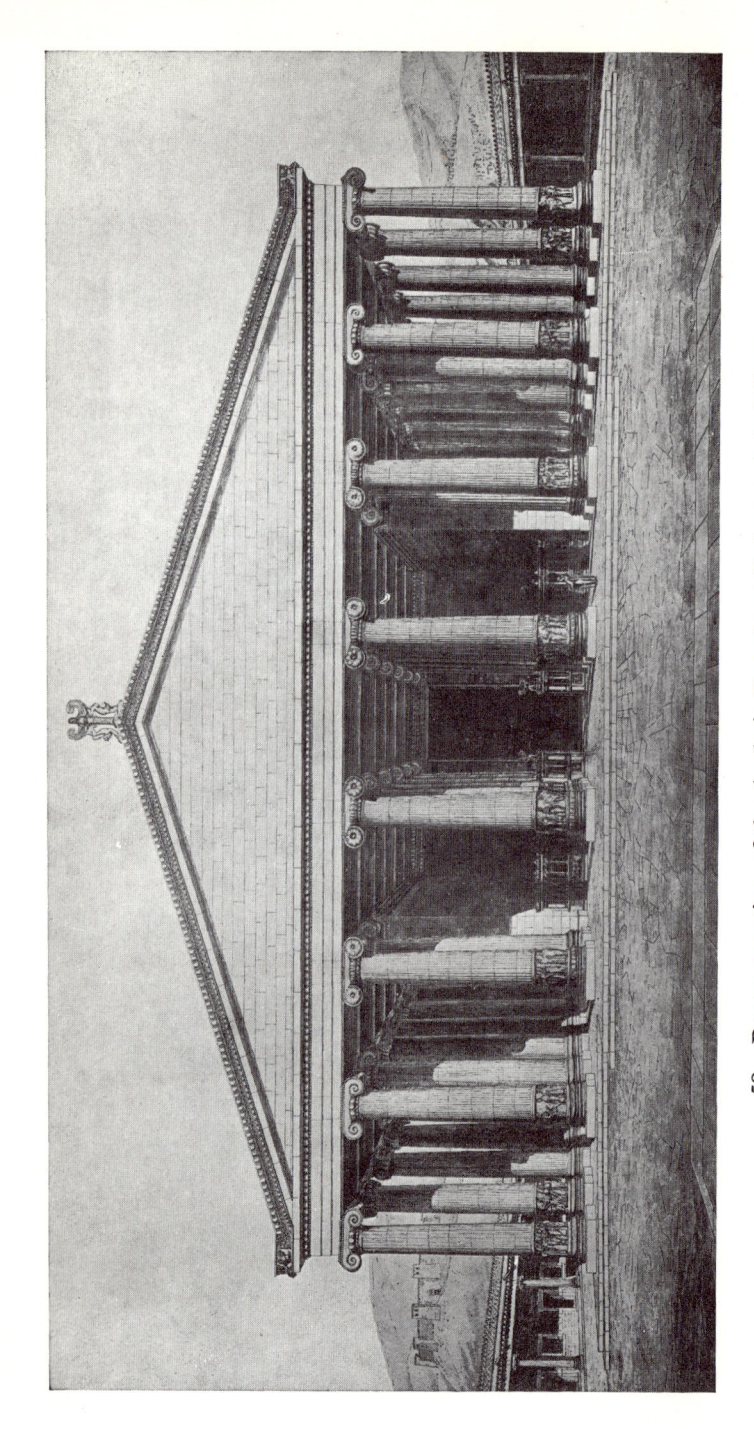

58 Reconstruction of the Archaic Temple at Ephesus, Asia Minor

would be on the west coast of Africa), where, when they arrived, they unloaded their wares, and set them out in an orderly fashion on the beach, and then returned aboard their ships and raised a great smoke. When the natives saw the smoke, they came down to the shore, and looking over the goods, put down as much gold as they thought they were worth, and then withdrew to a distance. The Carthaginians then came ashore, and if they thought the gold enough, took it and sailed away; if not, they retired aboard ship once more and waited for more gold, and so on, until both sides were content. The natives never ran away with the goods, nor did the Carthaginians take them back and run off with the gold.

The FIFTH BOOK gives the early history of Sparta, and details of the Persian expedition to Pæonia in Thrace. Here in the country to the north-east of the mainland of Greece the Persians found lake-dwellers. These people lived like the dwellers in the Swiss lake-villages which had many points of resemblance with our own Glastonbury lake-village. Herodotus gives details of these Thracian lake-dwellings—of how the piles were driven into the bed of the lake to support the platforms on which the huts were built, and approached by a single narrow bridge; how trap-doors gave access to the lake underneath, and the fish were so plentiful that all you had to do was to lower a basket into which the fish came and packed themselves, all ready to be drawn up. Not only the people, but the horses, ate the fish. The babies were tied up with a string by the foot.

During this campaign the Persians consolidated their powers in the Ægean. They took the islands of Lemnos and Imbros, and Herodotus notes that up till this time not one of the Cyclades (the islands in the Ægean Sea) was subject to King Dareius. It was told to him that Naxos was fertile, and containing much treasure and many slaves. Slaves, unfortunately, were an essential part of Greek civilisation. They supplied the man-power which was necessary before the days of "horse-power". So a Persian expedition was sent to annex Naxos. This was a failure because of the brutal treatment by the Persians of a captain of an auxiliary ship, whose friends, in consequence, warned the people of Naxos. Forewarned was forearmed, so that they were able to beat off the Persians and remain masters of the sea.

Before this a Persian general had advised the king, after he had conquered all the Cyclades, to send a hundred ships to annex Eubœa, the large island which nearly touches the east coast of the mainland of Greece, and had his advice been followed, the history of Western Europe would have followed a different course. The Cyclades are stepping-stones across the Ægean, and Eubœa a jumping-off place from where the subjugation of Greece itself could have been accomplished. Fortunately for us the advice was not followed.

The failure of the expedition to Naxos led to a revolt of the Ionian cities against the Persians. The conspirators chose a clever way to communicate with one another. The head of a slave was shaved and the message tattooed on the bare skull. The hair was allowed to grow, and the slave was sent with a message that his head was to be shaved and then read.

The Spartans were asked to render assistance, "inasmuch as the pre-eminence over all Greece appertains to you", and here it was that Aristagoras, pleading with Cleomenes on behalf of the Ionians, attempted to bribe the Spartan, and, offering at first ten talents, increased it step by step to fifty, when Gorgo, the daughter of Cleomenes, interrupted and said, "Father, get up and go, or the stranger will certainly corrupt you." And so Aristagoras was sent away, and no help given him. He then sailed to Athens, because "he knew that, after Sparta, Athens was the most powerful of the Grecian States". The Athenians voted that twenty ships should be sent to the assistance of the Ionians. As Herodotus points out, this was the beginning of the trouble which culminated at Salamis. The Ionian revolt failed, and Dareius asked who the Athenians were, and, on being told, took his bow and shot an arrow into the sky, and called on his god that he might be revenged on the Athenians. He also commanded a servant to say to him three times each day, when at dinner, "Master, remember the Athenians."

There are many interesting details in the FIFTH BOOK. We are told that it was the Phœnicians who introduced writing into Greece.

There is an interesting note on clothes. The Athenians sent an expedition to Ægina, which met with disaster, and only one survivor came back to Athens. The wives of all those who had been killed crowded round the man, and struck him with the brooches by which their dresses were fastened, asking him,

THE IONIAN REVOLT

59 From the walls of a tomb at Xanthos (*c.* 470 B.C.)

"Where is my husband?" And the man died. The Athenians thought the deed so horrible that they changed the dress of their women from the Dorian type (80), which required brooches, to the Ionian linen tunic, which was sewn, and so did not require brooches (81).

The SIXTH BOOK deals with the conditions after the revolt of the Ionians. Herodotus gives one very interesting detail. Phrynichus, a poet, produced a drama in Athens on the Capture of Miletus (one of the Ionian cities captured by the Persians). This so affected the Athenian audience that all the people burst into tears, and the unfortunate poet was fined 1,000 drachms for being too tragic an artist. The Persians, who at first treated the Ionians cruelly, after some time did them no more hurt, but summoning deputies from the cities, compelled them to enter into treaties not to quarrel with one another. Others sailed away—some to Zancle, the modern Messina. Like William the Conqueror, Dareius compiled a survey, measuring up their country in parasangs (30 furlongs).

Having finished with the Ionians, Dareius had time to deal with the Athenians, and we have heard the precautions that he took that he should not forget. We may be quite sure that every time Dareius sat down to dinner his servant said to him three times, "Master, remember the Athenians"—it was not advisable to forget the instructions of a Persian king. So an expedition was sent against them, 493 B.C., under Mardonius, who had married the king's daughter. The fleet skirted the land while the army marched to the Hellespont, crossing which, they proceeded through Thrace and Macedonia. A storm drove many of the ships against Mount Athos, and this expedition failed.

Dareius does not appear to have been perturbed. It must have been inconceivable to him that these Athenians, of whom he knew so little, could oppose him, so he made preparations for another expedition, and sent heralds to Greece to demand submission, but Themistocles had foreseen the trouble ahead and was already fortifying the Peiræus.

The second Persian expedition, under Datis, 491 B.C., remembering how their ships had been wrecked on Mount Athos the year before, embarked the troops and horses and sailed across to Greece by Samos and the islands of the Cyclades, their destination being Eretria, on the Attica side of Eubœa, the large island off the east coast of Greece—a much more dangerous threat. Ionians and Æolians were forced to accompany the Persians. The Athenians came to the rescue of the Eretrians, but, hearing that some were for flight, and others for betraying their country to the Persians, withdrew to Oropus. The Persians defeated the Eretrians, and then sailed to Marathon, on the mainland of Greece, not many miles from Athens itself. The Athenians, under Miltiades, sent the runner Pheidippides to Sparta to ask for help, and he took only two days to run 135 to 140 miles; but the Spartans had to wait until the full of the moon before they could help. Meanwhile the Athenians drew themselves up in order of battle in the Sacred Close of Heracles, with the Platæans who came to their aid on their left wing. Herodotus says that the Greeks charged the Persians at a run, and that this was the first time that the Greeks employed the charge. The centre of the Greek line was broken, but the two wings outflanked and outfought the Persians, and drove them back to their ships, and captured seven of these. The Greeks had won the first round against their great adversary.

In the SIXTH BOOK we are told of the honours accorded to the Spartan kings at death; of how, when the women heard the news which was carried by horsemen, they ran hither and thither, drumming on kettles, and when these were heard, in every house two free persons, a man and a woman, had to put on mourning, and the three types of people had to attend the funeral. These were the Spartans, descended from the Dorians and Heracles himself; the country people, descended probably from the dispossessed Achæans who had submitted to the Spartans; and the Helots, who were the slaves. They spoke of the Dorian Invasion (p. 87) as the "Return of the Heracleidæ".

There is another note on the use of wine. The Spartans thought the madness of Cleomenes was caused by his having learned to drink his wine without water from Scythians who came to Sparta. The Greeks always diluted their wine with water.

There is another note explaining the use of tallies. A certain Milesian came to Sparta, and brought half his money with him, because Ionia was insecure, while Sparta stood firm. He gave the money into the hands of Glaucus, with tallies, saying that he must not give the money to anyone unless they brought the fellows of the tallies. These tallies were short sticks which were notched and then split, the Milesian keeping one half and Glaucus the other, and he would know if the Milesian had really sent his half, because the notches on the two when put together would tally.

As to marriage, Callias was held to be remarkable, because he had three daughters, and when they came to be of marriageable age, he gave each of them a dowry, and allowed them to choose their own husbands. The usual practice seems to have been followed by Cleisthenes, another father, who had a daughter called Agarista, whom he wished to marry to the best husband that he could find in the whole of Greece. At the Olympic Games, therefore, having gained the prize in the chariot race, he caused public proclamation to be made that any Greek who deemed himself worthy to become the son-in-law of Cleisthenes, should come within sixty days to Sicyon; for within a year's time Cleisthenes would decide on the man to whom he should contract his daughter. Suitors began to flock in, and Cleisthenes had a foot-course and a wrestling-ground made ready, to try their powers. He kept them on tenter-hooks for a whole year, but the favourite appears to have been an Athenian, Hippocleides, the son of Tisander.

The day at length arrived when Cleisthenes had to declare his choice. First of all he sacrificed a hundred oxen, and held a banquet for all the suitors and the people of Sicyon. After the feast the suitors showed how well they could play and speak on a given subject, and then, as the drinking advanced, Hippocleides called for the flute-player, and began to dance. Cleisthenes, so Herodotus tells us, began to feel very unhappy. Then Hippocleides, not content, told an attendant to bring in a table, and, mounting upon it, danced first of all some Laconian figures, then some Attic ones, and then, throwing away discretion, he stood on his head upon the table and began to wave his legs about. This was more than Cleisthenes could stand, and he cried out, "Son of Tisander, thou hast danced thy wife away!" "What does Hippocleides care?" was the other's answer, and so the Greek proverb arose.

The SEVENTH BOOK opens with a note that when the news of the Battle of Marathon reached King Dareius, his anger against the Athenians waxed still fiercer, and he became more than ever eager to lead an army against Greece. He died, however, in 485 B.C., before he was able to do so, and the task was left to his son Xerxes. First a revolt in Egypt had to be subdued, 484 B.C., and Xerxes then reconsidered the question of the attack on Greece, the land of "the Ionians who live in Europe". His uncle tried to persuade him against the expedition. Xerxes first decided to go, then altered his mind, and finally was sent to meet his fate by a dream. He spent four full years collecting his host from all the nations in Asia. Detachments from the tributary nations were sent to cut a canal "beneath the lash of taskmasters", through the Isthmus of Acte, off the Macedonian coast, 13 furlongs long, in order to save the rough passage through the stormy waters rounding Mount Athos, where the fleet had been wrecked in the expedition under Mardonius. Herodotus tells us that only the Phœnicians understood what is meant by the "angle of repose" of material. They cut their part with sloping sides, so that the earth did not tumble in on them. A bridge of boats was built across the Hellespont, but a great storm broke the whole work to pieces. "When Xerxes heard of this he gave orders that the Hellespont should receive three hundred lashes, and that a pair of fetters be cast into it", and the bridge was repaired.

It was at Abydos, on the Hellespont, that Xerxes reviewed his troops. The whole Hellespont was covered with the vessels of his fleet, and all the shore and every plain about Abydos was full of troops. Xerxes, after reviewing his army, wept, saying to Artabanus, "There came upon me a sudden pity, when I

EXPEDITION UNDER XERXES

thought of the shortness of man's life, and considered that of all this host, so numerous as it is, not one will be alive when a hundred years are gone by."

After Xerxes had crossed the bridge of boats he stood to contemplate his army as they crossed "under the lash". The crossing took seven days and seven nights.

There is an interesting note on the difficulty which these early people found in counting. Xerxes wanted to count his army, and this is the way he went to work. Ten thousand men were made to stand as close together as possible, and then a circle was drawn round them. On the circle a fence was built about the height of a man's middle. Then the enclosure was filled continually with fresh troops, till the whole army had been counted.

60 Helmets and crests from black-figure vases, sixth-century B.C.

When the Persians reached the River Strymon in Macedonia, they sacrificed white horses to make the stream favourable to their crossing, and then arrived at a place called The Nine Ways (after Amphipolis). Here, learning the name of the place, they took nine of the youths of the land, and as many of their maidens, and buried them alive on the spot, as a sacrifice to the god dwelling underneath the earth.

The Persian navy, skirting the shore, sailed through the channel which had been cut by Mount Athos, and had brushes with scouting ships sent out from Athens, and the Persians succeeded in taking two of these. The news of the disaster was sent from the island of Sciathus to Artemisium (about 13 miles) by fire signals.

The ships were not very large, because Herodotus tells us how some of the Persians, on one occasion, saved both themselves and their vessels by dragging them up on the beach. A great storm destroyed part of Xerxes' fleet off Cape Sepias, and it took refuge in the Bay of Pagasæ.

On the recommendation of the men of Thessaly, the Greeks sent a force to guard the Pass of Olympus, where they occupied the defile of Tempe, but this force was recalled, so that the Thessalians were compelled to join Xerxes.

He sent heralds to many of the other Greek cities, demanding that they should send him earth and water as a sign of their submission. No heralds were sent to Athens or Sparta, and the Greek force was now drawn up at the Pass of Thermopylæ, their fleet being at Artemisium, on the north coast of Eubœa.

The SEVENTH BOOK closes with a description of the fight at Thermopylæ (the Hot Gates) and the end of the Spartans, who were seen by a spy of Xerxes combing their hair before the battle. The Persians, driven on by whips, were unable to take the Pass by frontal attack, but did so in the end, because they were shown a path over the mountains by Ephialtes. The main body of the Greeks retreated, and the Spartans remained to hold the Persians in check. Their last fight, under Leonidas, and how they defended themselves with swords, and then, when these were broken, with hands and teeth, until the last of them, surrounded on all sides, were overwhelmed and buried under showers of missiles, is one of the great heroic episodes of history.

Things had now reached a desperate pass for the Greeks, and all the comfort they had was a message from the Delphic oracle that

> *Safe shall the wooden wall continue for thee and thy children.*
> *Wait not the tramp of the horse, nor the footmen mightily moving*
> *Over the land, but turn your back to the foe, and retire ye.*

Some of the Greeks thought this meant they were to desert Athens and take to their ships. This was the view of Themistocles and this is what they did, the Greek navy by this time having retreated from Artemisium to Salamis.

After Thermopylæ, the main body of the Persians came down through Bœotia to Athens, which they burned. The Persian fleet by this time had come down south through the Euripus,

THERMOPYLÆ AND SALAMIS

the narrow strait between Eubœa and the mainland, to Phalerum, near Athens.

Now the stage was set for the last act of the great drama, and it seemed as if nothing could save the Greeks from the might of Persia. Yet Herodotus clearly thinks that the gods were on the side of the Greeks, because he tells us how, before Salamis, a cloud of dust such as might be raised by a crowd of 30,000 men was seen coming from Eleusis. From the cloud came the sound of voices, chanting the mystic hymn to Dionysus, which was sung at the festival to Demeter and Persephone at Eleusis, and the cloud sailed in the direction of Salamis, and rested over the Greek fleet. So, confronted by their gods, the Greeks braced themselves, and in the EIGHTH BOOK Herodotus reaches the peak of his history and tells how the Persians were defeated at the Battle of Salamis, 480 B.C. The Persians were not a seafaring nation, and their fleet, manned by Phœnicians, Cyprians, Ionians, and Egyptians, was no match for that of the Greeks in its own home waters. Still, the might of Persia had been so great that, when the sea fight was over, the Greeks, first setting all the wrecked and disabled ships together, prepared for another engagement, thinking that Xerxes would renew the fight with the vessels which still remained to him. But the king had no more heart left in him, and feared that the Greeks might sail straight to the Hellespont and break down the bridges there, in which case he would be blocked up in Europe, and run great risk of perishing. He therefore made up his mind to fly. At the precise moment that Xerxes came to this decision, the whole course of Western civilisation was altered, and it was left to the Greeks to steer the way. So we can take leave of the Persian king. Herodotus gives one amusing detail of him: a great banquet was given on his birthday, and gifts distributed, "and this is the only day in all the year on which the King soaps his head".

The NINTH BOOK deals with the fate of the remainder of the Persian army, left behind by Xerxes under the command of Mardonius, and how they were defeated at Platæa, 479 B.C. The folly of the whole enterprise was well shown by Pausanias, the Spartan commander, who captured the war tent of Xerxes, which had been left behind for the use of Mardonius. This was adorned with gold and silver; its hangings were of divers

61 A device on a shield

colours. Pausanias ordered the Persian cooks to make ready for him a feast in such fashion as was their wont for Mardonius. And this they did. The couches were of gold and silver, with rich coverings. The tables of gold and silver were laid with a feast which suited such magnificence. Then Pausanias ordered his own followers to prepare a Spartan supper. Then both suppers were served, and it was apparent how vast a difference lay between the two, and Pausanias laughed, and sent for the Greek generals, and pointed to the two boards, and said: "I sent for you, O Greeks, to show you the folly of this Median captain, who, when he enjoyed such fare as this, must needs come here to rob us of our penury."

Here our outline from Herodotus must end. We leave him with the Greeks triumphant. There must have been a period after Salamis when they rested to lick their wounds and get the ache of battle out of their bones. Perhaps they wondered how it had all happened. Their thoughts may have gone back to the time when their forefathers had been turned out of Greece by the Dorians. They may have remembered their wanderings and struggles in Ionia and the other Greek colonies, and the tales of the heroes, and the traditions of Mycenæan art which they took with them. They may have realised, as Herodotus did, that the Arts and Sciences were kept alive in these colonies, and in due course, when the colonists sent heralds to consult the oracles in Delphi, or athletes to compete in the Games at Olympia, these returning Greeks carried back with them something indefinable, which quickened the Greek genius again. Homer sustained them, and as they heard the *Iliad*, they remembered that they were descended from heroes, and the adventures of Odysseus sent them out in search of adventure themselves. They were quarrelsome, and not always helpful to one another—sometimes they were treacherous—they were undisciplined, and yet overthrew the disciplined host of Persia, and in a few short years after Salamis were able to raise a structure of art and science which was so wonderful and so

GREECE TRIUMPHANT

much in the highest class that we call it today "Classical". How this was done must always be one of the wonders of history. Perhaps it was because, for the first time, men were allowed to think and express their innermost thoughts in speech or writing—so the thoughts and ideas flowered, and formed Classical Greece. But we shall never enjoy the beauty of the flowering unless we are prepared to take some little trouble in finding out how the plant itself grew, and the qualities of the soil which nourished its roots.

Chapter VI

THE TEMPLE AND THE HOUSE

WE will now examine the architectural accomplishments of the Greeks in the Archaic period, which came to an end with the Battle of Salamis in 480 B.C.

The first thing to be noted is that they had two patterns of building, one we call Doric and the other Ionic, and these correspond with the two great divisions of the Greek race. The Spartans were the typical Dorians, and the Achæans, who fled to Asia Minor, were the Ionians.

We will deal with the Doric type of architecture now, and take the temple first, because it was in housing their gods that the Greeks expended their greatest energies.

To understand the temple, we must realise that the religion of the Greeks was quite different from that of the Christians. Herodotus noted (p. 91) how the Persians did not think of the gods as having the same nature as men, as the Greeks did. The Christian believes that "God said, Let us make man in our image, after our likeness" (Genesis, chapter i, verse 26).

This is the essential thing about Greek religion, that instead of man being made in the image of God, the gods were like men, only being stronger, cleverer, and braver, they were better able to look after themselves, and settle all the difficult problems which arise when man himself seeks to interpret the Universe.

So when the lightning flashed, and the thunder rumbled and echoed in the mountains, the Greek called on Father Zeus, who lived on cloud-capped Olympus. Or, if he was at sea in one of his fragile boats, and the waves arose, then Poseidon would help him. If his lady-love would not smile, Aphrodite would know how to soften her heart. Hera, the wife of Zeus, was capricious and feminine. Hades was the god of the dead. Hestia guarded the hearth, and Demeter was the corn spirit. They were the brothers and sisters of Zeus. Then he had children, just as the Greeks had. Athene was the goddess of the arts; Apollo the god of light; Hermes the messenger; Dionysus the god of the vine; Aphrodite of love; Hephæstos of fire; and Ares of war.

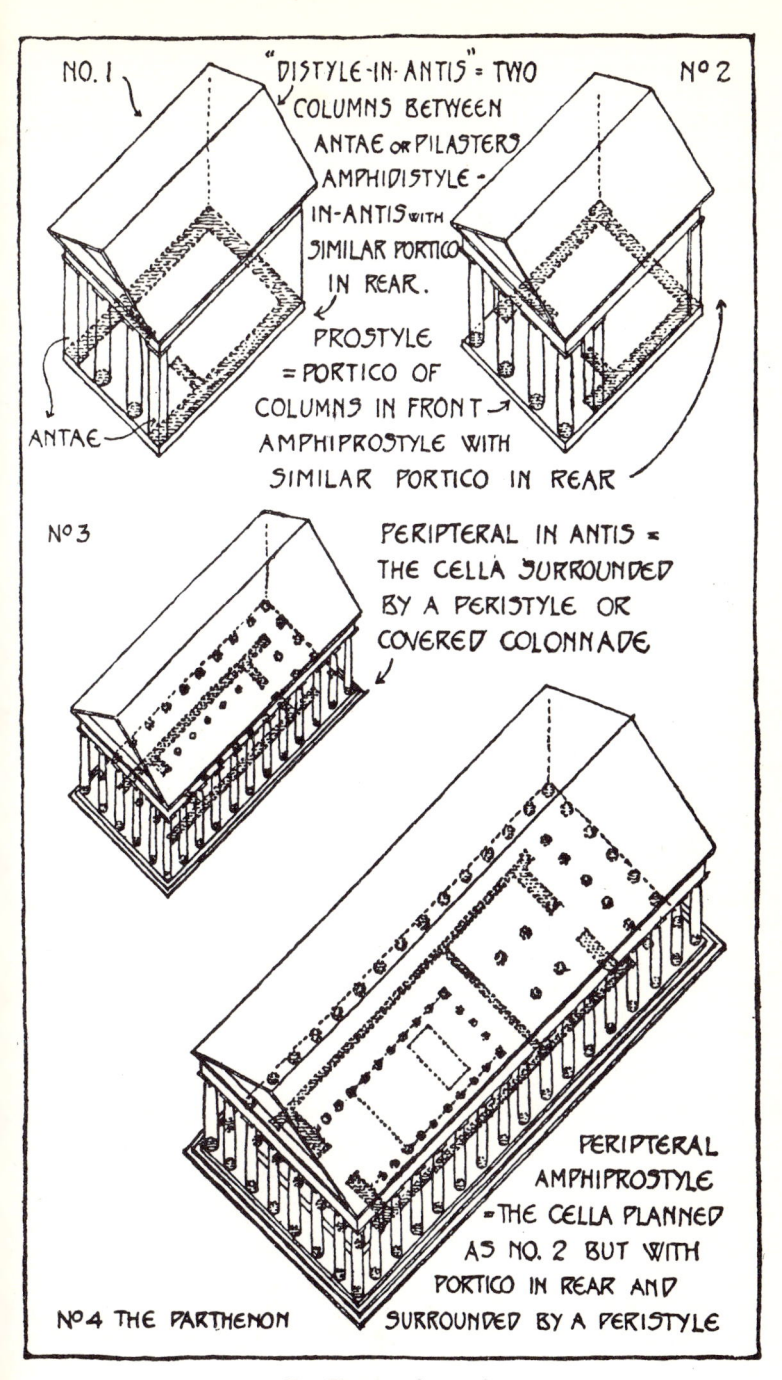

62 Types of temples

THE TEMPLE AND THE HOUSE

All these relationships were regularised by Hesiod between 750 and 700 B.C. (see p. 78). So the Greek had gods on whom he could rely for help on any occasion, and they were fellow Greeks, and, as such, understood the nature of a bargain. All the gods demanded was that they should be propitiated by sacrifice. This done, the Greek was safe. He was not oppressed by any feeling of sin, or that he need save his soul.

The first thing to remember, then, is that the temple was the house of the god they worshipped, and, as such, it had to be finer than the house of man. It was not a church, as we understand it, used for a congregation of people worshipping inside the building.

We can now consider the various types of temples, and here we cannot do better than turn to Vitruvius, a Roman, and the first of the writing architects, who published his book on architecture in the time of Augustus, 27 B.C. to A.D. 14. It is obvious that he had made a study of Greek architecture, and as one of the Roman architects he would have to do so, because their inspiration came from Greece. So far as Western Europe is concerned, only Greek and Gothic architecture have been primary styles; all the others have been derived from these. Vitruvius probably invented the technical terms. Fig. 62 will show the meaning of some of these. The simplest type of temple had the célla, which contained the image of the god, with a porch before it, as No. 1, Fig. 62. Nos. 2 and 3 show how this was developed. In the fully developed temple, as the Parthenon, No. 4, there was the porch (pronaos) in front of the cella, which faced east, and a chamber at the back, which was used as a treasury where offerings to the god could be put, and this had another porch (opisthodomus), the whole group being surrounded by a colonnaded walk.

If reference is made to the plan of the Men's Hall at Tiryns (37), built by the Achæans who invaded Greece about 1450 B.C., and again to the Argos Hut of the eighth century B.C. (p. 77), it will be seen that the Greek temple of the Archaic period was clearly a descendant of the early homes of men. This continued in Greek and Roman Classical times; the gods continued to live in halls, as did the Achæan chieftain, long after their descendants had altered the patterns of their own houses. Similarly, because the first figures of the gods were cut in wood, they continued to

THE TEMPLE PLAN

be made in this way; even in the Parthenon, the great figure of Athene was made of wood, though it was sheathed with gold and ivory.

To go back to the temple plan. We see the ruins of one today set in solitude; a few columns support a broken architrave against the blue sky, and we walk amongst the scattered stones and find it difficult to reconstruct it as a centre of life. Originally a wall surrounded the sacred enclosure. There was a great altar outside the east porch where sacrifice could be offered, and the god worshipped by the people, standing with raised arms and the palms of their hands uppermost. If they prayed to the gods of the underworld, the hands were reversed. If the temple was in a great shrine, sacred to all the Greeks, as at Delphi, then the various other cities would have their own treasuries in the enclosure, where the vestments they used at festivals could be stored, and the precincts would be beautified by statues and all kinds of works of art sent as offerings to the gods. We shall attempt to describe Delphi in Part III; meanwhile we are concerned with the development of Doric architecture.

First, we must try to understand the principles which guided the Doric architects.

It is obvious that the actual ground on which the temple stood was sacred. Greek architects were frequently hampered in this way. Their buildings often had to be placed in a certain spot, or were cut short because they might encroach on another sacred area.

Then the actual form of the temple became sanctified by use. As we have pointed out, the Megaron at Tiryns, and the Argos Hut, are obviously in the same building tradition, and this form became established as the temple type. One of the earliest Doric temples of which ruins remain was that dedicated to Hera, at Olympia; this dates from about 700 B.C., and there were two earlier temples on the same site. The cella walls had stone bases of great thickness, faced on the outside with vertical slabs (orthostates) as a dado. On this stone base the upper walls were built of sun-dried mud bricks. It was these bricks which preserved the Hermes of Praxiteles, which is now in the museum at Olympia; this statue was found at the foot of its pedestal, buried in clay formed out of the brick walls which had fallen in and covered it. The columns of this early temple at Olympia

THE TEMPLE AND THE HOUSE

were formed of wood, as they were at Tiryns.

Pausanias, a native of Lydia, who travelled extensively, and wrote his *Description of Greece*, between about A.D. 150 and 175, writes that in his time one of the pillars of the back chamber of the Temple of Hera at Olympia was of oak. From this it is conjectured that the entablature, and the columns which supported it, were originally of wood, the latter being replaced with stone as they decayed. Fig. 63 has been drawn to show this timber construction of the early Doric temples, and Fig. 64, of the Temple of Theseus in Athens, shows how the timber forms survived even when stone and marble were used for building. Let us take Fig. 63 first, and we will start with the timber shaft cut from a sturdy oak. It would have been a reasonable thing for a carpenter to place a circular pad on the top of the shaft, with a good square block of wood over it. These became the Echinus and Abacus (64). The purpose of the vertical columns was to support beams, bridged across horizontally from column to column; these became the architraves. Then other beams were placed across the building with their ends resting on the architraves. These tied the whole building together and provided it with a ceiling. The ends of the beams were chamfered off, and so one arrived at the triglyphs (64). One of these crossbeams always came over the top of the column under, and one between the columns, so that spaces were left between the beams on the top of the architrave.

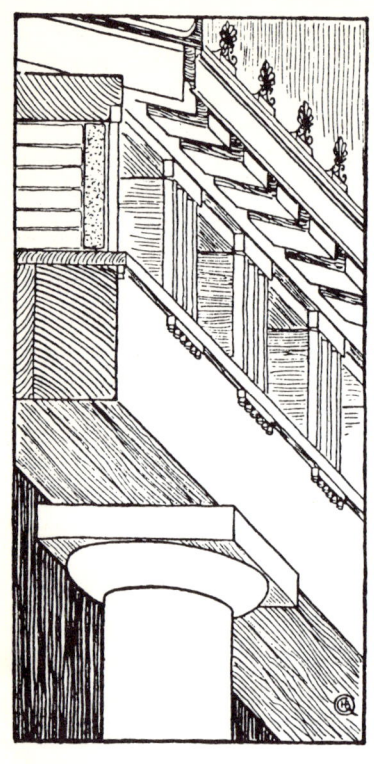

63 The timber origin of the Doric style

THE DORIC STYLE

These were filled in with brick at the back, and at first terra-cotta panels were placed in front of the bricks; later beautifully carved marble panels were inserted, as at the Parthenon, and became the metopes. On the top of all this another beam was placed, to give good fixing for the ends of the overhanging rafters. Later these became part of the marble cornice, and were called mutules (64), but the little wooden pegs used when they were of wood continued to be shown in the new material, and the mutules still sloped as they had when they were the feet of rafters. It is the architrave, frieze, and cornice which together are called the entablature.

Sometimes the wooden mouldings of these early temples were sheathed with gaily decorated terra-cotta plaques.

At the ends of the building the sloping roofs were finished with flat gables, called pediments. Along the tops of these a gutter, or sima, ran, which finished at the feet with a lion's head. The roof was covered with thatch in the earliest times, and then, later, with terra-cotta and marble tiles resting on the rafters; these were flat, with turned-up edges at the sides which were placed together, and covered with a small tile which had an ornamental termination at the eaves, called an antefix. In the later Ionic temples the sima was continued along the sides of the building, as a gutter, with lions' heads as water-spouts. Acroteria were the ornaments placed on the apex and at the feet of the pediments. The temples had ceilings inside, because Pausanias tells us that the body of a soldier was found at the

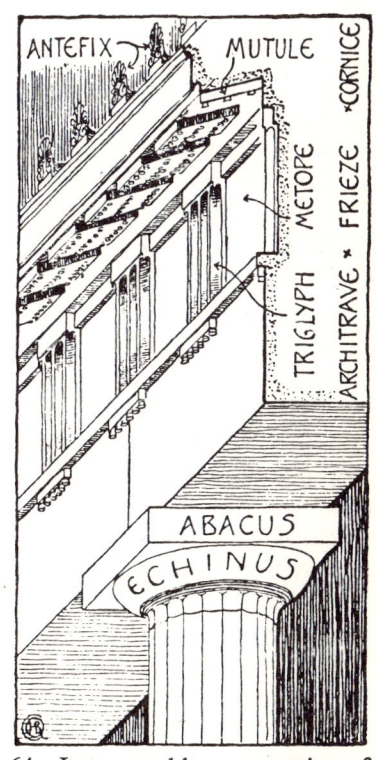

64 Later marble construction of the Doric style

THE TEMPLE AND THE HOUSE

Temple of Hera, between the ceiling and the roof, where he had taken refuge.

Vitruvius says that "Proportion is that agreeable harmony between the several parts of a building, which is the result of a just and regular agreement of them with each other; the height to the width, this to the length, and each of these to the whole." He points out that proportion is as necessary to the beauty of a building as it is to the human figure. Today we have not the faintest idea of the importance which these old architects attached to proportion. Vitruvius goes on to measure up the human figure and says that

> from the chin to the top of the forehead should equal one-tenth of the height of the body;
> from the chin to the crown of the head should equal one-eighth of the height of the body;
> from the upper part of the breast to the roots of the hair should equal one-sixth of the height of the body;
> from the upper part of the breast to the crown of the head should equal one-fourth of the height of the body;
> the length of the foot should equal one-sixth of the height of the body;
> the length of the forearm should equal one-fourth of the height of the body;

and so on. As well, that "The navel is naturally placed in the centre of the human body, and, if in a man lying with his face upward, and his hands and feet extended, from his navel as the centre, a circle be described, it will touch his fingers and toes."

Vitruvius suggests that the sturdier Doric column was founded on the proportions of a man's figure, and the slenderer Ionic on that of the woman's (see p. 117).

In another place Vitruvius points out how useful it is for the architect to know something about octaves, fourths, and fifths, because "music assists him in the use of harmonic and mathematical proportions".

Syracuse, in Sicily, was one of the great Dorian colonies. A temple to Apollo, and the Olympieum, were built there in the sixth century B.C., and a later one of the fifth century is now the Cathedral Church. It is an extraordinary experience to go into this Christian church and find Doric columns and caps, and

PROPORTION. SICILIAN DORIC

then think that when they were newly cut it was Athene who was worshipped in the building.

At Selinus in Sicily there were no less than six temples, but all are in ruins. These were built in limestone, which was covered with a very fine stucco to take painted decorations, and by this time all the walling was of stone, and the sun-dried bricks were no longer used.

There are more temples at Acragas (Agrigentum or Girgenti) on the south coast of Sicily. The town in the sixth century B.C. must have been a very important place. It stands back now about $2\frac{1}{2}$ miles from the sea, on a raised table-land, bounded on the east by the River Acragas, and on the west by the Hypsa. The walls of the ancient city were 10 miles in circumference. The acropolis, which is now the modern city, was at the northern extremity, and here was a temple, which, like the one at Syracuse, has been incorporated into a Christian church.

We are more concerned with the range of temples which was built on the southern boundary of the city looking towards the sea. At the eastern end is the Temple of Hera Laconia. Then moving west we come to the Temples of Concord, Heracles, Zeus Olympius, Castor and Pollux, and Hephæstos. If we think of these temples, as they must have been at one time, decorated with glowing colours, and set up on the top of the city wall hewn out of the rocky face of the hill on which they stood, with broad terraces, and flights of steps leading up to the temples, and adorned with the greenery of trees and fine statues, we may be able to gain some faint idea of the beauties of Archaic Greece, and the splendid vision of her builders.

We have selected one of the southern temples, Zeus Olympius, for particular attention. The first thing to be noted is its great size. It stood on a platform, or stylobate, measuring 173 ft. by 361 ft. Imagine seven Doric columns set up at each end of this, and fourteen on each of the sides, and you will be able to form some idea of the scale of the building. The columns are not free standing as at Pæstum (56), but have a wall filled in between them.

There would, of course, have been a pediment at each end of the building. Its technical description would be that it is heptastyle pseudo-peripteral (62). This only means that it had seven columns at each end, and that its peristyle, or colonnaded

THE TEMPLE AND THE HOUSE

65 The west pediment of the Temple at Ægina (*c.* 480 B.C.)

walk, was a false one, because it was blocked by the walls between the columns. These walls may have been necessary to support the entablature over, and here it is that we come to the tremendous figures which have given the temple its name of the House of the Giants. The figures are now broken and scattered on the ground. One has been roughly reconstructed and found to be 27 ft. in height. Many suggestions have been made as to their position in the building, and the most reasonable one seems to be that they acted as supports. Atlantes is the Greek term for male figures used in this way, and caryatidæ for female ones. The columns are on such an enormous scale that a man's back fits quite comfortably into one of the flutings.

There was another Greek colony at Pæstum, in Western Italy, and here there are two early temples, and one later (about 460 B.C.), dedicated to Poseidon, which is so well preserved that it is about the best illustration one can have of the Doric temple. (See Fig. 56; in plan it follows No. 3, Fig. 62.) Some idea of its size can be gained when you know that the diameter of the columns is 6 ft. $9\frac{1}{2}$ in.

This temple will help us to understand another at Ægina, an island to the south of Salamis (65). This was dedicated to Artemis Aphæa, and dates from about 480 B.C. Its plan is shown in No. 3, Fig. 62. It is famous because of the wonderful sculptures of fighting Greeks and Trojans which once graced its pediments. Our drawing (65), shows how the sculptures were placed in the pediment.

DORIC AND IONIC

The lion's head (66) is a superb example of architectural sculpture. It formed part of the temple at Himera, built about 480 B.C., and destroyed by the Carthaginians in 409. The ruins were excavated in 1929 by the Italian Government. Forty of these lions' heads were found.

ARCHAIC IONIC

Just as we find the best examples of the early Doric temples in the Dorian colonies, so we must go to Ionia in Asia Minor for the early Ionic temples. If Syracuse was the most important Dorian colony, then Ephesus and Miletus led the way in Ionia.

66 A lion's head, from Doric temple at Himera, Sicily

Fig. 67 shows that the Ionic Order was very different from the Doric. Vitruvius says the Ionian architects "used the female figure as the standard", and made their columns eight times the diameter in height, and placed a base under it, like a shoe, and added volutes to the capital, like graceful curling hair, and sunk channels on the shaft, as the folds on a matron's garment.

Perhaps the most celebrated Archaic Ionic temple was that at Ephesus, dedicated to Artemis (Diana of the Ephesians).

St. Paul must have known nearly all the places of which Herodotus wrote. In the Acts, chapter xix, we find that Paul "having passed through the upper coast came to Ephesus". It was during this visit that a silversmith named Demetrius, who made silver shrines for Diana, called together his fellow-craftsmen, and pointed out to them that Paul's preaching would turn away people from the worship of the great goddess, and they would find their occupation gone. "And when they heard these sayings, they were full of wrath, and cried out, saying, Great is Diana of the Ephesians."

The temple Paul knew was the later one, built after the fire, in 356 B.C., which destroyed the one we are now going to

THE TEMPLE AND THE HOUSE

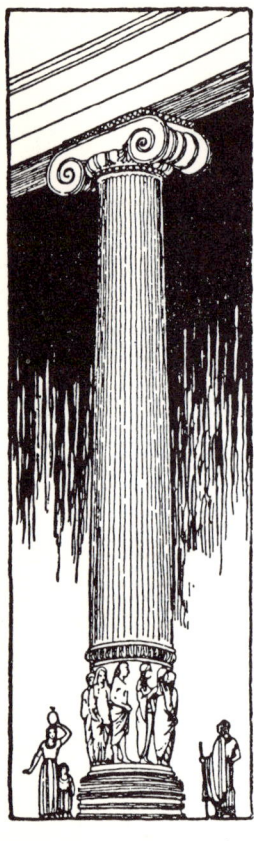

describe. This was dedicated to Artemis, who was the same goddess as the Roman Diana. Crœsus assisted in building this, before his overthrow by Cyrus in 547 B.C. His name is actually cut on a base from the temple in the British Museum. It was a vast building, the top of the platform measuring 180 ft. by 360 ft. (58). The cella, with its front and back porch, was surrounded by a double row of columns. The technical term for a double peristyle is dipteral. There were eight columns across the main façade (octastyle) and nine in the rear (enneastyle), and there were twenty-one along the sides. Herodotus tells us that Crœsus gave golden heifers as an offering, and most of the columns. These columns were of unusual character. Ionic columns had moulded bases, unlike the Doric, which sprang directly off the stylobate without any base. Then above the base mould at Ephesus the lower drums of the columns themselves were sculptured with figures. The Ionic columns were more slender, eight or nine diameters high to the Doric four or five. An Ionic capital from Ephesus is shown in Fig. 67, and it should be noted how oblong it is in shape, and not square, as in the later Ionic caps. It probably, like the Doric, started life as a long pad of wood, cantilevered over each side of the column to pick up the weight of the architrave, and then to ornament it the carpenter cut a spiral on each end, and this became the Ionic cap. The Ionic architrave is triply divided into three faces, and it is thought that this started as three wooden beams, each projected a little forward. The Ionic cornice was decorated with dentils, and these are thought to have been the ends of the cross-ceiling joists.

67 A reconstruction of the Ionic Order of the Archaic Temple at Ephesus

The general form and plan of the Archaic Ionic temple was

ARCHAIC IONIC

much like the Doric one. It was the details which varied. Beyond this we cannot say much, because there are no very complete ruins of an Archaic Ionic temple, nothing as complete as the Doric ruins of the Temple of Poseidon. Fig. 58, reproduced from a drawing by the architect to the excavations of Ephesus, gives the best idea we have of an Archaic Ionic temple.

Vitruvius tells us how the marble for the temple was discovered by a shepherd. During a fight between two rams of his flock, the horns of one, glancing against a rock, broke off a splinter, which showed that it was marble. We are given as well details of the troubles which the architects of the temple, Chersiphron and Metagenes, had in transporting the marble from the quarries to the site. Finally, they found a solution by making it into a gigantic garden-roller, or, as Vitruvius says, "the rolling stone used for smoothing the walks in palæstræ [gymnasia]".

If there is no very complete Archaic Ionic temple, there is a very valuable reconstruction, in the Delphi Museum, of a Treasury built at Delphi by the Siphnians. Siphnos is an island in the Cyclades. These treasuries were built in the form of small temples, at the great shrine, as the headquarters for the people sent to Delphi during the festivals. This Siphnian Treasury is Ionic in character, of the distyle-in-antis type, as No. 1, Fig. 62. It has caryatidæ (or maidens, as the Greeks first called them) instead of Ionic columns. The treasury was built about 525 B.C., of marble, brilliantly coloured, so that it is very interesting as a forerunner of the Erectheum built on the Acropolis at Athens. As examples of Archaic Ionic sculpture we may study the bas-reliefs (about 500 B.C.) from Xanthos in Asia Minor, now in the British Museum. Two of these, a fighting cock and a lioness, are illustrated in Figs. 53 and 55; see also Fig. 114. The sculptors were equally skilled in the working of bronze and other metals: the statuette of a lady shown in Fig. 82 (though it may be later) is inlaid with silver and has small diamonds for the pupils of the eyes.

HOUSES

Having dealt with the temples or houses of the gods and their adornments, we can pass on to the homes of men, and here we are at once in difficulties, because there are so few remains of

68　A Minoan house

THE MINOAN HOUSE

the early types. From the earliest times there seem to have been two types, a northern and a southern, and of these the southern was much more advanced. This from the earliest times was a rectangular building, with a flat terraced roof made of logs, covered with a layer of clay. An example of the New Stone Age has been found at Magasa, in Crete. Here, even before 1700 B.C., we find it developed into a town house, with two or even three stories. Fig. 68 illustrates one of these, and is a reconstruction from one of the faience plaques, showing house fronts discovered at Cnossos. The bases of the walls were rubble masonry, and on these timber framing was erected, filled in with sun-dried brick, which was plastered and in all probability gaily decorated with colours. Generally at the ground-floor level there was only the door from the street. The windows over are quite modern in appearance, divided up with mullions and transoms. The small projection on the top obviously screened a staircase up to the roof. Staircases offered no difficulty to the Minoan architects.

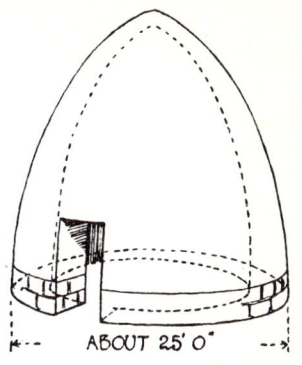

69 A house at Orchomenus, Bœotia, Greece

The northern type of house seems to have developed from the circular hut, formed by leaning saplings against a central post with a covering of thatch, until the shape was like that of the bell-tent. This must be nearly as old as man himself. In the Old Stone Age the Aurignac and La Madeleine drawings suggest this hut form. Again, in the New Stone Age in England, we find the same circular hut, with its conical roof, but vertical walls have been added under to give more height inside. This circular hut was the forerunner of the beehive domed house. This type was built first of wattle and daub, and then of sun-dried bricks (69). Ruins of this type have been found at Orchomenus, in Bœotia, and it must have been the inspiration for the "Tomb of Agamemnon" at Mycenæ. This was a beehive house, built underground as befitting a home for the dead.

A terra-cotta urn, found in the island of Melos, shows the way that man goes to work. He needed a larger type of house than

THE TEMPLE AND THE HOUSE

the single hut, and obtained it by placing seven huts together so that they enclosed a courtyard, the open end of which was closed by a wall with a gate and porch (70).

This type of plan must have proved rather inconvenient, wasteful of material, and difficult to roof. Still, the architects had discovered that it was possible to group parts into a whole. The next step seems to have been a type of plan, as Fig. 71, of the apsidal house at Korakou, Corinth, where the walls between the huts have been done away with and the sides straightened. Here the plan appears to have been based on two and a half huts. Half a hut became the apse at the back, used as a bedroom (thalamus); the hall occupied one and a half huts; the porch (prodomus) another half hut, squared up for convenience. This offered a much less difficult roofing problem, and the thatch could then be laid in two plain slopes. The next step was the fully developed hall plan of the Megaron at Tiryns, which was illustrated in Fig. 37.

70 A reconstruction based on a hut urn from the island of Melos

A small terra-cotta model of a house found in an eighth-century B.C. burial at Argos is evidently a descendant of the apsidal house at Korakou, and then the evidence becomes scanty.

One reason for this was that the Greeks did not pay much attention to their houses. Their climate allowed them to live out of doors, and as there was nothing they enjoyed more than good talk, they passed much of their time in the agora, or market-place, where they could be sure of meeting their fellow-men. Their houses were used for feeding and sleeping. Demosthenes in one of his orations said: "The great men of old built splendid edifices for the use of the State, and set up noble works of art which later ages can never match. But in private life they were severe and simple, and the dwelling of an Aristides or a Miltiades was no more sumptuous than that of an ordinary Athenian citizen." It is to their credit, then, that they paid more

GREEK HOUSES

attention to building the Parthenon to house Athene than their own dwellings.

Again, the climate had something to do with the apparent simplicity of the Greek house. It looked inwards on itself, not outwards on the world, because it was necessary to shut out the glare of the sun and the dust of the narrow streets. Unless the Greek builders were prepared to plaster meaningless ornament on the outside walls, the exteriors of the houses of necessity had to be very simple.

The actual detail of the houses of the fifth century B.C., are exhibited in the remains of one at Dystus in Euboea. Vitruvius said that the Greeks did not have an atrium, meaning, not a complete court, with colonnaded walks roofed over and open in the centre. The entrance passage (of no great breadth) from the entrance gate had the stable on one side and porters' rooms on the other, next the inner gate. From this one enters into the peristylium, with a portico on three sides. "On that side facing the south are two antæ, at a considerable distance apart, which carry beams, and the recess behind them is equal to one-third less than their distance from each other." This was the porch (pronaos). This led to the house-place, or living-room (œcus), where the mistress sat with the spinsters. To the right and left of this porch were two bedchambers (thalamus and antithalamus). Round the porticoes are dining-rooms (triclinia) for common use, the bedchambers and other apartments for the family.

Though Vitruvius' description must apply to later Greek houses, we can still find the various parts in the (fifth century) house at Dystus (72): 1 was the entrance, and 2 appears to be the porters' room. Apparently horses were not kept, but if they had been, the stable would have been on the right-hand side of the entrance passage. According to the fourth book of the *Odyssey*, the chariot, which was a very light affair, was kept "tilted up against the shining walls of the entry".

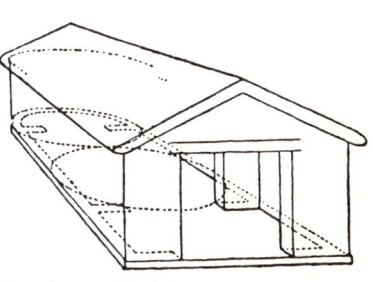

71   An apsidal house at Korakou, Corinth

THE TEMPLE AND THE HOUSE

72 Plan and reconstruction of a house at Dystus, Eubœa, Greece

3 was the court or peristylium; 4 was the hall, or house-place; 5 the bedchambers. The other rooms were used for general family purposes—one would have been the kitchen. At 6 was the exedra, or recess, where people could sit out in the summer. There may have been an upper floor for the women, approached by a staircase, at 7. We saw in Part I how Penelope had an upper chamber that she retired to when the suitors in the hall were a nuisance.

In Part III we shall be able to give rather fuller details of the Greek house.

Chapter VII

LIFE INSIDE THE HOUSE

THE sixth-century Greek architect, like the English one in the Middle Ages, had a very much simpler task than his successors of today. In the Greek and medieval houses one had to provide a hall, and various other rooms which had traditional positions. If one had to pass across one room to get to another, nobody was worried, or talked about privacy being disturbed; in the same way, one might have to cross a courtyard.

A simple house such as the one at Dystus (72), probably housed a larger family than it would have done today. The two bedchambers must have been for the family—the maids and children would have gone upstairs to the rooms over the exedra, and here the women may have retired when the menfolk were entertaining their friends. The slaves and any other folk would have slept in any odd corner.

Vitruvius gives us one indication of the use of the hall, when he says that here "the mistress of the family sits with the spinsters". The married women did the weaving, and their daughters the spinning—hence spinster for an unmarried woman. However, the Greek climate is so pleasant that the hall door would have been open most of the time, and a great deal of the work done in the open court, or under the exedra—here we may be sure that vine and fig trees added colour to the scene.

FOOD

From the point of view of the housewife, the most constant need of man has always been his food. Vitruvius, writing of some of the later and larger houses, says that separate apartments were provided for guests, like the "lodgings" in an Elizabethan house, and that the guests were provided "with poultry, eggs, herbs, fruit, and other produce of the country". The Greeks in late Archaic or Classical times were not mighty eaters of meat, like the heroes of the Trojan War. This in a way is an indication of the northern extraction of the latter. Meat

LIFE INSIDE THE HOUSE

73 The fountain
From a black-figure vase

was not needed in a climate like that of Greece, or only occasionally, when a beast had been sacrificed to a god. Then, after the proper portions had been offered on the altar, the family feasted on the remainder.

In some late fourth-century houses at Priene, near Miletus, in Asia Minor, hearths were found in a central position in some of the halls, like that in the Megaron in Tiryns (39). Here, perhaps, slices of meat were grilled before the fire, or black puddings, like the one Odysseus won by beating Arnæus. Cooking utensils were found in some cases in the porches outside the halls at Priene, where they would have been close at hand for use in the hall. One of the smaller rooms in the house at Dystus (72) may have been used as a kitchen, for the preparation of vegetable dishes. On a raised hearth small charcoal fires were made, and the food stewed over them in saucepans, or fried in olive-oil.

Bread seems to have been baked in a portable pottery oven. It would have been simple to make a wood fire in one of these, and then rake the ashes to one side and imprison the heat to bake the bread by putting on a lid. It is the same principle as the cooking-pit of the New Stone Age and the brick oven of old farm-houses.

The people who lived in the house at Dystus were fortunate;

FOOD. POTTERY

they had a well in their courtyard from which they could draw water. But the black-figure vase painters frequently drew women going to the fountains, so that we can assume that this was the general source of supply. The builders of the city would have chosen a site where there was a good spring, and then conducted the water by pipes to a fountain in the market-place, where it could be discharged through lions' heads, so that the women could fill their jugs (73).

POTTERY

From kitchens, cooking and water supply, we pass naturally enough to pots and pans. Pottery is one of the oldest arts, and has been practised here in England since the New Stone Age. Pottery is like glass-blowing—the maker has only his hands and a few simple tools, but a material which lends itself very readily to shaping. Shape must be considered, and our illustrations will show how beautiful and varied the shapes can be. Then pottery has to be handled, so the quality of the surface should be pleasant. Pottery lends itself to decoration, and every conceivable type has been used. The Minoans, who were wonderful potters, and could draw the figure admirably, did not use it to decorate their vases. The Greeks did, and so their vases have become almost of as much importance as historical documents in showing the feats of the heroes and the details of everyday life. Then pottery is nearly indestructible, and the archæologist uses the potsherd to date the strata through which he digs.

Like everything else, the Greek vases have a long history. Excavations in Northern Greece (Bœotia, Phocis, and Thessaly) have unearthed richly painted vases, decorated with line ornament in red and white, which date from the New Stone Age. Northern Greece appears to have been in advance of the South during this early period.

In the Early Bronze Age this pottery gave way to

74
A Kamares vase

75
A late Minoan vase

coarse unpainted ware. At Hagia Marina, in Phocis, after the New Stone Age, they had a hand-made ware with a black or red glaze, and rectilinear ornaments. This was followed at Orchomenus by Minyan ware, of dark grey or yellow, turned on a wheel. Then there came what is known as Creto-Mycenæan, dating from the first late Minoan period, at the end of the Bronze Age. This must have been imported from Crete, and was found by Schliemann in the shaft graves at Mycenæ in conjunction with the local Minyan ware.

76 A late Mycenæan vase

It is obvious, then, that we must go back to Crete to discover the beginnings of Greek pottery. The New Stone Age pottery, found in Northern Greece, was in advance of that found in Crete, probably because that period lasted longer in Thessaly. Crete seems to have become prosperous suddenly. By the middle Minoan period (2200–1600 B.C.) they were making pottery with a good black glaze, and decorating it with many colours.

The Kamares ware (74), from Cnossos and Phaistos, followed, and here both in shape and the decorations in white, red, and yellow on black, it is easy to see that the potters had made wonderful advances. It was exported to the Ægean Islands and Egypt.

This was followed by middle Minoan III and late Minoan I (75), and now for a short period the potters revelled in a more naturalistic treatment, and employed seaweed and other marine plants, and cuttlefish, among others, as decorative symbols. This would be about 1500 B.C.

In the second late Minoan times there was a return to a more rigid style of decoration, called the Palace style, and then disaster fell on Crete, and the interest shifts to the mainland of Greece. We have come to the Achæan people of whom we wrote in Part I, and the work they did, called late Mycenæan, cannot compare with the Minoan work. Fig. 76 shows one of their vases, in yellowish clay decorated with red. After this came the Dorian Invasion, and the potters had to start again. It is now that we come to the start of Greek vases proper, and

STYLES OF POTTERY

Fig. 77 shows one in the geometric style, 900–700 B.C. At the end of the period we come to the Dipylon ware, so called because very fine examples have been found in a cemetery near the Dipylon Gate in Athens. The decoration is geometric in character, and figures are introduced. Looking at these quaint figures is a good reminder of how knowledge can be lost. In the frescoes at Cnossos and Tiryns, and the sculpture of the Lion Gate at Mycenæ (48), great anatomical knowledge was displayed, and this had all been forgotten, and a beginning made again in these quaint little figures.

77 Types of Greek vases

About the seventh century B.C. there were new developments. By this time the Greek colonies in Asia Minor were firmly established, and they served as a half-way house between the East and Greece. They collected Oriental fabrics and metal ware, and traded them back to their homeland. Here they served as an inspiration to the potters, and the new style of pottery came to be called Corinthian, doubtless because Corinth was a great trading centre.

The decoration advances, and the palmette, or honeysuckle pattern, is employed, and well-drawn animals are painted in continuous bands, in black and purple on yellow backgrounds, the outlines being incised by lines scratched on the surface of the clay. In the later Corinthian vases the animals give way to the human figure. In the British Museum there is a plate with a fine drawing on it of the fight between Hector and Menelaos.

LIFE INSIDE THE HOUSE

Work like this prepared the way for the black-figure vases of the sixth century B.C.—so called because the figure and ornaments were painted directly in a black varnish on to the orange-red clay of the background. Detail was given to the figures by incised lines; sometimes purple and white were added for the same purpose. These black-figure vases are contemporary with the Archaic architecture and sculpture, and have the same charm, and it is these which would have been used in the house at Dystus The design on the bottom of the cup of a kylix by Exekias (see Fig. 77 for shape of kylix) is founded on the legend of Dionysus, the god of the vine, given in one of the Homeric Hymns. The god was once by the seaside when pirates who were sailing by spied him, and coming ashore seized, bound, and carried him to the ship, thinking to sell Dionysus as a slave. But his bonds fell away, and the pirates were afraid, and hoisted their sail, thinking that the god could not escape when they were at sea. But fragrant wine flowed through the ship, and a vine sprouted and twined round the mast; meanwhile the god was changed into a roaring lion, and a bear, and the pirates leapt overboard and were changed into dolphins.

78 Athenian feeding-bottle (*c.* 500 B.C.)

Fig. 77 gives the types of Greek vases in general use, and their technical names. The fine pieces would have been used for table purposes, or to decorate the sitting-rooms. The vases we see in museums have generally been found in tombs, where they were placed for the use of the dead in the spirit world. Plain, undecorated ware was used for kitchen and storage purposes. The big jars (pithoi), with

79 An oil flask (askos), Athenian black figure

BLACK-FIGURE VASES. DRESS

pointed ends, were supported by being driven into the earth.

COSTUME

Having considered cooking, and pots and pans, we can now think about dress. If, of the three primary occupations, feeding comes easily first, the second

80 The Dorian chiton

must be given to dressing. We may be sure that the Greek woman, with a roof over her head, after she had fed her family, turned her attention to clothes.

Taking her own garments first, she wove on her loom (25) what we should call a dress-length, about 6 ft. wide by 11 ft. long. This she made into her principal garment, the chiton, without any cutting or waste of materials; and this is a very important detail to note in the drawings. Herodotus has told us (p. 99) of the two types of chiton, the Dorian and Ionian. The Dorian was made very simply, by taking the length of material and folding over about a quarter of its width. It was then arranged and fastened on the shoulders by brooches, as at A, Fig. 80, and fell into the familiar folds as at B. In the earlier styles the open side was not sewn up, but it was secured by a girdle at the waist, and the material pulled out and pouched over the girdle. The turned-over piece which hung down at back and front, looks, in some of the vase drawings, as if it were a separate tunic, but this is not so. The later chitons were sewn up at the sides.

The Dorian chiton was fastened, at first, on the shoulders, by pins made of the leg bones of small animals, fibulæ, and later, when

81 The Ionian chiton

LIFE INSIDE THE HOUSE

82 A bronze statuette

they came to be made of metal, they were still called by the same name. The earliest garments were woven in fine wool.

The Ionian chiton was introduced early in the sixth century. This was much more like a dress, and did not have the turned-over piece, so it was more economical so far as the material was concerned. The width was about 4 ft. 6 in., and the length twice the span of the arms, say 11 ft. The material was folded and sewn as C, Fig. 81, leaving holes for the head and arms, and it then fell into folds as D. Finely crinkled linen, like crape, was used, and sometimes muslin. The chiton was girdled and pouched. Sometimes the material was striped, and had fringes added. Saffron and red seem to have been favourite colours. Under the chiton the woman may have worn a little slip, and probably a broad belt to support the figure.

The vase drawings show varying fashions, especially in the use of the mantle, or himation. This, again, was a plain oblong, but of many sizes, and worn in different ways. A small himation might be thrown over the shoulders and worn indoors on chilly

DRESS

days, and a larger one as a cloak when going outdoors. Sometimes they are shown under the left arm and over the right shoulder, or a fold might be drawn up as a head covering. They have decorative borders, and are shown hanging in such cunning folds that it almost suggests the himation was sometimes pleated. These are well shown on the Archaic bronze (82) of one of the female Archaic figures which were discovered in excavations on the Acropolis site. They were there when the Persians destroyed the Acropolis in 480 B.C. (p. 104), and afterwards must have just been shovelled into the ground to assist in building up a new level.

83
End of sixth century B.C. A warrior blowing a trumpet through the mouthpiece
From Athenian fabric

Women had various ways of doing their hair, and wore caps and veils. Our illustrations, which have all been made from black-figure vase drawings, show as many types as we have been able to find. Indoors the Greeks do not seem to have worn shoes, and sometimes not out of doors.

When we come to man's costume, we find that the most important garment was a plain tunic, which could be short in the case of the peasant, or much longer where one had a draughty job, like the charioteer (106).

Sometimes the tunic was short and tight, and worn under the armour (83). Another useful garment for the working man was a short double apron, as Fig. 107. Men of high rank appear to have worn white, and the peasants a natural wool colour. There were conical caps and useful high boots (85). When travelling, men wore

84 Sixth century B.C. An archer in Asiatic costume blowing a trumpet through the mouthpiece

LIFE INSIDE THE HOUSE

a wide-brimmed felt hat called petasos (Fig. 170).

FURNITURE

The principal pieces seem to have been the couches used by the men to recline on when dining. The women did not use them in this way, but sat on a chair when taking their meals. The food was served and brought in on the light three-legged tables, one to each person (86). These were low enough to be pushed under the couches when not in use. The couches served as beds at night, and had a mattress supported by interlaced cords, or leather thongs stretched between the wooden frame. Fig. 87 shows a baby's cot from a black-figure vase. There were chairs and stools; clothes were kept in chests, as they were in England until the beginning of the seventeenth century, and the other things were hung on nails in the wall. There were many beautiful types of chairs—no less than three are shown on the Harpies' Tomb in the British Museum. This dates from about the middle

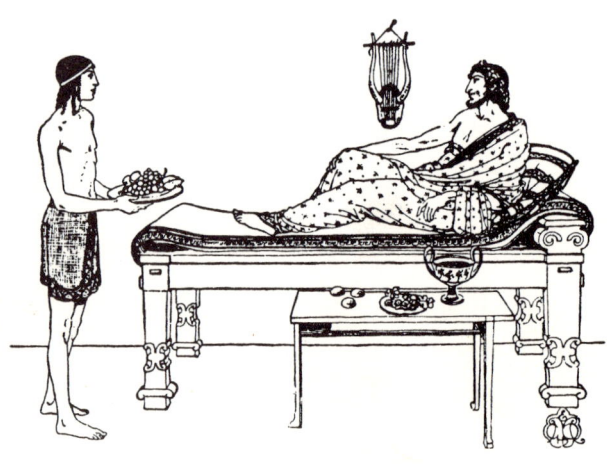

85
Hermes, sixth century B.C.
From a black-figure vase

86 A couch and table
Reconstructed from black-figure vase drawings

FURNITURE

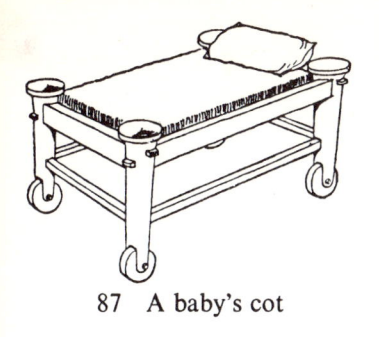

87 A baby's cot

of the sixth century B.C., so we are given admirable details of Ionian furniture of that period. The three chairs are seats of honour (thronos), and footstools were generally used with them. Fig. 88 has square-cut feet, with terminals of a swan's head on the back, and the front and the back legs have been framed up so that the wider and more ornamental face came at the side of the chair. In Fig. 92 it comes in the front. The actual seat of the chair was probably of leather thongs, to support the loose cushion which hung over a little in front and at the back. Fig. 89 has turned legs, and Fig. 90 claw-and-ball feet. This is not by any means the first appearance of this type of foot. Tutankhamen's throne had animal's feet.

It should be noted that we did not add the tenons shown in our reconstruction; the sculptor cut them in the original marble. The same thing occurs with the figures from Branchidæ in the British Museum. These figures, seated on their thrones, and cut out of marble, once stood along a processional way leading to the Temple of Apollo at Didyma, near Miletus, in Asia Minor. Herodotus says that there was an oracle there from very ancient times which the Ionians and Æolians consulted. These figures date from 580 to 520 B.C. Fig. 92 shows one of the thrones. Figs. 91 and 93 show stools.

Greek women had all kinds of small ornamental objects such as trinket-boxes, wicker-work baskets in which to keep their wools, mirrors, pins for their hair, and brooches for their dresses.

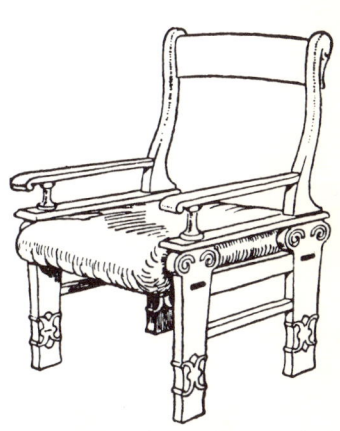

88 A chair from the Harpies' Tomb

135

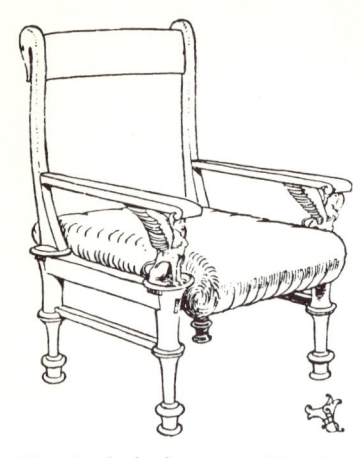

LIFE INSIDE THE HOUSE

89 A chair from the Harpies' Tomb

90 A chair from the Harpies' Tomb

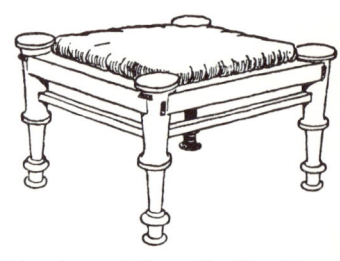

91 A stool from the Parthenon frieze

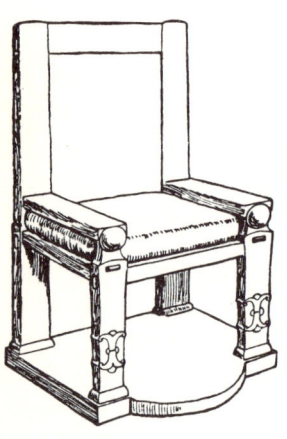

92 A chair of figures from Branchidæ

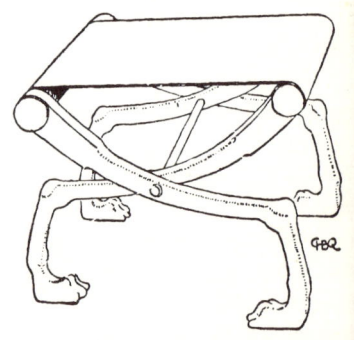

93 A folding stool

89–93 Chairs and Stools.

EDUCATION

We may be sure that the Greek mother was not too much occupied with her housekeeping to find time to superintend the education of her children, and she could then, as now, send them to school. In the sixth book of Herodotus we are told that the roof of a schoolhouse had fallen in upon their boys (Chios), who were at lessons. This was about 494 B.C., and there were 120 pupils in the school. Herodotus seems to have mentioned the school not as a rarity, but because of the tragic result of the roof falling and killing nearly all the pupils. We can take it, then, that there were schools in Greece in the Archaic period before Salamis.

The boys were sent to school when they were about seven, and went accompanied by an old slave, who appears to have gone inside with them, perhaps to help maintain order. On the vases, the boys are shown standing before their masters, who are seated on stools. This must be a convention, because there can hardly have been one master to each boy. On a red-figure vase one master plays a flute, another looks at a written exercise, the third master and pupil each have a lyre, and the fourth reads from a roll.

Writing was done on wax-coated tablets. These were made of wood, and the central panel was surrounded by a flat, raised edge, which served to protect the wax coating on the panel. Several tablets were strung together on strings, passed through holes bored in the edges. The writing was scratched on the wax surface with the sharp point of a stylus. At the British Museum there is a tablet which has a multiplication table and a reading exercise on it, and a beautiful ivory stylus found in a fifth-century B.C. tomb at Eretria in Euboea. The stylus is flattened at the other end so that mistakes could be scratched out.

Paper made from papyrus, and pens and ink, were used for important documents.

In arithmetic, the Greek boy was handicapped by a most inadequate set of symbols. His numerals followed the alphabet, so he had letters instead of numbers. This was in reality a great help, because he was thrown back on his fingers to count with (hence, digit, a finger, for a number under 10), or pebbles (hence, calculate, from calculus, a pebble), or the abacus or

LIFE INSIDE THE HOUSE

reckoning-board. The abacus must have been a very useful implement. Here it is at A, in its simplest form of pips, or beads, on wires.

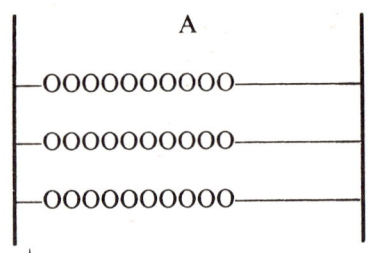

```
          A
—OOOOOOOOOO——
—OOOOOOOOOO——
—OOOOOOOOOO——
```

The ten beads on the top line count as 1 each, and
added together . . . . . . = 10
The ten beads on the second line count as 10 each, and
added together . . . . . . = 100
The ten beads on the third line count as 100 each, and
added together . . . . . . = 1000
                                                    ―――
                                    All the beads = 1110

How the Greek boy used the abacus we cannot say; but obviously addition would not be difficult.

```
        B1                              B2
—OOOO———OOOOOO—          —OOOOO———OOOOO—
—OOOOOOOOO———O—          —OOOOOOO———OOO—
—OOOOOOOO———OO—          —OOOOOOOO———OO—
```

Supposing you wished to add 216 and 15 and 4. The two 100's would be slipped to the right as B1, then one 10 and six 1's for the 16. Then comes 15. You want one 10 and five 1's, but you have only four 1's left. However, you can get over this by adding two more 10's to the right, and slipping back five 1's to the left, but you must return four of these to add the 4, and complete the addition. Your abacus, as B2, will then have two 100's at the bottom, three 10's above it, and five 1's, or a total of 235.

B2 will serve to illustrate subtraction. If you wished to subtract 235 from 1110, by moving these pips to the right you can read

ARITHMETIC

off that there will remain on the left eight 100's, seven 10's, and five 1's, or a total of 875. Multiplication could have been turned into an addition.

The great advantage of the abacus must have been that the Greek boy could experiment with numbers, and discover the difference between odd, even, and prime. He ceased to think of them as numbers; they came to life, became things, and he saw them. This is proved by the names he gave them. The root of a square number was called its side. The gnomon, originally the upright pointer of a sundial, was employed to indicate a square, which was shown arithmetically thus, ⌐: : the square root here was literally the side of the diagram. Or the Greek boy could build up a square of pips on his abacus, and find the root quite simply.

In the same way, in geometry, the words used show that the Greeks saw these things: isosceles comes from Greek words for equal and leg; equilateral from equal-sided; parallelogram from contained by parallel lines; parallelepiped, from parallel and plane, and hypotenuse from to stretch under.

Thales of Miletus (624–546 B.C.) in Ionia, Asia Minor, was one of the first philosophers who was interested in arithmetic. He travelled in Egypt, and probably saw there the methods of the Egyptian land surveyors to which Herodotus referred in his Book II (p. 93). The famous Rhind Papyrus in the British Museum (about 1700 B.C.) gives rules for measuring areas. The Egyptians knew that a triangle having its sides of lengths of 3, 4, and 5 is right-angled, and used this method of setting out right angles. Probably they did not know the proof, and this was left to Euclid (323–283 B.C.).

It is thought that Thales invented the theory of geometry. Pythagoras of Samos, like Thales, travelled, and was interested in numbers. He is known to schoolboys by his famous proposition, that the square on the hypotenuse of any right-angled triangle is equal to the sum of the squares on the other two sides, and he probably did this by making models.

Greek schoolboys knew no algebra: this was not invented until the third century B.C., by Diaphantes of Alexandria.

The education of Greek girls was entirely domestic. In Xenophon's *Œconomicus*, to which we shall refer later, the young wife of Ischomachus had passed her girlhood "under the strictest restraint, in order that she might see as little, hear as little, and ask as few questions as possible".

MUSIC

We can now consider music, and the great importance which the Greeks attached to it. Plato, later on, was to point out that education should have two divisions, gymnastic for the body, music for the soul—and music included literature, because poetry was chanted to the accompaniment of the lyre. Lyric poetry has the nature of a song, in which the poet tells us his thoughts. Epic poetry is a recited narrative of the doings of a hero perhaps, and dramatic poetry would be acted.

Plato said that music should be considered for its words, melody, and rhythm. Certain harmonies he disliked very much. The Ionian and Lydian are instanced as being relaxed and soft, and more suitable for drinking parties than the education of the young. For this latter purpose the Dorian and Phrygian harmonies were preferred, because these had a strain of courage and temperance. Perhaps Plato summed up the whole matter when he said that "Beauty of style and harmony and grace and good rhythm depend on simplicity—I mean the true simplicity of a rightly and nobly ordered mind and character, not that other simplicity which is only an euphemism for folly."

Passing to instruments, he condemned the flute for its "composite use of harmony". The lyre and harp were allowed for use in the city, and pipes for shepherds in the country. We will consider the lyre first, and here we can turn to the Homeric Hymns, which, if not composed by the same hand as the *Iliad* and *Odyssey*, are of great age. In the hymn, or lay, to Hermes, we find that it was the messenger of the gods to whom the Greeks credited the invention of the lyre. When young, he found a tortoise feeding on grass, and, choking the creature, scooped out its inside with a gouge of grey iron. He then "cut to measure stalks of reed, and fixed them in through holes bored in the stony shell of the tortoise, and cunningly stretched *round* it the hide of an ox, and put in the horns of the lyre, and to both he fitted the bridge, and stretched seven harmonious chords of sheep-gut".

Fig. 95 shows the back, or carapace, of the tortoise, and what is more important, the belly, or plastron, and the fact that it is

MUSIC

attached to the carapace. This seems to have been lost sight of by many writers, who assume that Hermes stretched the oxhide across the belly, as if the lyre were like a banjo. The hymn is explicit, that the oxhide was stretched round the shell, obviously with the idea of closing the holes in it fore and aft, used by the tortoise for projecting his head and legs. The stalk of reed may have been drilled across from edge to edge of these holes, as supports for the oxhide, and to add to the resonance.

94 The music lesson

There are in the British Museum the remains of an early lyre found in a tomb at Athens. The horns are of sycamore, on to which the top bar is jointed (95). This precluded tightening the strings by tuning, as with violin pegs, so it seems as if each string was pulled as tightly as need be round the bar and then tied. This is suggested by some of the vase drawings. The small drawings in Fig. 95 are from black- and red-figure vases.

The kithara must have been developed from the lyre. It seems to have been the instrument used by professional musicians at public festivals, while the lyre was used in the home. It represents the same idea, but the body of the instrument was made of wood instead of tortoise-shell.

This leads us to Pythagoras' interesting discovery, that the musical intervals correspond with certain ratios in the lengths of strings at the same tension. Thus the fourth, fifth, and octave of the note are produced by stopping the string at three-quarters, two-thirds, and half of its length. One assumes that the Greek musicians must have had some scale before the time of Pythagoras, as primitive people of today have, but it was not a scientific one. Pythagoras (572–497 B.C.), philosopher, mathematician, and geometrician, hoped to find the key to beauty and harmony in some subtle combination of numbers.

The pipes were said to have been invented by Pan, the son of Hermes, who had goats' legs and horns, and whose friend was Echo. One of the Homeric Hymns is dedicated to Pan:

LIFE INSIDE THE HOUSE

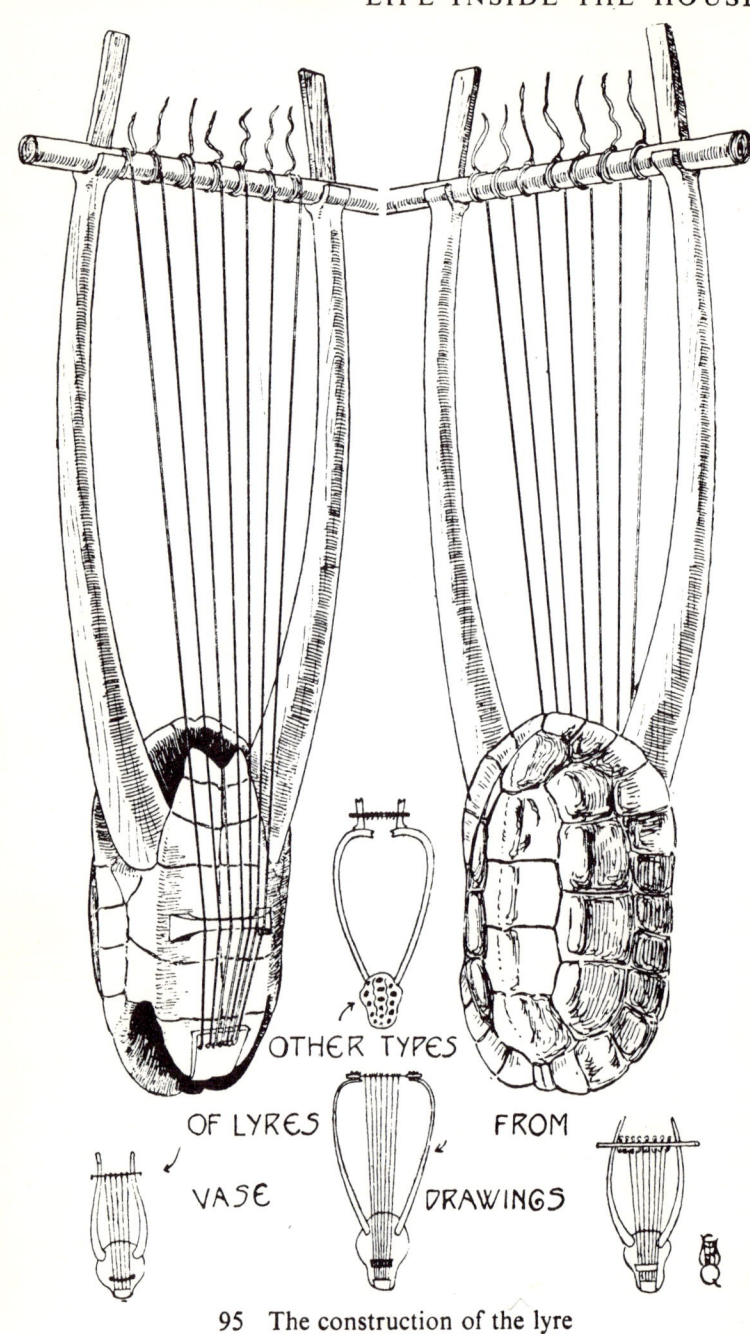

OTHER TYPES
OF LYRES   FROM
VASE   DRAWINGS

95 The construction of the lyre

MUSIC AND DANCING. GAMES

Tell me, Muse, concerning the dear son of Hermes, the goat-footed the twy-horned, the lover of the din of revel, who haunts the wooded dells with dancing nymphs that tread the crest of the steep cliffs, calling upon Pan the pastoral God of the long wild hair.

Pan's pipe, or the syrinx, was made of graduated reeds, fastened together with wax and cords. He was the god of the country, and protected flocks, but wandered in the forests, and led dances of the nymphs. If you heard his pipes, then there was no saying what might happen. Echo would take up the refrain, and you be cast in panic fear.

DANCING

The flute was used to accompany dancing; it was played in pairs, by the help of a mouth-band. The dancers often used castanets. Dancing with the Greeks had a religious character. A dance would be performed at a public festival in honour of a god or goddess. Women danced at home for their amusement, but not men and women together as with us. It is curious, but men and women seem to have been much better companions in the *Iliad* and *Odyssey* than they were in Archaic or Classical Greece. Perhaps this was because in between these times many had emigrated to Asia Minor and rubbed shoulders with Oriental peoples. The Greek men do not seem to have danced. The tale of Hippocleides, on p. 101, shows that the guests were shocked at his performance. It was more usual for professional dancers to perform at the symposia or banquets. Judged by the vase drawings, Greek dancing consisted of a series of graceful rhythmic movements of the body and arms, assisted by the swing of the draperies. There is a beautiful drawing of girls dancing, on a vase shaped like a knuckle-bone, in the British Museum.

GAMES

Knuckle-bones was a game played by women as well as by boys. Knuckle-bones came from the ankle joint of cloven-footed animals. The five small prettily shaped bones were thrown into the air, one at a time, and had to be caught and retained on the back of the hand. We have seen, on p. 91, how Herodotus gave the credit to the Lydians for inventing this game.

LIFE INSIDE THE HOUSE

In the Metropolitan Museum in New York there is a terracotta group of two girls pickaback. This, apparently, was a kind of forfeit for failure in a ball game. In the same place there is a toilet-box with a drawing on it of two girls: one stands behind a wicket in exactly the same attitude as a wicket-keeper, and the other girl is throwing a ball in; the batsman or batswoman is absent, otherwise it looks exactly like an early game of cricket. Women are shown on another vase in New York whipping tops. On p. 40 we have seen how Nausicaa fell to playing ball. Hoops are often shown on the vases.

Chapter VIII

LIFE OUTSIDE THE HOUSE

THOUGH we think of the city-State as being typical of Greek civilisation, the city was very small judged by modern standards. The people were not huddled together in a mass of houses, with the country miles away, and only to be reached by a long journey through suburbs. The Acropolis at Athens was at one time the actual town, a city on high, with the country coming right up to its walls, and even in the time of Pericles the area of the city was not large.

Each city was the centre of a much larger agricultural district, so the Greek was very fortunately placed. He could civilise himself by living in the city and rubbing shoulders with his fellow-men in the market-place and gymnasia, or retire to the quietude of his farm in the country if he needed rest and peace.

We gave details in Part I of eighth-century B.C. country life from Hesiod's *Works and Days*, and in Part III we shall use Xenophon's fourth-century *Œconomicus* for the same purpose. In the Archaic period the life of the Greek countryside was probably just as pleasant as that described by these authors.

FARMING

Hesiod, however, paints a picture of rural life as being very laborious. His Bœotian farmer wrests a living from the soil only by persistent labour. But by the time Xenophon was writing, conditions had become much easier, and slaves were employed to do the hard work. Slavery seems to have started with the enslavement of the natives by the Dorians when they invaded Greece. The position of the slaves does not seem to have been worse than the English villeins of the Middle Ages. They were attached to the land, and had to work for their masters. As many of them were prisoners of war, they were not regarded as a race apart.

The black-figure vases frequently show country-life scenes. Men beat down the olives from the trees, and women pick them up, just as they do today, and ploughing is another subject.

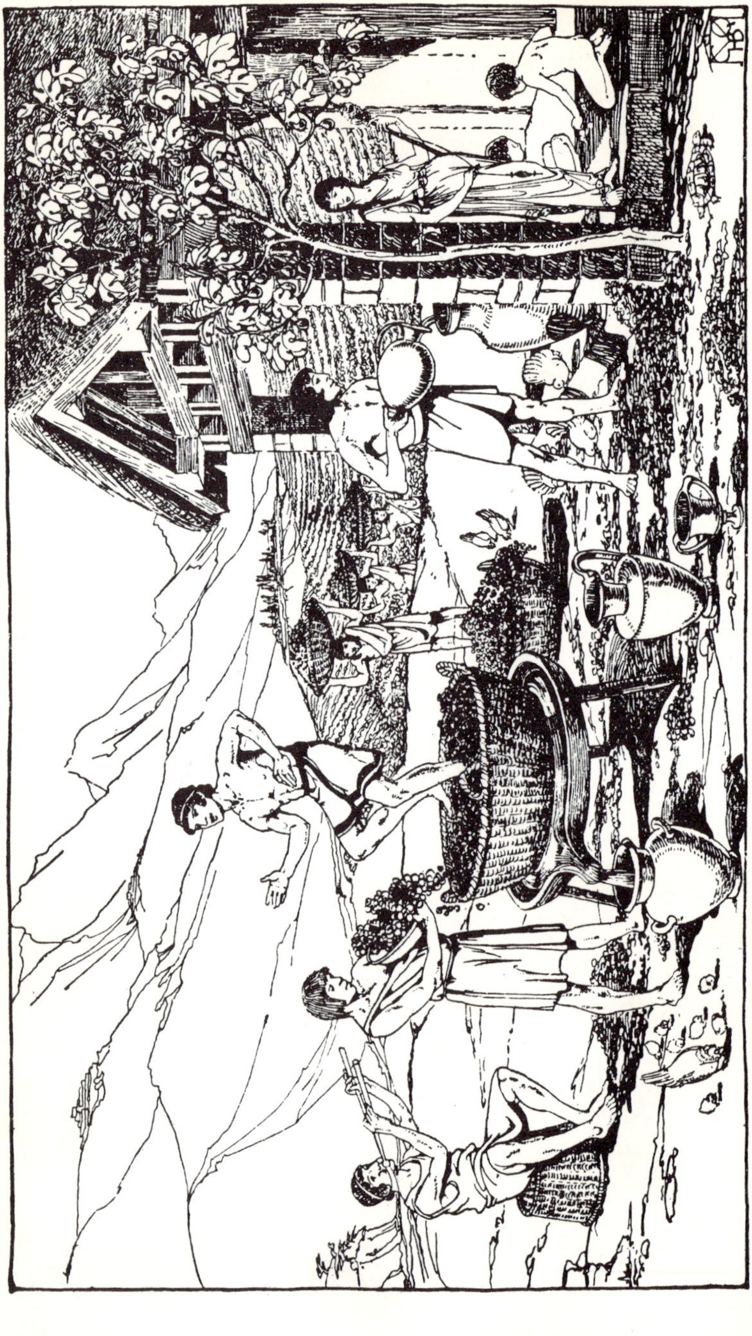

THE HARVEST: WINE AND CORN

Fig. 96 shows a vintage scene which has been reconstructed from a black-figure amphora. The grapes are being trodden out in a large wicker-basket, mounted on a three-legged stool, with a spout to it to conduct the wine into a jug. In the original the work is being done by satyrs, who were attendants on Dionysus, the giver of wine.

97 A satyr with a wineskin, *c.* 500 B.C.

The satyrs, and their female companions the mænads, are often shown on the vases. They laugh, dance, skip, and indulge in the most irresponsible gambols, and their habits are not polite. Dionysus and his attendants represented, not so much wine and pleasure, as the life and fertility of vegetation. The satyr is always shown with a tail like a horse and pointed ears.

Demeter was the corn spirit. In one of the Homeric Hymns, we hear how she brought famine to the land. Persephone, the daughter of Demeter, was stolen by Hades, the god of the dead, for his wife, by Zeus' permission. Demeter, in revenge, prevented the growth of the crops until the gods gave her news of her daughter. Hermes, the messenger, was then sent to Hades, to tell him that he must send back Persephone to her mother, but,

98 Dionysus, end of sixth century B.C.
From Athenian fabric

LIFE OUTSIDE THE HOUSE

before doing so, he gave her sweet pomegranate seed to eat. This is the food of the dead, and whoever eats it must return to Hades; and this was Persephone's fate—for two-thirds of the year she was free to live with her mother, but for the remaining third she had to go back and reign as Queen of the Shadows.

In this hymn we hear of a drink made of meal mixed with water, and flavoured with the tender herb of mint.

So much for the Greek as a farmer. His own simple needs were corn for his bread, olive-oil instead of butter, and goat's milk to drink, or wine diluted with water. At a festival he could sacrifice a heifer or kid and eat its flesh. He grew beans and peas, and kept bees to provide honey for sweetening purposes.

It was when he wished to dispose of this surplus produce that he was confronted by the problem which turned him into a sailor. The fertile plains in Greece, like those in Norway, are often cut off from one another by mountain ranges in between, so it was much easier for the farmer to load his produce into a boat, and, hugging the shore, sail to the next township to barter his wine for pottery. In this way he early learned the usages of the sea, and by the Archaic period he was trading all round the Mediterranean, and learning the details of the craft which was to stand him in such good stead at Salamis. Herodotus tells us in his third book that "twice a year, wine is brought into Egypt from every part of Greece"—in earthen jars.

SHIPS

We have seen in Part I how the Greeks sailed in their ships to the Trojan War, and Hesiod's eighth-century farmer was quite prepared to go to sea. In Part I we reconstructed a boat from a vase in the British Museum, which dates from about 800 B.C.(52). This boat was still used in the Archaic period, and seems to have been referred to as a "long boat".

The next development seems to have been the penteconter, or fifty-oared galley. We have seen how Herodotus gives the credit for the first long voyages to the Phocæans of Asia Minor. He says they used the long penteconter, and not the round-built merchant ship, and that they explored the shores of the Mediterranean as far as Tartessus, near Cadiz. This was very different from sailing through the Cyclades to Asia Minor (2).

We have attempted a reconstruction of a penteconter in

THE PENTECONTER

99 The penteconter

Fig. 99 from various vase drawings. It seems to have been the long boat, with a boar's head added as a ram and small decks fore and aft. In addition to the fifty oars, it carried one square sail.

If we refer to Fig. 99, it will be seen that horizontal lines run from the edge of the sail, and that in between these each section is bellied out—also that from the yard eight lines are shown coming down to the bulwarks. From this it is thought that the sail, made of thin canvas, was divided up into squares by leather or webbing strips (99). On to the intersections of the strips a ring was sewn, and the buntlines being passed through these, the sail could be triced up to give the steersman a better outlook forward, and reefed when it blew hard. On some vase drawings these buntlines are shown coming from the foot of the sail. It was really very much like the old-fashioned Venetian blinds, made of thin laths of wood, which could be drawn up by cords. It remained on ships till Roman times. Down-hauls may have been used to set the sail.

In addition, the penteconter, of course, had forestays and backstays to secure the mast, halyards to haul up the yards, sheets to secure the sail, and braces to pull round the yards.

Herodotus writes in the third book of an expedition of the Spartans against Samos, in the time of Cambyses, and says that this was the first time they went into Asia; also, that all ships in these early days were painted with vermilion.

LIFE OUTSIDE THE HOUSE

100 The merchant ship
From a black-figure vase

As to the round-built merchant ships, these are shown on the black-figure vases, and there is a good drawing on one in the British Museum. This we have reconstructed in Fig. 100. Obviously the hull is rounder, and not so long and snaky as the pentecontor. It did not carry any oars, and depended solely on the one square sail. The rigging of this was much the same as the pentecontor, and all this is very clearly shown. It is when we consider the superstructure of the hull that the trouble begins. Over the gunwale comes a long band of diagonal sloping lines, above this is another band of cross-hatching lattice, and above this again, supported on posts, a balustrade made up of three horizontal lines, with other vertical ones at intervals. Some writers have thought this was a ladder, but the ship is already provided with the one which was used for getting on or off, and shown in the usual place on the stern. Obviously there was no need for a second ladder, especially one nearly as long as the ship, so we take it that it really is a balustrade to a walk fore and aft (100).

We assume that this was necessary, because the boat was not decked, and if this was so, then the band of diagonal lines becomes a cloth which could be stretched along to protect the cargo, and the band of criss-cross is rope-lacing to secure the cloths.

MERCHANT SHIPS, TRADE AND INDUSTRY

TRADE AND INDUSTRY

All cargo boats, however, were not undecked. Fig. 102 shows a reconstruction of a very beautiful design on the inside of a black-figure Spartan drinking-cup (kylix). It shows Arkesilas of Cyrene watching the loading of silphion into a merchant ship. Cyrene was a Greek settlement on the north coast of Africa (p. 96); the vase painter put in

101 A carpenter with an adze (*c.* 500 B.C.)
From a red-figure goblet

the monkey to set the scene in Africa. Herodotus, in book three, tells us that silphion (a carrot-like plant, 3 ft. high) was grown in North Africa, and used both for food and medicine.

In the design, we see how the silphion has been dried and baled up, and is being weighed before the king, and then, packed in sacks, is being taken down into the hold. The yard has been lowered, and swung inboard to support the scales, and the sail forms an awning for the working party. It is interesting to find that the balance-type of scale was used and not the steelyard of the Romans.

So far as industry is concerned, the building trade must have been in a prosperous condition in Archaic Greece. With all the temples to build, there could not have been much unemployment. Fig. 101 shows a carpenter using an adze.

Another important trade must have been that of the smith. How to provide himself with weapons or tools with a keen cutting edge has always been a matter of prime importance to man. He first used flints, which he flaked to an edge. He then discovered bronze, and this metal was used in the Homeric period. Homer, writing the *Iliad* and *Odyssey*, about the tenth century B.C., mentions iron, which was then taking the place of bronze in Greece.

As iron has been of so much use to man, it is worth while

102 The loading of silphion at Cyrene, Africa

103 Winter 104 Summer

Bas-Reliefs from the Ludovisi Throne, now in Rome (early fifth century B.C.)

105 (*left*) A Tanagra figure of a
wearing a sun hat, made about 300

106 The life-size figure of a chario
The eyes were of onyx and enamel,
lids inlaid with copper, and the h
band with silver. The original stoo
a chariot drawn by four horses. (M
about 480 B.C.). (Now in the De
Museum)

IRON SMELTING, MONEY

taking some trouble to find out how he smelted the ore. One of the earliest illustrations must be the drawing on a black-figure wine jug at the British Museum, which is Athenian ware of the end of the sixth century B.C.; we have reconstructed the drawing in Fig. 107. It is really a blast-furnace, embodying the same design that is used today. A tower was built up, probably

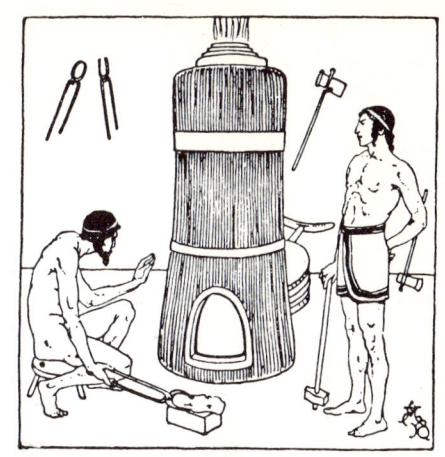

107 Iron smelting
From a black-figure vase

of bricks, with a lining of clay, and banded round to give greater strength. In the tower were placed layers of charcoal and ore, and a fire being kindled, the door in front was closed up, and a blast sent into the furnace from the bellows behind. This had the same effect that bellows have on an ordinary fire. The heat was maintained by closing the top of the furnace up. When the ore had melted, and the charcoal consumed itself, the metal slowly trickled down into a lump at the bottom of the furnace. This "bloom", as it was called, was reheated, and then forged into shape.

This type of furnace did not, of course, generate enough heat to make the iron run so that it could be cast. Bronze, however, melts at a much lower temperature, and there are vase drawings of foundries where bronze figures were cast from similar furnaces.

MONEY

Trade and industry lead us naturally to money. Unless the traders do their business by barter, they need money as a medium for the exchange of goods. This is the only function of money, and the real basis of trade; it also explains why money has sometimes taken such strange forms: flat iron currency bars were used in England in the Early Iron Age before the Romans came. So long as these were recognised as currency, and not counterfeited, trade could go on.

LIFE OUTSIDE THE HOUSE

Again, in small communities, where everybody knew everybody, it was usual to give credit to trustworthy people. The settlement took place after the harvest. They all totted up their tallies, and found out how they stood. The hard-working, far-seeing man might find that he was better off than the thriftless one. If some were one up, others were one down. A few currency bars or coins would enable them to settle their differences, and start level again. But they had not made or lost money —they had made, or failed to make, goods.

There remains the question of price, which was, and still is, settled by supply and demand. If a majority of the Greek traders made wine, and only a few pottery, up went the price of the latter. The intelligent man would try to arrange his trading so that he could buy cheap and sell dear. If, however, a criminal began to buy up money, and gamble in currency, then he committed a crime against the community, because he hampered trade.

We saw, on p. 91, how Herodotus gave the credit to the Lydians for being the first people to use gold and silver coins. The Greeks adopted the money habit from the Lydians, and made their coins so beautifully that all the later coinages have been modelled on them. You can see them at the British Museum with the early gold staters of Crœsus.

TRAVEL

When the old Greek wished to travel on land he used the chariot. In the fourth book of the *Odyssey* there is a fine description of the chariot drive of Telemachus from Pylos to Sparta.

A fine Corinthian krater shows the departure of Amphiaraos, who was one of the heroes of Argos. He was persuaded by his wife Eriphyle, who had been bribed by a necklace, to join in an expedition against Thebes, in which he knew he would be killed. The vase painter has depicted the warrior's departure. Just such a scene must have occurred in old Greece when any soldier went off to the wars, or the father of a family left on business travel. We have attempted a reconstruction in Fig. 54.

The chariot has been brought out of the entry, and the horses have been yoked to it. We described the chariot in detail on p. 74. A groom stands at the horses' heads, a stirrup-cup

COINAGE, TRADE, TRAVEL, GAMES

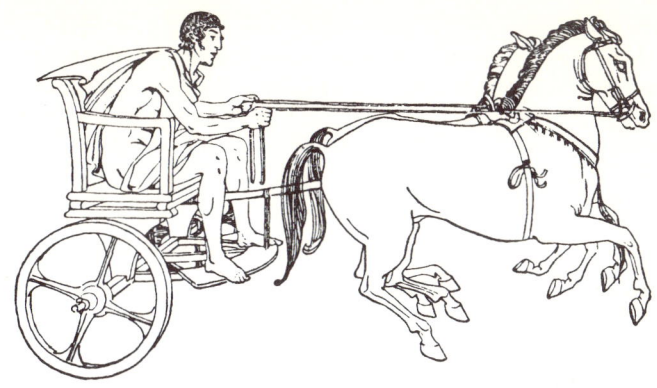

108 A cart
From a black-figure vase

is being handed to the charioteer, and he is shown on the vase, clothed in a long tunic, like the Delphic charioteer (106). This was the equivalent of an overcoat, and a more comfortable driving garment than the shorter tunic. The family all stand round, and a little dog jumps up to say good-bye to his master. Lizards run up the wall; there is a scorpion, and what looks like a hedgehog.

In the Archaic period chariots were no longer used in war.

The Greeks were good horsemen, and there are many fine vase drawings of them as such. Another mode of conveyance was a small two-wheeled cart (108) drawn from a black-figure vase.

GAMES

When we come to the amusements of men, the first place must be given to their organised games. These date from a very remote antiquity. The Greeks thought that they were originated by Heracles himself. In Part I we noted how, in the twenty-third book of the *Iliad*, Homer describes the games held after the funeral of Patroklos. Chariot-racing, boxing, wrestling, and running were included.

Again, on p. 93, we saw how the dead Phocæans were honoured with "solemn games both gymnic and equestrian". This does not mean that all the games were always solemn, or only associated with funerals. In the eighth book of the *Odyssey* we are told how the Phæacians entertained Odysseus. There

LIFE OUTSIDE THE HOUSE

was a sacrifice, then a feast, followed by games of running, wrestling, boxing, dancing, and casting a great stone. Like every other Greek activity, the games were held under the patronage of the gods, and after sacrifice had been made to them. Fundamentally, the games kept men fit and prepared them for war; also they satisfied the Greek ideal—that a healthy body was necessary for a well-balanced mind. The Greeks, being artists, must have derived great pleasure from watching beautifully proportioned bodies in action.

It must have been at the games that the sculptors gained their inspiration, and saw the models which they translated into terms of beauty in marble. This was possible because in the early days and the best periods there was no trace of professionalism, or the specialist, and the Pentathlon was introduced as early as 708 B.C. This consisted of five events—running, jumping, discus and javelin throwing, and wrestling. The prize, only a crown of wild olive, was given to the best all-round man; brain had to be added to brawn, and beauty to both. All over Greece we may be sure that every boy practised these five parts of the Pentathlon, hoping that he one day would be able to represent his city at Olympia. This great festival was first held in 776 B.C., and then every four years until A.D. 393.

Another useful purpose which the games served in Archaic Greece was that they helped to keep the peace. We have seen that the people were quarrelsome. The small city-States, which fostered genius, bred a strong local patriotism, which expressed itself in fierce inter-city jealousies. Sparta and Athens were generally at loggerheads, and their dissensions are bound up in, and almost constitute, the history of Greece. Just as William the Conqueror introduced a Truce of God to stay his turbulent barons from killing one another, so the authorities at Olympia, every four years, sent heralds, wearing crowns of olive, to all the Greek States to proclaim a Truce of Sport. So for a time all the Greeks forgot their quarrels and engaged in friendly contests.

Visitors to the Games came from all over the Greek world, and camped on the plain. Competitors arrived at Olympia some while before the festival, and went into training; they had also to satisfy the judges that they were of Greek birth.

The festival lasted for five days. All the competitors sacrificed to the gods, and swore that they had been properly trained,

GAMES. OLYMPIA

and would not cheat in the contests. The games opened with chariot- and horse-races, and then followed the Pentathlon. The sacred enclosure was situated on level land at the foot of the Hill of Cronos at the junction of the Rivers Cladeus and Alpheus. The enclosure was called the Altis. On the north side was the temple to Hera, to which we referred on p. 111. This dates from about 700 B.C., and there were two earlier ones on the same site. The great Temple of Zeus, on the south side of the Altis, was not built until the fifth century B.C., nor, probably, the treasuries of the various Greek cities which formed the headquarters of the deputations sent to Olympia. It was then that Pheidias made his great statue of Olympian Zeus. In his workshop have been found clay moulds for its gold drapery. An earlier dedication of the same century was a Persian conical helmet, perhaps from the battle of Marathon in 490 B.C., inscribed, "Given to Zeus by the Athenians who took it from the Medes." In Archaic times all would have been much simpler: the temple set in an enclosure —an altar for sacrifice—simple buildings for treasuries—pleasant gardens and colonnaded walks, with statues set up to celebrated athletes. The stadium was to the east of the Altis, with earth banks for the spectators to sit on. The elaborate stone seats found at some places were added at later times.

109 Heracles, sixth century B.C.
From a black-figure vase

The stadium was so named because its length was 1 stadion, or about 606 English ft., and its width about 30 yds., not quite so long as an English furlong of 10 chs. or 660 ft. Heracles is supposed to have stepped it out. The competitors raced up and down, and did not run round as we do. The track was covered with white sand. At Olympia you can still see the starting- and finishing-lines of the fourth century B.C. These were formed by letting stone slabs, about 18 in. wide, into the ground right across the course. In these, parallel grooves are cut about 7 in.

LIFE OUTSIDE THE HOUSE

apart, which appear as if they had been used by the runners to get a toe grip. Again, at 4-ft. intervals, there are square sockets which must have taken wooden posts. The posts suggest that lines were stretched along the course. These would have been very useful for the short race of one length of the stadium. In longer races the posts alone would have served to fix the turning-points, the Greeks had races of 7, 12, 20, and 24 stades.

Herodotus gives us an idea that, notwithstanding his oath, the Greek athlete needed watching. In the eighth book, Adeimantus says: "Themistocles, at the games they who start too soon are scourged." "True," rejoined the other, "but they who wait too late are not crowned." This explains why, on all the vase drawings, the referee, instead of being provided with a whistle, is always armed with a good strong rod.

We can now discuss the Pentathlon.

Jumping.—Greek jumping was a running long jump, as ours, except that the jumper was assisted by weights, which he held in his hands and swung forward to assist him in his flight through the air. The weights weighed about $2\frac{1}{4}$ lb., and the jump was made on the forward swing of the arms. The jumping-ground was dug up, and the jumps marked by little pegs. On a red-figure vase in the British Museum a flute player is playing, and the jumper may have regulated the swing of his weights by the music. Apparently the Greeks did not have high jumps.

Throwing the Discus.—We read in Part I how at the Phæacian Games Odysseus threw a great stone, and at the funeral games of Patroklos, in the *Iliad*, Polypoites flung a pig of iron "as far as a herdsman flingeth his staff". By Archaic times this had been regularised into a circular metal plate, from 6 to 11 in. in diameter, and weighing from 3 to 9 lb. The thrower stood on a space marked off by lines in the front and at the sides, and his endeavour was to throw the discus as far as possible, not, as in quoits, to hit a mark. The discus was held above the head, the left hand holding the lower edge and the right hand the upper edge; it was then swung down in the right hand, and back again on the forward swing, to be thrown with all the weight of the body behind it. Myron's "Discobolus" (484–440), shows the moment when the discus has been swung back, and is just going forward again. The record throw in the modern Olympic Games is 180 ft. $6\frac{1}{2}$ in. (1952); the world record throw (1953) is recorded as 194 ft. 6 in.

THE PENTATHLON

Throwing the Javelin.—The Greek javelin was about the height of a man, and was thrown by the assistance of a leather thong (the amentum) bound to the centre of the shaft, and into which the first two fingers were put. If the amentum was slightly twisted on the javelin, a rotary movement was given to it.

110　The pankration

Xenophon, in his work on Horsemanship, writes of javelins of cornel wood thrown from horseback. The rider advances his left side, and draws back his right, and, rising on his thighs, launches the weapon with the point directed a little upwards.

Wrestling.—Wrestling is one of the oldest sports. With the Greeks a fall on any part of the body counted. If both wrestlers fell, there was no count. Three falls gained the victory, and tripping was allowed. In one vase drawing, one man has played a clever trick on his opponent. He has seized his arm, turned, pulled him on to his back, and then pitched him over it.

Boxing.—Boxing is described by Homer in the funeral games of Patroklos, and in Part I we wrote of the fight between

111　A cock-fight: Corinthian ware, sixth century B.C.

LIFE OUTSIDE THE HOUSE

112 A huntsman with fox and hare: kylix (goblet), about 520 B.C.

Polydeuces, the champion of the Argonauts, and King Amycus. Greek boxing-gloves, until the end of the fifth century, consisted of thongs of oxhide bound round the hands. Apparently there was not any ring, or rounds, or body-blows, or classes. They aimed at each other's heads. Though the heavyweight might score in the boxing, he would not have had any chance of winning the Pentathlon.

The Pankration.—This event first instituted in 648 B.C. was a regularised rough-and-tumble fight to the finish. Wrestling, strangling, arm-twisting, hitting, kicking, and jumping on one's opponent were allowed. Apparently one could do everything with, or to him, except bite him, or gouge out his eyes. It was drawn on the vases (110), and may have been rather comic in reality.

Sport.—Apart from the regularised games, there were other sports. Fig. 111 shows a cock-fight, which is an example of an unpleasant subject treated in a delightful way.

Hunting was not so much a pastime as a means of stocking the larder. Figs. 112 and 113 are animated little pictures from black-figure vases.

Having dealt with Life and Work, we come to Death and Funeral monuments.

Fig. 114 is a reconstruction of the Harpies' Tomb, from Xanthos, Lycia, in Asia Minor. The sculptured panels which formed the actual sides of the sepulchral chamber are now in the British Museum. Originally this chamber was set upon the top of the tall shaft, as shown in our drawing. There was a small door into this chamber on the west side, closed by a slab of stone.

113 Olpe (ware jug): Attic Corinthian fabric, sixth century B.C.

114 The Harpies' Tomb, from Xanthos, Lycia, Asia Minor

LIFE OUTSIDE THE HOUSE

Its name was given when it was thought that the figures in the frieze were harpies carrying off the dead.

Now it is thought that the winged figures in the frieze show the Genius of Death carrying away, in a kindly fashion, the soul of the deceased person—the soul being shown by a miniature figure.

PART III
Classical Greece

III. CLASSICAL PERIOD

B.C.	CURRENT EVENTS	B.C.	SCIENCE AND ART
480.	Battle of Salamis.	484.	Birth of Herodotus.
479.	Battles of Platæa and Mycale.	480.	Birth of Euripides and Antiphon.
478.	Wall of Athens rebuilt and port of Peiræus completed.		
477.	Confederacy of Melos.	477.	Myron of the Discobolus.
475.	Capture of Eion.		
		474.	Pindar.
474–472.	Conquest of Scyros.	472.	Pheidias begins. Æschylus at Court of Hieron.
471.	Ostracism of Themistocles.	472–465.	Polygnotus painting.
469.	Pericles comes to the front.	471?	Thucydides born.
		469.	Socrates born.
465.	Greeks attack Persians in Pamphylia and conquer Thasos. Death of Xerxes.	468.	Sophocles.
		462.	Anaxagoras at Athens.
460.	Greeks assist Libyans against Persians.	460.	Hippocrates born.
457.	Long Walls built.		
456.	Athenians conquer Bœotia and Phocis.	456.	Death of Æschylus.
454.	Common funds moved from Delos to Athens.		
450.	Truce between Athens and Sparta.		
448.	Congress at Athens to decide on rebuilding temples destroyed by the Persians.	448.	Birth of Aristophanes.
		447–438.	Parthenon built. Ictinus and Callicrates, architects. Pheidias, sculptor.
433.	Beginning of the quarrel between Sparta and Athens.		
432.	Revolt of Potidæa.	437–432.	Propylæa built. Mnesicles, architect.
431.	Outbreak of Peloponnesian War.		
430.	Outbreak of plague in Athens.		
429.	Death of Pericles.		
		427.	Birth of Plato.
		426.	Temple of Athena Niké. Callicrates, architect.
425.	Fortification of Pylos and capture of Sphacteria. Spartans propose peace.		
424.	Thucydides banished.		
423.	Truce between Athens and Sparta.		
422.	Expedition to Chalcidice.		
421.	Renewed truce.	c. 421.	Erechtheum begun.
420.	Alcibiades comes to the front.		
416.	Athenians conquer Melos and massacre the inhabitants.		
415.	Athenian expedition to Sicily.		
413.	Spartans invade Attica and fortify Decelea, and total destruction of the Athenian forces in Sicily.		
		409.	Work on Erechtheum resumed, finished about 406.
		406.	Death of Euripides and Sophocles.
		405.	Aristophanes' *Frogs*.
404.	Surrender of Athens. Destruction of the Long Walls.		

Chapter IX
GREEK ARCHITECTURE

IF we are to deal with things, Greek architecture must be allowed to take the first place.

The Romans took their architectural ideas from the Greeks, and whether they built at Rome, or Timgad in North Africa, or Bath in Great Britain, they used the same Classical details to clothe their buildings. In the Renaissance in Western Europe in the fifteenth and sixteenth centuries these old Classical details were reborn, and have continued in use down to our own time.

The work done in Greece twenty-five centuries ago still influences architecture today.

THE ACROPOLIS AND ITS TEMPLES

We will make a beginning with the work at Athens. The town stands back from the sea some four miles, and Peiræus was its port; the walls of Athens were continued down to the port as a corridor, so that the town was safe, and could not be cut off from its wooden walls on the sea. When we think of Athens as a city, it is generally a picture of the Acropolis, its rocky crags crowned with old buildings, as Fig. 115, which first comes into our minds. This is just as it should be, because the Acropolis was the first city. Thucydides tells us, "Before this [the union of Attica under Theseus, the legendary hero who fought the Minotaur] what is now the Acropolis was the city, together with the region at the foot of the Acropolis toward the south."

Athens, then, must have started life as a place very much like Tiryns, which we illustrated in Figs. 36 and 38. Acropolis comes from two Greek words for high and city, and the first Athens was placed on this high rocky crag, so that the early Achæan chieftains could feel safe and secure, and keep watch and ward over the country below. Fig. 115 shows the Acropolis from the west. It is about 1,000 ft. long from east to west, by 500 ft. from north to south, and the slope being more gradual on the west, here is the entrance, which we shall discuss presently.

GREEK ARCHITECTURE

115 View of the Acropolis, Athens, from the Hill of the Pnyx

Pausanias, in his description of Greece, between A.D. 150 and 175, says, "there is but one entrance to the Acropolis: it admits of no other, being everywhere precipitous and fortified with a strong wall".

Fig. 115 has been taken from the Hill of the Pnyx to the west of the Acropolis. This was the place of assembly for the people, where they were addressed from the bema, or platform. Slightly to the north of a line from the Pnyx to the Acropolis is the Areopagus, or Hill of Ares, so called because he was the first to be tried there. This was the great Court of Justice, cut out of the rock itself, in the form of three sides of a quadrangle, surrounded by a bench. The accused and accusers stood on unwrought stones—the stone of injury for the accused, and the stone of ruthlessness for the accusers. Near by was a sanctuary of the goddesses called the Benevolent Ones. This was a polite and safe way of talking of the Furies, who punished crimes and were feared by both gods and men. Persons who had been acquitted in the Court of the Areopagus celebrated their escape by sacrificing to the Furies in this sanctuary.

Having sketched in the general outline, we can now go up on to the Acropolis. The principal buildings were not built in the same order that we have described them. The Parthenon, which we have left till the last, was the first to be built, between 447 and 438 B.C. The Propylæa followed in 437–432, Athena Niké in 426, and the Erechtheum, begun in 421, was not finished until about 406.

ATHENS. THE ACROPOLIS

THE PROPYLÆA

We enter by the Propylæa (116). This is a descendant of the simple type of entrance we first saw at Tiryns in Part I, p. 64. This latter is called a Propylon. Propylæum is the term used for the gate into the Temenos, or sacred enclosure of a temple. At Athens the whole Acropolis, which was at first the actual town, came to be used as a sacred place, and as there are five doors, the plural form, Propylæa, is used. It was built between 437 and 432 B.C., just at the beginning of the Peloponnesian War, and the architect was Mnesicles. It is as pure in its detail as the Parthenon, without any hint of the over-elaboration we shall find in the Erechtheum. The Propylæa follows the Tiryns type of a front and back porch, with a dividing wall between, in which are the actual doors (119). Fig. 116 gives a reconstruction of the west, or entrance front, which the Athenian saw as he climbed up from the town. It should be noted how skilfully the six Doric columns of the central portico are arranged. To appreciate this, we must remember the original timber construction of the Doric Order which we discussed in Part II. The beam over the columns is the architrave, and the ends of the original cross-beams, which rested on the architrave, gave rise to the triglyph design, which is a distinctive feature of the Doric Order. The spaces between the triglyphs, often beautifully sculptured slabs, are the metopes; this part is the frieze. The architrave, frieze, and the cornice over it is the entablature. It is the setting out of this which settles the spacing of the columns under. One of these always comes under a triglyph, except at the angles, where, as the column is wider than the trigylph, it is moved in a little, so that the outside of the column and the entablature above are in line. This had the advantage of giving the angles an appearance of greater strength, because the two outer columns are closer together than the others. Generally there is one triglyph between the columns, but at the Propylæa a wider central entrance was desired, so here there are two triglyphs instead. On the left of the Propylæa was a building which is called the Picture Gallery, and on the right the architect appears to have contemplated a corresponding building. This was never completed, perhaps because it would have encroached on the sanctuary of the little Temple of Niké Apteros, which comes

116 The entrance front of the Propylaea, Athens

117 Restoration of the Erechtheum, Athens; from the North-west

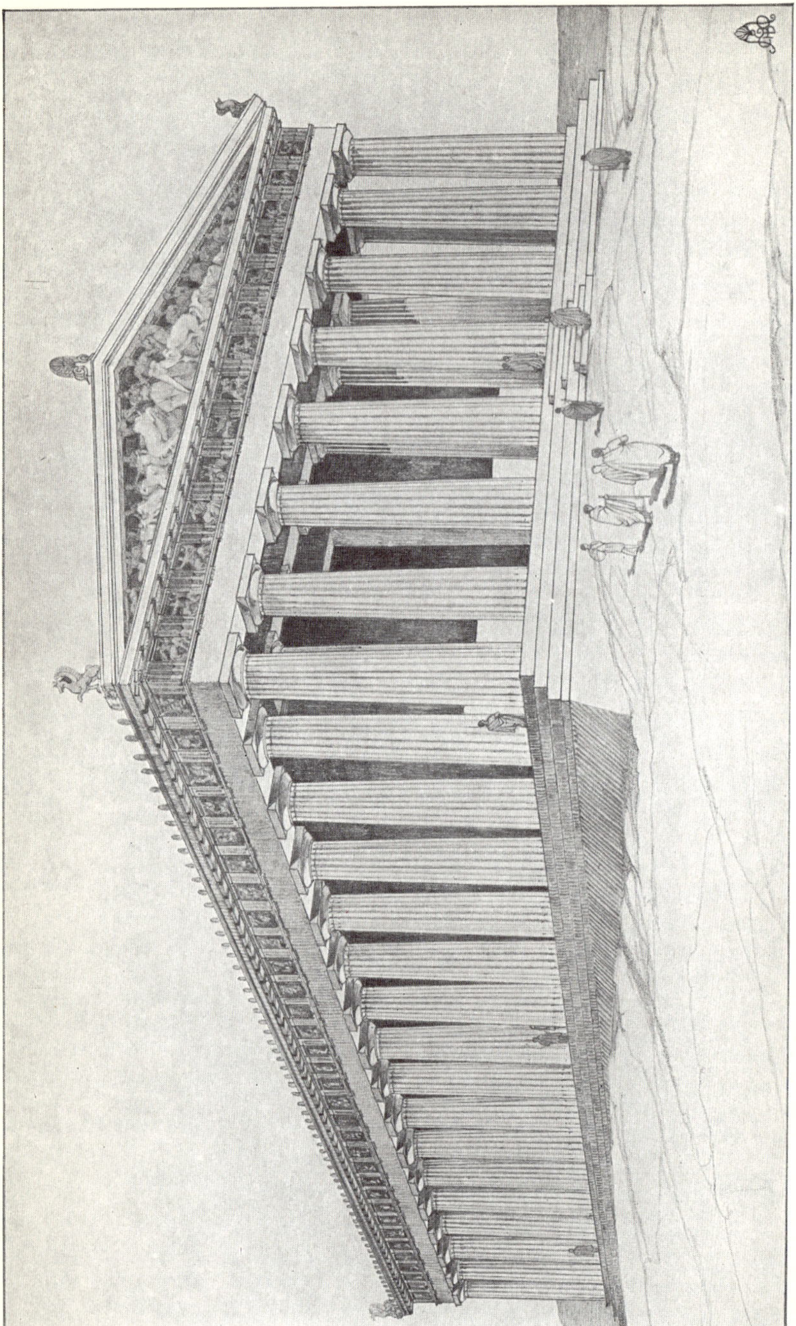

PROPYLÆA

on this side of the Propylæa, or perhaps because the Athenians were now more inclined to war than building.

On the Acropolis side of the Propylæa, at each side of the gateway, were halls, which would have

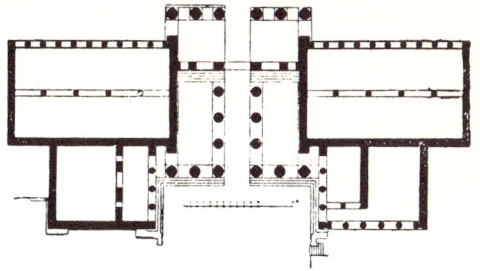

119 The Propylæa of the Acropolis
Restored by Dörpfeld

been useful as gathering places for pilgrims to the temples. A lower gate, discovered in 1852, was built about A.D. 250.

Today, one approaches the Propylæa by wide marble steps. The lower ones were added in Roman times, and form an interesting comparison between the later and the original work. The joints to the Roman steps are visible, and the work comparatively rough. The joints to the steps of the stylobate, or base of the Propylæa, are nearly invisible: apart from the design, the Greek builders got an exquisite finish into their work that no other craftsmen have ever approached.

Originally the path up to the Propylæa was on the actual rock face, and as it was steeply sloping, the architect had to build up a platform of four steps for the building to stand on, but these were broken in the middle, so that the beasts for the sacrifices could pass through the central gateway, 14 ft. wide by 24 ft. high (1). This rise in the ground meant that the floor of the back portico was five steps higher than the front one, as was its roof. The internal columns, which were necessary to carry the wider ceiling of the front portico, and which were placed at the side of the central processional way, were of Ionic design; we saw the beginnings of the Ionic Order in the Temple of Artemis, at Ephesus (67). There the caps were oblong in shape and a little clumsy; here, in the Propylæa, they are square and of the most beautiful proportion and finish. This double row of Ionic columns was necessary to carry the marble ceiling: all construction was of the post and lintel type, the columns being the posts and the ceiling-beams the lintels. Pausanias was struck by the beauty and size of the blocks of which the ceiling was constructed, and said they had never been matched. These are

GREEK ARCHITECTURE

shown in Fig. 1, and a reminder must be given of the size of the building. This outer porch of the Propylæa is 59 ft. 6 in. wide between the walls. The width from centre to centre of the Ionic columns over the processional way is 17 ft. 6 in., and from the centres of the Ionic columns to the wall behind, 21 ft. These were the lengths of the marble ceiling-beams, which not only carried the coffered marble slabs that formed the actual ceiling, but had to support the timber roof above them. It says a good deal for Pentelic marble as a building material.

120
The kithara

Fig. 1 shows the coloured decorations on the ceiling of the Propylæa. These were carried out in gold and blue, and green and red.

The effect must have been superb, as the colours glowed on the translucent surface of the marble in the light reflected from the marble pavement under. We do not know if anything was done with the plain surfaces of the walls. Now, these are of the most mellow loveliness, stained an orange tint here and there by the passing of time; when new they must have been of a glaring whiteness. The walls of the portico of the Propylæa do not appear to have been covered with fresco painting, otherwise Pausanias would have mentioned them when he visited the Acropolis. He does tell us of the pictures in the Picture Gallery at the side. He mentions, among others, Orestes slaying Ægisthus, and Odysseus approaching Nausicaa washing clothes with her maidens (p. 40). This was by Polygnotus, and must have been transferred from an earlier building, because he was painting between 473 and 465 B.C. All these paintings have long since vanished. Probably they resembled the vase paintings in which beautifully drawn figures express the painter's intention, and the background is only slightly suggested.

In Fig. 1 the figures we have shown have been drawn from the Parthenon frieze (p. 179), and show the victims for the sacrifice passing up through the Propylæa. The oxen have gone on ahead and are followed by sheep. Then come tray-bearers carrying small cakes, and youths with jars of wine for the libations. Then there are pipe players, and men playing on the

PROPYLÆA. ATHENA NIKÉ

kithara. This was a form of lyre which in its simplest type had a sounding-box made of a tortoise-shell (see p. 141). In the kithara this was beautifully shaped in wood (120). The instrument was supported on the left hip and held in position by a band passing round the left wrist, which left the fingers of this hand free to stop off the strings at the proper intervals to produce the notes. All the strings seem to have been fastened on to the one yoke at the top, and not on to separate pegs like a fiddle. The strings were struck with a plectrum held in the right hand. The kithara appears to have been used by professional musicians, and the lyre in the home.

TEMPLE OF ATHENA NIKÉ

Fig. 121 gives the position of the little Ionic Temple of Athena Niké, built about 426 B.C., from designs by the architect Callicrates. Its skewed position, on the bastion on the right-hand side of the approach to the Propylæa, was probably due to the fact that it replaced an earlier shrine. It is a small building, the stylobate or platform on which it stands only measuring about 18 ft. 6 in. by 27 ft. The front wall of the central cella, in which the figure was placed, was open save for two square pillars, and in between these a metal grille was fixed. There was a portico in front of this, and another at the back. Technically, this plan is described as tetrastyle amphiprostyle (62). Tetrastyle means having four columns. The Ionic caps shown in Fig. 135 should be noted. Their form is like that of a sheet of paper whose ends are rolled up. The curled shapes of these ends, which are called volutes, show on the front and the back; this did not matter until the architects came to the angle columns, where they were confronted with the problem of making both faces the same. They solved this by making the angle volute on a diagonal line, which was not quite satisfactory. The later Roman architects made all these volutes in this diagonal way, so that all four faces of the cap were the same.

This little temple, sometimes called Niké Apteros (Wingless Victory), doubtless served a similar purpose to that of a side chapel, dedicated to some particular saint, in a medieval cathedral: it was a place at which the pilgrims could offer a special prayer.

Pausanias tells us that the sea is visible from the bastion, and

GREEK ARCHITECTURE

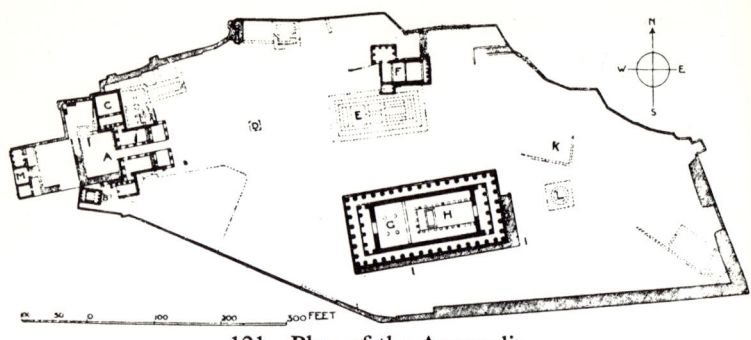

121 Plan of the Acropolis

A Propylæa.
B Niké Apteros.
C Picture Gallery.
D Athene Promachos.
E Earlier Parthenon.
F Erechtheum.
G, H Parthenon.
M Beulé Gate.

it was here that Ægeus, the father of Theseus, waited for his son's return, and when he saw that the sails of the returning ship were still black, threw himself down on the rocks below and was killed. In his time the Athenians had to send each year to Cnossos a tribute of youths and maidens to be sacrificed to the Minotaur (p. 11). Then Theseus went one year to kill the monster, and told his father that if he were successful he would, on the return journey, change the black sails with which the ship set out to white, and this he forgot to do.

The sculptured slabs (152) are supposed to have formed a parapet round the bastion on which the temple stands.

ATHENE PROMACHOS

When the pilgrim had passed through the Propylæa the first thing that he saw must have been the great statue of Athene Promachos (the champion) (121). This was designed by Pheidias, and cast in bronze from the Persian spoils of Salamis. The gilded helmet of the figure was 53 ft. above the ground, and just as today it is thrilling to pick up the outline of the Acropolis when coming to Athens by sea, in the old days the Athenian sailors would have seen, in addition, the rays of light gleaming from the helmet of Athene guarding their town.

The Erechtheum is on the left hand as one enters the Acropolis, and the Parthenon on the right; the statue of Athene was on the open space in front, and here were many others, and trophies

ATHENE PROMACHOS. ERECHTHEUM

set up to remind the Athenians of their famous men and heroic past. Pausanias mentions, among the other things he saw on the Acropolis, a bronze figure of the so-called Wooden Horse, but says that all except simpletons know that it was only an engine for breaking down the walls of Troy (p. 42). One piece of sculpture showed Heracles strangling the serpents, another the birth of Athene from the head of Zeus.

PRECINCT OF ARTEMIS BRAURONIA

The space on the right-hand side of the Propylæa, in front of the west end of the Parthenon, was the precinct of Artemis Brauronia, who was the goddess to whom the women of Athens appealed, and the little girls served her before marriage. Once upon a time Artemis was very angry because a she-bear had been killed: she was the protectress of game. Because of the death of the bear, a feast was held once a year when a goat was sacrificed, and little girls appeared as she-bears in saffron-coloured dresses.

THE ERECHTHEUM

The Erechtheum, a very interesting building, shows that the Athenian architects could not only build simple types, like the larger temples, but were quite able to grapple with the complications of a difficult site, varying levels, and the grouping of several parts into a whole. Work was started 421 B.C., and resumed in 409, to be finished about 406. This was after the total destruction of the Athenian forces in Sicily in 413, and just before the surrender of Athens and the destruction of the Long Walls in 404. The Athenian Empire had come to an end, and Athenian pride had been humbled in the dust of the quarries at Syracuse (p. 247). This is reflected in the architecture of the Erechtheum. Though the workmanship is beautiful, there is much unnecessary ornament. Take one example—the Ionic columns are not really helped by the collar of ornament added under the volutes of the capitals—in fact, they are rendered less beautiful than those of the Propylæa shown in Fig. 1. The archæologists have had a difficult task in reconstructing the building, because it has had many uses, and has been altered from time to time. It has been a temple, a Christian church, and a pasha's house during the Turkish occupation.

GREEK ARCHITECTURE

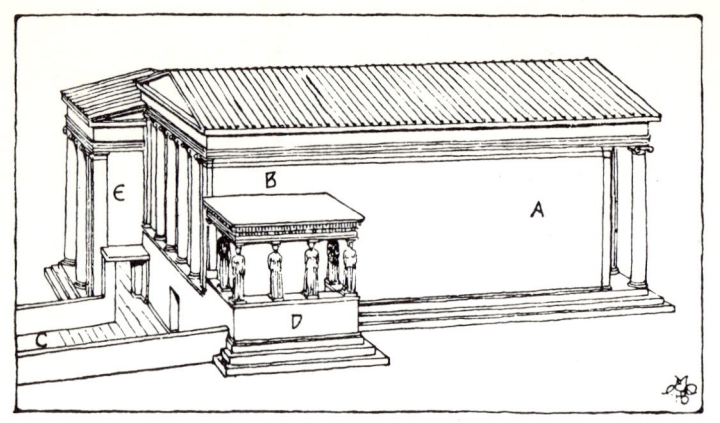

122 A bird's-eye view of the Erechtheum; from the south-west

    A Cella of Athene.   C Sanctuary of Pandrosos.
    B Shrine of Erechtheus. D Porch of the Maidens.
                 E The north portico.

Fig. 122 gives a bird's-eye view of the building from the south-west. On the high level, at A, was the Cella of Athene, with a portico before it. Behind this to the west, on a lower level, at B, was the Shrine of Erechtheus, and here there was a salt spring under the floor. This part of the building is of the usual Greek temple type, except that on the west end the Shrine of Erechtheus was lighted, either as shown in Fig. 117, by leaving out the upper part of the walls between the columns, or by windows. To the north was another beautiful portico which led into the Shrine and the Sanctuary of Pandrosos. In a crypt under this portico was a trident mark. To the south is the Porch of the Maidens, which led from the higher ground to the south down into the Shrine of Erechtheus; one of these Maidens is in the British Museum.

On the west was the Sanctuary of Pandrosos, where the sacred olive tree grew. This was burned during the Persian invasion, but new green shoots appeared and put hope into the hearts of the Athenians. The Erechtheum marks the spot where once the traditional contest took place between Athene and Poseidon for the lordship of Athens. Athene had produced as her symbol the olive tree, and Poseidon the salt spring. The Erechtheum enshrined these, and the mark of Poseidon's trident on the rock.

ERECHTHEUM. PARTHENON

The legend is that Erechtheus was the son of Hephæstos, and was reared by Athene. She left him in charge of Agraulos, Pandrosos, and Herse, concealed in a chest which they were forbidden to open. They did open it and saw the child in the form of a serpent. Erechtheus became King of Athens, and when Athene and Poseidon had their contest, he decided in favour of Athene. Homer referred to Athens as the "strong house of Erechtheus". He became a god after his death, and the building which commemorates the contest was called after him. When the Erechtheum came to be built, it had to be a museum as well as a temple, and this is the explanation of what appears to be the somewhat haphazard planning of it as a whole —the buildings had to be built on the sacred spots.

Pausanias wrote of the Erechtheum that there was an altar of Zeus before the entrance, but no animals were sacrificed, only cakes laid on it. Inside the building there were three altars— one to Poseidon, on which they sacrificed as well to Erechtheus; one to Butes, a hero; and the third to Hephæstos. There were paintings on the walls. Within, "for the building is double, there was sea-water in a well, and when the south wind blew the well gave forth the sound of waves". Pausanias tells us also of the mark of the trident on the rock, and how Poseidon brought these details forward as evidence in support of his claim to the country.

The Maidens of the Erechtheum exhibit the elaborate dressing of the Athenian woman's hair: this can be studied on the one original in the British Museum (centre of Fig. 123; round it are other fashions from red-figure vases).

THE PARTHENON

Now we can turn to the Parthenon itself. An earlier temple to Athene, built about the middle of the sixth century B.C., and another which had only just been begun, were destroyed by the Persians in 480 B.C., and the stone from these was used to rebuild the north wall of the Acropolis. Ictinus was the architect, and he was assisted by Callicrates. Pheidias was the sculptor. The Parthenon took ten years to build, 447–438 B.C., and it marks the culmination of the Greek Doric style, and is one of the most famous and purely beautiful buildings of the world. We dealt with the timber origins of the Doric style on p. 112, and

GREEK ARCHITECTURE

here in the Parthenon these can still be traced in the marble.

We gave a smaller plan in Fig. 62: it is the type called by architects octostyle peripteral, because it has eight columns in front and rear, and is surrounded by a colonnade or peristyle. Fig. 124 is a plan to a larger scale.

The central chamber or cella (naos hecatompedoscella of 100 ft.) faced east, as was usual. Here stood the figure of Athene, 40 ft. high, carved in wood, and plated with gold and ivory. There is a porch (pronaos) before the cella on the east end. At the back of it is a chamber which gave its name to the whole building, the Parthenon, or chamber of the Virgin, used as the treasury, in which the offerings were stored. This again had its own porch at the west end (opisthodomus). The cella itself had aisles on each side formed by the columns which supported its roof.

123 Greek hair-dressing

Ictinus, taking the simple type of plan which can be traced back to the Megaron at Tiryns (37), worked into it every subtlety and refinement. If Fig. 118 is referred to, it will be seen that the Parthenon stands on a platform, or stylobate, of three steps. Ictinus evidently thought that if he made the top of this stylobate quite flat, and then built the temple on it, it might look as if the great weight had caused the stylobate to sink down in the middle, or become concave. To correct this, he made the top, about 100 ft. by 230 ft., rise up from each corner, $2\frac{3}{4}$ in. to the centres of each end and $4\frac{3}{8}$ in. to the centre of each side, so that it was convex.

The architrave, frieze, and cornice, called the entablature (64), followed the same line. In the same way, the shafts of the columns not only taper upwards, but, in doing so, have a delicate outward curve, called entasis. Again, to prevent any appearance of top-heaviness, the columns all lean inward a little. It has been estimated that if the axes of the columns were prolonged upward, they would meet about $1\frac{1}{2}$ miles above the

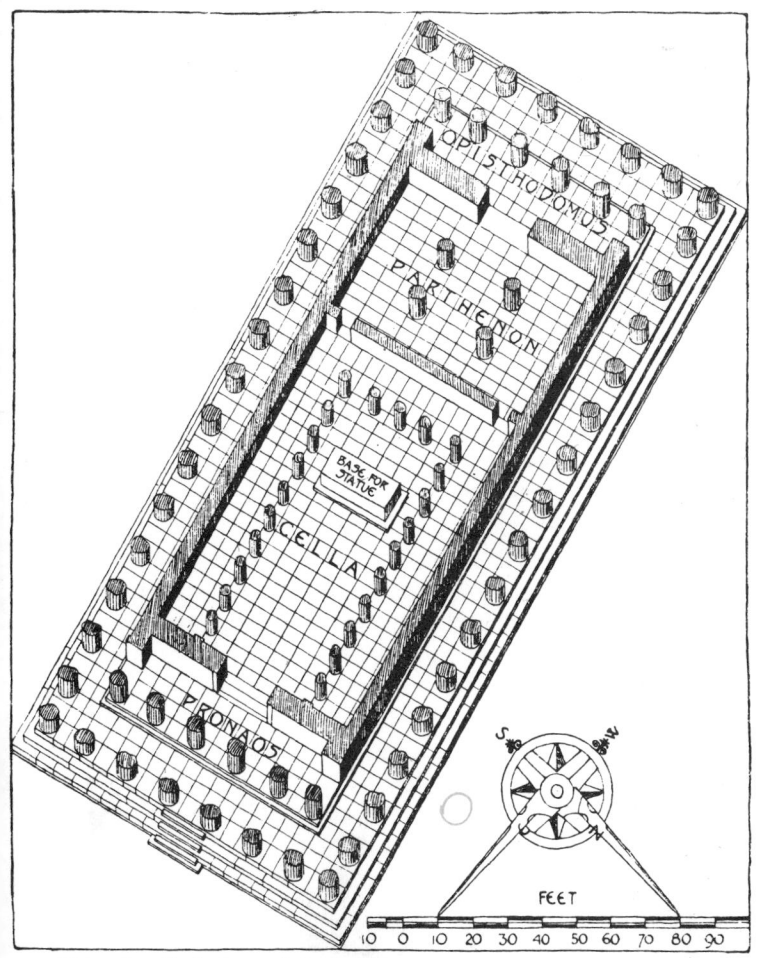

124 A relief plan of the Parthenon, from Penrose's survey

building. Only the most beautiful workmanship made this possible. The Parthenon was built of Pentelic marble, and no mortar was used, the various blocks being fastened together with iron dowels and clamps. Even today the joints are barely visible.

The whole interior of the Parthenon is now bare and open to the sky, but the positions of the internal columns which supported the roof are visible. About the roof-over itself and the method of lighting, nothing is known. Possibly openings were left in the coffers of the timbered ceiling, so that sufficient light could filter through these from the semi-transparent marble tiles of the roof-over. The opening of the east door, 16 ft. wide by 33 ft. high, was immediately opposite the gold and ivory statue of Athene, and though some part of this opening would have been taken up by a frame, and the door was under a portico, still a large area would have been left for the strong southern sunshine to stream through. The cella would have been decorated in gold and with carved mouldings, and perhaps another frieze like the one outside (see p. 180).

We can now consider the Parthenon sculptures, and as many of these are in the British Museum, we had better give an explanation of how they came to be there. The building was a temple of Athene the Virgin, from the time it was built until A.D. 450, and then it became a Christian church, dedicated to the Virgin Mary, and so remained until A.D. 1458, when Athens was captured by the Turks, who turned the Parthenon into a mosque. In 1687 Athens was besieged by the Venetians, and one of their shells struck the Parthenon and ignited gunpowder stored there by the Turks, and the sides of the building were blown out. Small huts were then built among the ruins. It was at the beginning of the nineteenth century that Lord Elgin, who was British Ambassador to the Turks, obtained their permission to remove the sculptures, which were gradually being ruined by neglect. They were then bought for the nation in 1816.

Unfortunately, nothing remains of the central figure of Athene herself, which once stood in the cella, but various small copies survive, which enable us to follow Pausanias' description. He said the figure was of gold and ivory. The helmet was surmounted by a sphinx, with griffins on either side. The figure stood upright, with a garment reaching to the feet, and on its breast Medusa's head was wrought in ivory. A Victory, 4 cubits high, was held in one hand and a spear in the other. At her feet were a shield and serpent "which may be Erichthonius" (the son of Hephæstos, reared by Athene, and seen by Pandora in the form of a serpent). The pedestal of the figure had a relief of the birth of Pandora, the first woman on earth, who brought with her a box containing all the human ills.

Pheidias was the sculptor of the figure of Athene, and he made it of wood, because this was the traditional material, but because

PARTHENON SCULPTURES

it had to be especially beautiful, it was plated with gold and ivory. It stood 40 ft. high with its base. In the second book of Thucydides' *History*, Pericles gave an inventory of the wealth of Athens at the beginning of the war. Among other things, he mentioned the statue of Athene in the Parthenon, which was sheathed with pure gold plates weighing 40 talents, and all this was removable.

Other sculptures from the Parthenon are now in the British Museum. Those in the east pediment over the entrance, Pausanias says, all relate to the birth of Athene. On the left-hand side, Helios, the Sun god, rises with his team of four horses out of the sea. Next came the beautiful seated figure, which may be Theseus, the great Greek hero who was the son of Ægeus, King of Athens, or possibly Heracles himself. Next came two figures of goddesses, seated on chests like those used by Athenian ladies for storing their clothes. Then a single figure moves outward from the central group, which has disappeared. This must have dealt with the birth of Athene, which was a favourite subject with the vase painters. On the right-hand side of this east pediment come the three Fates who settle the destinies of men. In the far corner of the pediment, Selene, the Moon goddess, sinks with her horses into the sea.

The sculptures of the west pediment, in the British Museum, are not so complete as those of the east pediment. Pausanias tells us that the subject here was the contest between Athene and Poseidon for the possession of the land.

The British Museum possesses a wonderful series of metopes from the Parthenon. These are the sculptured panels which were inset between the triglyphs in the frieze of the entablature (64). The subjects concern the battle between the Centaurs and Lapiths. The Centaurs were half-horse and half-man, and lived on Mount Pelion, in Thessaly. When they were invited to a wedding-feast by the Lapithæ, a tribe living near by, they disgraced themselves by first getting drunk, and then trying to run off with the bride. The battle which arose was a favourite subject with Greek artists, perhaps because, as in the case of the Satyrs, it pointed the moral of what happens if you become half-animal and half-man.

The most delightful thing which has come down to us is the frieze, the position of which, on the outside of the cella walls,

GREEK ARCHITECTURE

is shown in Fig. 125. In the British Museum are 247 ft. of the original, and another 176 ft. of casts out of the total length of 524 ft. It is not possible to exhibit the frieze at the Museum in the same position that it occupied in the Parthenon. There it was on outside walls, in the Museum on inside ones. Readers who go to the Museum can buy an excellent little guide on the *Sculptures of the Parthenon* for 2s. 6d., and in the ante-room to the Elgin Rooms there is not only a good model of the Acropolis, showing the position of the Parthenon, but a larger one of the temple itself, showing the frieze. If a start is made by studying these, then the frieze on the walls explains itself, not only as beautiful fragments, but as a living part of a great work of art. Again, beyond this is the fact that it illustrates the Panathenaic Festival, which was a central event in the life of the Athenians.

Since the Parthenon was dedicated to Athene, and she was the protecting goddess of Athens, it was right that her people should honour her, so that every four years a new robe (peplos) was woven for the image in the cella, and this was carried through the streets of the lower town, stretched on the yard-arm of the mast of a ship drawn on rollers. Pausanias says that near the Areopagus he was shown a ship made for the procession, and that it was very large. It would have to be if on its yard could be suspended the robe to fit Pheidias' Athene.

It is this procession of the Panathenaic Festival which is shown on the frieze. The people have come up on to the Acropolis, through the Propylæa, and then turned to the right and passed across the west end of the Parthenon until they reached the right-hand side, or the south-west angle of the building. Here the procession divides, and horsemen, chariots, elders, musicians, traybearers, victims for the sacrifice, marshals, and maidens divide, and one part go along the south frieze and the other across the west end and up the north side, until both arrive at the east end; here, over the entrance to the cella, where the figure of Athene was, are gathered together the magistrates and citizens, with the seated figures of gods and goddesses come to see this central incident of the peplos. This has been taken down from its mast, and is being folded up, and received by a priest and attendant.

The frieze, then, is not only an architectural enrichment but a

THE PARTHENON FRIEZE

fine illustration of a very important happening in the lives of the Athenians, and it is packed with interesting detail. Cows and sheep walk to the sacrifice, and are followed by attendants with trays of offerings; others have jars of wine. Maidens carry libation bowls for pouring the wine. There are pipe and lyre players, charioteers, and Athenian cavalry. The frieze is 3 ft. 4 in. high, and as originally fixed it was 39 ft. from the floor to the peristyle (125) up to its lower edge. The sculptor dealt with this position in a skilful way. The general face of the sculpture is vertical, but the background slopes away from a very slight relief at the bottom of the frieze to about $2\frac{1}{4}$ in. at the top. Horizontally the relief is arranged by cutting back from the face in flat waves, like the ripples left in sand on the seashore, yet with this slight relief the Athenian cavalry advances, as in rows of five, six, or seven abreast. Rivet holes in the marble show that the reins and bridles were added in bronze. The frieze was probably quite well lighted by reflection from the floor below. A very poor view of it would have been obtained from the peristyle (125); an Athenian, standing on the level ground outside the temple, 29 ft. away from the bottom step of the stylobate, would have been able to see the top of the frieze, just under the bottom of the main architrave outside, but his view would have been broken by the outer columns. As the columns are just over 6 ft. in diameter, with only just over 8 ft. in between them, it is obvious that this colonnade must have been a very considerable obstruction to the view of the frieze from outside the temple.

This position of the frieze is very interesting. It is amazing to us that the sculptors were content so to hide their light under a bushel; but then the gods see everywhere. You find the same modesty in Gothic work. The bosses on the nave roof of Norwich Cathedral are carved with a complete record of Bible history, from the Creation to the Last Judgment, each one a masterpiece, yet suspended aloft, and hardly to be seen without a good glass; perhaps, like the Parthenon frieze, they were so placed that the pilgrims might have the joy of discovering them.

This brings us to another question: Did the Athenians regard their architecture and sculpture from a point of view quite different from ours? There is no evidence that the Greeks of the Classical period thought that there was anything remarkable

GREEK ARCHITECTURE

about their building. Consider Plato, who was born about 429–427, just after the outbreak of the Peloponnesian War, and died in 347. He was a boy in 413 when the Athenian forces were destroyed in Sicily, and a young man when Athens surrendered in 404. He saw the Empire fall in pieces, and his *Republic* is really a plan of how a better and more stable State could be built up. It was a forerunner of other books, with the same object, written in troublous times, like St. Augustine's *City of God* and Sir Thomas More's *Utopia*. Jowett points out in his translation of the *Republic* that "there is hardly any mention in Plato of the creative arts; only in two or three passages does he ever allude to them. He is not lost in rapture at the great works of Pheidias—the Parthenon, the Propylæa, the statues of Zeus or Athene."

Probably it never occurred to Plato that you could have cheap and shoddy work, so there was no need to provide against bad building in his *Republic*.

Delphi.—And now, having written of the Acropolis as the sacred part of a Greek city where the houses of its gods were built, we must go to Delphi, because this was the Acropolis for the whole of Greece. It was regarded by the Greeks as not only the very centre or navel of their earth, and a peculiarly sacred place, but it occupied a very important position from the political point of view. In the Homeric Hymns, which, if not actually written by Homer, are of very great age, in the lay to Apollo, we find that he it was who first marked out the foundations of Delphi beneath snowy Parnassus. Delphi is perhaps the most lovely of all the lovely places in Greece. Pausanias wrote of it—"the city of Delphi stands wholly on a slope, and not only the city, but also the sacred close of Apollo".

It came about in this way. The god of light and youth and music and the lord of oracles, the son of Leto, who was born in Delos, was once upon a time disporting himself in the upper air, when he spied beneath him certain Cretans from Minoan Cnossus, who were sailing their ship along the western coast of Greece to Pylos. Apollo determined that he would make them ministers to his shrine at Delphi, so he swooped down and jumped into their boat in the guise of a dolphin. He then caused the south wind to blow the ship past Pylos, and then a west wind, which took them into the Gulf of Corinth, to Crisa, the land of

DELPHI

vines. Here the god flew off, and returned soon after as a man, lusty and strong, and told the Cretans that he was Apollo, and that never again would they return to wooded Cnossos. The Cretans were not afraid or unhappy, but realising their high destiny built an altar on the sea-strand and sacrificed, and Apollo, harp in hand, led the way to Delphi, and the Cretans followed, dancing in his train.

This is the tale that was told to the boys and girls of Classical Greece, and they would have known as well, that before Apollo marked out the foundations of Delphi beneath snowy Parnassus, he had to kill a great dragon, or python, who lived in the caves there. It was this victory which was celebrated by the great Delphic festival of the Pythia, held in the summer of every fourth year, and gave as well the name of Pythoness to the priestess who was the medium for the oracles. In the second book of the *Iliad*, Delphi is referred to as "rocky Pytho". We must now explain the very important part which the shrine played in the Greek scheme of life. We saw (p. 89) how Crœsus, who was not a Greek, consulted the oracle at Delphi as to his chances of success against the Persians, and again (p. 104), how the Greeks consulted the same oracle. Again we are told by Thucydides that the Spartans sent an embassy to Delphi (432 B.C.) to find out if they should go to war with the Athenians, and the god replied that it would be to their advantage.

Now we will see what happened to a deputation sent from Athens to consult the oracle at Delphi. First, the officials had to be consulted and the case of the applicants stated to them and arrangements made for the ceremony; meanwhile they would have made use of what is now called the Treasury of Athens (136) as their headquarters, and deposited there the offerings which were very necessary—the god did not look with favour on people who arrived empty-handed. On the actual day, the pilgrims washed in the Castalian spring, outside the Temenos or Sacred Close of Apollo, and then assembled in the court by the principal entrance on the east side. Here by the gate were holy-water basins, so that they could sprinkle themselves. The pilgrims then joined up in procession and walked up the Sacred Way (127) until they came to the Great Altar. This stood just outside the door of the temple, so that the scent of the

GREEK ARCHITECTURE

sacrifice could be wafted in to the god, and the door of his house, or temple, was wreathed with laurels, because that tree was sacred at Delphi. Then sacrifice was offered to invoke the help of the god. This was a preliminary to almost every action in Greece—at every meal portions were offered to the gods. At Delphi the fullest ceremonial would have been employed. The victim, a goat, sheep, or ox, its horns gilded and garlanded with flowers, was brought to the altar; if it struggled it was a bad omen, but to bow and shake its head was a good one. The altar and people were sanctified by being sprinkled with water from a bowl into which a torch lighted at the altar had been plunged. There were prayers, and the victim was sprinkled with barley-meal. Hair was cut from it and burned on the altar, and then the beast, after being stunned with an axe, had its throat cut, and the blood, caught in a bowl, was poured on the altar. It was then disembowelled and its entrails examined for omens, then skinned and cut up; the portions reserved for the god being burned on the altar, the remainder was cooked on spits and eaten by the worshippers.

After the sacrifice the pilgrims cast lots as to which of them should approach the Adyton, or holy of holies, in the cella inside the temple. Here they found the Pythoness seated on a tripod and clad in festal raiment. Before the ceremony the Pythoness, who was always a free-born woman of Delphi, had fasted and bathed in the sacred spring.

In the Adyton there were benches for the other worshippers, and a staircase led down to a vault under which the sacred spring, Cassotis, ran. This has now dried up, and the only one remaining is the Castalian outside the precincts. The underground position of the sacred spring may have given rise to the legend that the Pythoness worked herself into a frenzy by inhaling vapours from a cleft in the rocks, or these vapours may have come from the spring, or the frenzy been induced by the fumes of burned laurel. It must have been an awesome moment when the Pythoness in her frenzy descended the stairs into the cavern, and so became the medium for the message from Apollo himself. This message was interpreted by the priests from the ravings of the Pythoness, and put into the cryptic form in which it reached the applicants.

The oracle was established by the time of the *Iliad*, and

125 Restoration of the South Peristyle of the Parthenon, Athens

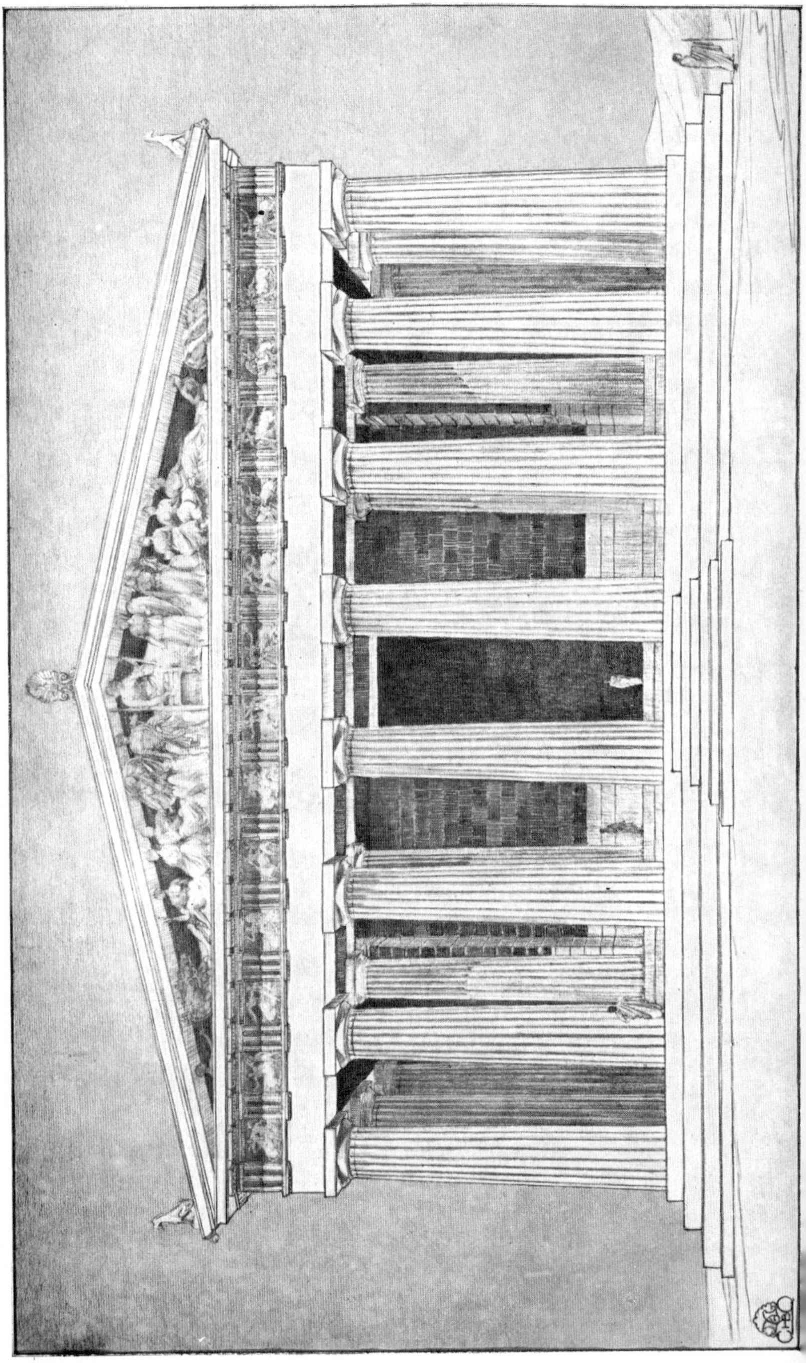

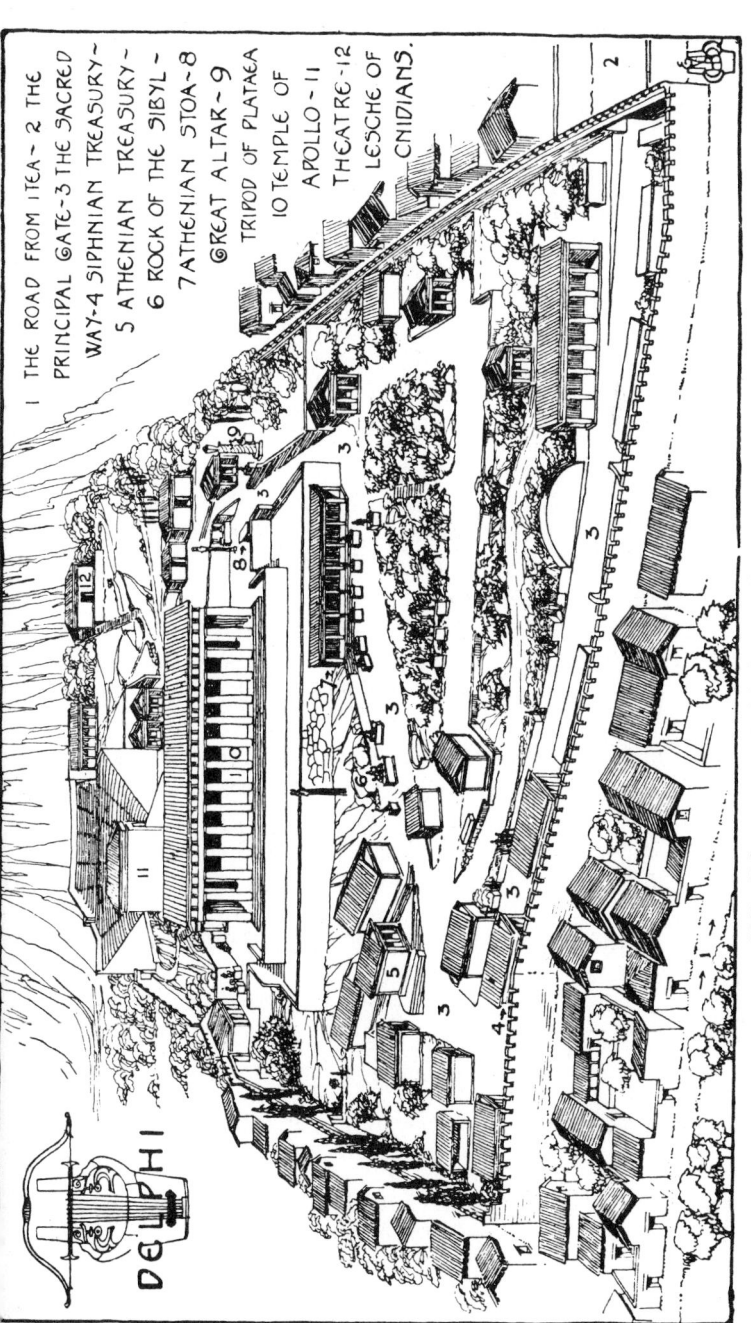

127 Diagrammatic bird's-eye view of Delphi

GREEK ARCHITECTURE

continued well on into the Roman Empire. The priesthood does not seem to have abused the enormous power which was placed in its hands. The officials at Delphi must have known many political secrets; at their bidding the Greeks went to war, or made peace, founded cities, and built temples or houses for their gods.

Fig. 127 is a diagrammatic view of the central sacred Close of Apollo. The road from the port of Itea is at the bottom. To the east, on the right hand, was the Gymnasium where the athletes trained for the Pythian Games. Towering over the city on the north comes Parnassus, 8,036 ft. high. The stadium is to the north-west up the mountain-side. Inside the Temenos, or enclosure, the path of the Sacred Way zigzags from the entrance on the east up to the Great Altar. It was lined with the Treasuries of the various Greek States and cities, and many kinds of memorial. Fig. 136 shows the Treasury of Athens built in 490 B.C. It is in the form of a small Doric temple of distyle-in-antis type, that is, its two columns stood between antæ, or pilasters (62). Xenophon dedicated a statue of Apollo to celebrate the deliverance of the 10,000, and this was set up in the Treasury. The Athenians also built the Stoa, or colonnaded walk, under the terrace wall of the temple. This would have been a pleasant place for the visiting Athenian to rest in the shade, and admire the lovely view over valley and plain.

We mentioned another of the treasuries on p. 119. The richness of this is explained by the fact that the island of Siphnos had gold-mines in ancient times.

Another very interesting building was the Lesche of the Cnidians. This was near the source of the spring Cassotis, and served as a club-house. It was adorned with paintings by Polygnotus.

The position of the theatre is shown in Fig. 127. In the centre of the Temenos came the great Temple of Apollo. The one which the Greeks of Classical times knew was finished about 510 B.C. and destroyed 373 B.C.

Opposite the Great Altar a famous monument was set up, the column of which was formed by the wreathed bodies of three snakes, who carried on their heads a tripod. This was to celebrate the victory of Platæa.

Just to the west of the Athenian Stoa was the rock of the

128 The Greek horses at St. Mark's, Venice

GREEK ARCHITECTURE

Sibyl. Pausanias wrote of this, "above the earth rises a rock, on which it is related that the first Sibyl took her position, and gave warnings in song". The Naxian Sphinx rose on her Ionic column just above this.

The charioteer, illustrated in Fig. 106, was found on the north side of the temple. Like the Hermes of Praxiteles at Olympia, the charioteer fell and was buried in rubbish, which preserved it for us. The Emperor Nero, in the first century A.D., is said to have removed not less than 500 bronze statues from Delphi, and yet when Pausanias went there in the second century, he still found many to describe. If after studying Fig. 127 our readers will turn to Pausanias' *Description of Greece*, they will derive great pleasure from his details of Delphi, and gain a better idea of the glories of Apollo's shrine than any we can give.

Fig. 128 shows the Greek horses of St. Mark's, Venice. These have a very travelled history. They are about 5 ft. in height, and originally must have formed part of a quadriga, set up perhaps as an offering at a Greek shrine. Then they found their way to the Imperial Hippodrome at Constantinople, where they were taken by the Venetians as spoils of war. In the same way the French took them to Paris in 1797, and then they were returned to Venice in 1815.

The Parthenon was the culmination of Greek architecture, and inspired the Roman architects who followed. The Northern peoples when Rome fell did the rough building we call Romanesque, out of which the Gothic cathedral developed. At the Renaissance, Greece again came into her own, so that many modern buildings still show Greek and Roman details. Thus the Parthenon, begun nearly 2,400 years ago, has influenced builders throughout the centuries, and Greek architecture is still a living force today.

Chapter X

THE TOWN AND ITS PUBLIC BUILDINGS

HAVING dealt with the Acropolis and its temples, we can pass on to the towns, and it should be remembered that there are two kinds of town—one which has just grown, and the other which has been planned. At Athens the Acropolis was at first the town, then it became the sacred place, and the houses were built outside on the south side. Gradually the town spread, and the houses were built alongside the lanes leading up from the country to the temple; enclosing walls were built, and these were extended to the port of Peiræus by the sea.

In just such a way many an English town started life, with the peasants' houses built for protection under the walls of a Benedictine monastery, or a village we know may have begun as the settlement of a Saxon chief, his hall as its centre, and its houses the huts of the churls. Close by, the chapel, built when the community was converted to Christianity, has now become the Parish Church. The winding lanes were the tracks between the common fields, and the common, the waste on which the pigs were fed. This is the way that many of the old towns of Europe have grown, and it is this slow growth through the ages that gives them their great interest; but the old towns which have survived, like Athens, do not help us to find out how the Greeks would have gone to work if they had to build a new town. Here in England we have such a town in Silchester, built during the Roman occupation, and then deserted when the Saxons came, and left to moulder away, until its ruins were excavated in the nineteenth century, to give us a good idea of a Romano-British city.

Town planning is a modern art with us, and dates back no earlier than 1909, when John Burns introduced his Town Planning Bill into Parliament, to try to persuade us to plan towns before we build them. To find the beginnings of town planning we should have to go back a very long way indeed. Hippodamus of Miletus had laid out the port of Peiræus, in the fifth century, on a rectangular plan. Herodotus tells us in his

129

A Agora, or Market-place.
B Temple of Asclepius.
C Prytaneum, or G
D Ecclesiasterion.

(From a Drawing by A. ZIPPELIUS.)

ne

    E Gymnasium.   G Temple to Demeter.
    F Theatre.   H Temple to Athene.

THE TOWN AND ITS PUBLIC BUILDINGS

first book that Babylon was on the same lines, so that the chessboard plan came from the East.

The Greeks of the Macedonian Age, between 330 and 130 B.C., were great town planners. Alexander conquered the East, and wherever he went new cities were founded and planned in the Greek manner. We know from Vitruvius that architects travelled in his train. One of them, Deinocrates, later on was ordered by him to plan the town of Alexandria in Egypt.

We have selected Priene, built during the Macedonian period, near Miletus, in Asia Minor, as our example of Greek town planning.

When it was excavated, it was found to be a perfect example of the chess-board plan. The type commended itself to a soldier like Alexander, because straight streets can be controlled, and do not lend themselves, like tortuous lanes, to street fighting. Again, they mark an advance in civilisation—the barbarian cannot set out things on a straight line.

The beautiful drawing (129), which we reproduce, shows how Priene was built on land sloping to the south. The broad streets, some 23 ft. wide, go from east to west, and the steeper ones, from north to south, are not more than 10 ft. The town was walled for defence.

Markets.—The principal street seems to have been the one which ran from the west gate, and came out on the north side of the Agora, or market-place (A, Fig. 129). This was the centre of the town, and it was more or less surrounded by colonnaded walks with shops behind. These would not have been much more than openings in the wall, with the counter in the opening. In the centre of the Agora were the stalls of the peasants who brought in their vegetables and fowls and eggs for sale. Here the household slaves, not the women of the household, bought their provisions. In the centre of the market was an altar for sacrifice, and bases have been found where memorials and statues were set up. Probably there was a fountain here, because water was laid on to the city from springs in the high ground to the north, and brought underground in stoneware pipes, a safer method in times of siege than the overhead Roman aqueduct.

There was another market on the west side of the Agora, which was devoted to the sale of fish and meat. We know this because the marble slabs on which these were exhibited have

PRIENE

been found. The market must have presented a busy scene, because not only were there the buyers and sellers, but the citizens met in the arcades around to talk and discuss the latest news.[1]

Hospitals.—One of the most interesting buildings discovered at Priene was the Temple of Asclepius, on the east side of the

130 A Greek surgeon

Agora (B, Fig. 129). This consisted of a courtyard, with an altar in the centre, and colonnades on the north and south. The west end was occupied by the temple, with its portico facing east. There can be little doubt but that the building served the same purposes as a hospital today. Asclepius was the god of healing. He was a son of Apollo, and was brought up by Chiron, the centaur, who was very wise, and a friend of the Argonauts. Asclepius was served by an order of priests called the Asclepiadæ, and their knowledge of medicine was handed down as a sacred trust. Side by side with this, there appear to have been other doctors (130). In the fourth book of the *Iliad* we read that the Greeks had doctors (see p. 18): the battlefields of the Trojan War must have been a good school for the surgeons.

Hippocrates, the great name in Greek medicine, was born as early as 460 B.C., and seems to have practised his profession as a doctor does today, with an outlook which was scientific and free from quackery. The Doctors' Oath is ascribed to him. This oath continued in use in Western Europe for many centuries, and was revised in Christian times. Its pagan form[2] was:

I swear by Apollo Physician, by Asclepius, by Health, by Heal-all and by all the gods and goddesses, making them witnesses, that I will

---

[1] The Athenian Agora, which has now been excavated by the American School of Archaeology at Athens, was also the centre of public life: it contained the Council House, the Tholos or Rotunda, the Prytaneum, and the Law Courts, as well as Magistrates' and Record Offices. See R. E. Wycherley, *How the Greeks Built Cities*, Chapter IV, for a description and plans.

[2] W. H. Jones, *Hipppcrates*, 3 vols., Loeb Classical Library.

THE TOWN AND ITS PUBLIC BUILDINGS

carry out, according to my ability and judgment, this oath and this indenture:

To regard my teacher in this art as equal to my parents; to make him partner in my livelihood, and when he is in need of money to share mine with him; to consider his offspring equal to my brothers; to teach them this art, if they require to learn it, without fee or indenture; and to impart precept, oral instruction, and all other learning to my sons, to the sons of my teacher, and to pupils who have signed the indenture and sworn obedience to the Physicians' Law, but to none other.

I will use treatment to help the sick according to my ability and judgment, but I will never use it to injure or wrong them.

I will not give poison to anyone though asked to do so, nor will I suggest such a plan.

The oath goes on to state that the doctor must never carry out any illegal operations, and that in "purity and in holiness" he must guard his life and art. As well it points out that as he will enter many other people's houses to help the sick, he must not betray their confidence, and must keep himself free from any wrong-doing. If in the course of his practice, or social intercourse, he comes to know "what ought never to be published abroad", he must regard such things as "holy secrets". The finale is

Now, if I keep this oath and break it not, may I enjoy honour, in my life and art, among all men for all time; but if I transgress and forswear myself, may the opposite befall me.

This is the beginning of the professional man's outlook, that his work is more important than its reward.

Galen, born A.D. 130, comes at the end of this great epoch in the history of medicine, and after that darkness descends for more than a thousand years.

There can be no doubt that the patient who attended the hospital at Priene would have stood a much better chance of recovery than a patient in Anglo-Saxon England. One of the medical treatments mentioned by Bede was to gather, from his tomb, some of the mortal dust of St. Chad and put it into water, and give it to "sick cattle of men to drink".

At Priene the invalid would have been brought to the Temple of Asclepius, and after consultation with the officials, sacrifice would have been offered on the altar, and prayers for recovery.

MEDICINE, PUBLIC LIFE, DRAMA

He might sleep on the skin of a sacrificed ram, and dream dreams and see visions of restored health, and these would be interpreted for him by the priest. This would have been the spiritual side of the healing, and then a doctor would have ministered to the patient to cure his bodily ills. He would probably have been helped by the fact that all Greeks indulged in physical exercises, and so had healthy bodies for a start. We may imagine the patients on their beds in the cloisters, with plenty of fresh air and sunlight, and a good chance of recovery.

There was another famous sanctuary of Asclepius at Epidaurus, in Argolis, on the east of the Peloponnesus.

Prytaneum.—The Stoa, or colonnaded walk on the north side of the Agora, was extended to the east, so that it overlapped the Temple of Asclepius. Just above this eastern end of the Stoa (C, Fig. 129) came the Prytaneum, or Government House. In Part II, p. 88, we noted how Herodotus tells us that when the emigrants left Greece they took fire from the sacred hearth to the new settlement, where it was kept alight in the Prytaneum, and so symbolised the life of the State. Here the head of the city would, if the necessity arose, have made sacrifice and prayed to the gods on behalf of the citizens.

Ecclesiasterion.—To the west of the Prytaneum came the Ecclesiasterion (D, Fig. 129). This was a square building to hold about 700 people. There was the usual altar in the centre, surrounded by rising tiers of seats, rather like a modern lecture theatre.

Gymnasium.—Behind the Prytaneum and the Ecclesiasterion came the Gymnasium (E, Fig. 129). Here the Greeks could not only practise their physical culture, but meet to discuss their affairs.

Theatre.—Again, behind these buildings, and slightly to the north-west (F, Fig. 129), was the Theatre, which played a great part in the life of the Greek.

"Drama" comes from the Greek word, "to act, or do", so that it consists of a picture of human life with action; it began, many hundreds of years ago in old Greece, as a dance given at a vintage festival to thank Dionysus, who was the god of fertility and the vine.

"Tragedy" comes from the Greek word for "goat". The goat was an enemy of the vine, and apt to eat and destroy it, so at

THE TOWN AND ITS PUBLIC BUILDINGS

131 The goat-dance

these Dionysiac festivals it is thought that a goat was sacrificed; the plays then started as an act of worship and a religious duty. There must have been a procession, sacrifice, and dance. Fig. 131, drawn from a black-figure vase in the British Museum, shows a goat-dance.

"Comedy" comes from a Greek word for revel, and was based on the lighter side of the festivals. "Comic" is related to comedy, and we can be quite sure that in these old village festivals, after the tragic dances concerned with the death of the goat, as the good wine circulated, then some of the revellers had to make the people laugh and keep them happy, and the dances became gayer.

Still, there was nothing as yet of what we now understand by drama. The dithyramb, which was a wild and enthusiastic song, sung by the dancers in chorus, is first spoken of about 650 B.C. The Dithyrambic chorus often personated satyrs, because they were the personal attendants of Dionysus. Mummers, where they still survive, are probably descended from these satyr dancers.

Thespis, a native of Icarus in Attica, at the Dionysia of 534 B.C., produced a dithyrambic chorus of satyrs, with an additional person, who talked with the leader of the chorus. "Actor" comes from the Greek word, "to lead", and we talk today of the Thespian art, meaning drama, because of this idea of Thespis—but really he had only arrived at dialogue, which stops just short of drama. "Two is company and three none" can be rendered in this connection, as two make a dialogue, but three give the possibilities of drama. The third person in the background, who may spoil the plans of the other two, add the touch of salt, which is the tang of drama.

Then comes Phrynichus, of whom Herodotus wrote (p. 99), that when he produced the *Capture of Miletus*, in Athens, his audience was moved to tears, and the author was fined 1,000 drachms for making them unhappy.

Æschylus, born 525 B.C., was the real inventor of the drama, because Aristotle, in the *Poetics*, tells us that "Æschylus first

TRAGEDY AND COMEDY

132 The bird-dance
From a black-figure vase

introduced a second actor; he diminished the importance of the chorus, and assigned the leading part to the dialogue." With this limited cast, Æschylus was able to produce *Prometheus Bound*.

The next great name is Sophocles, born about 496 B.C.; according to Aristotle, he added a third actor, and used some form of scene painting. Seven of his plays survive, and his work should be studied by readers of this book, because it is typical of the age of Pericles. Euripides was born in 480 B.C.; his work, though slower to win fame, became after his death the most popular of all, and nineteen of his plays have come down to us.

After Euripides there were no more great masters of Greek tragedy, and we hear more of comedy. If tragedy was concerned with the heroic legends, comedy could take notice of everyday life. Magnes (*c.* 460), and a little later, Cratinus, are early names, but Aristophanes, born about 448, is the first great one. Eleven of his plays survive. In *The Birds* (414 B.C.), produced just before the Sicilian disaster, two Athenians persuade the birds to build a cloud-city, to which they can fly from the troubles on earth. The early comedies satirised political conditions. Fig. 132, showing a bird chorus, has been drawn from a sixth-century black-figure vase in the British Museum, and so is much earlier than Aristophanes' play.

Plays in Greece were performed in the daytime, and in the open

THE TOWN AND ITS PUBLIC BUILDINGS

air. The early plays were given on a circular dancing-place for the chorus. This was called the orchestra in later theatres, from the Greek word "to dance". The people sat round on the grassy slopes above the orchestra, and stone seats were not added until the fourth century at the Theatre of Dionysus at Athens. The plays were produced, and the choruses hired and paid for, by a wealthy citizen as one of his duties to the State. He was called the choregus. Victories gained in the competitions were celebrated by building monuments, such as the choragic monument of Lysicrates, in Athens (133), which originally supported a tripod, won in the theatre there in 334 B.C. This monument is interesting, because it shows the Corinthian Order, which was the third of the Greek Orders of architecture. Vitruvius tells us an old legend of how this Order originated. A Corinthian virgin died, and her nurse collected some of the things of which she was fond, and placed them in a basket and carried it to the tomb and placed it there, with a large square tile on the top of the basket to keep its contents safe. Then an acanthus plant grew all around the basket, and when it reached the tile, its fronds turned over and formed volutes, and Callimachus saw the basket, and from it designed the Corinthian Order.

The open-air performances in the Greek theatre necessitated the use of various conventions. An actor today, who wishes to move his audience, would plead that the theatre should not be too vast, and that the huge scale of the sky should be shut out. This question of scale was one of the great difficulties which the Greek actors had to contend with. They wore shoes with thick soles, and huge masks of stiffened linen, with wigs, which added to their height, and padded their bodies to increase their girth. The masks saved them the need of torturing their faces into expressions which might have been ludicrous in the sunlight, and these masks were pierced for the eyes to see through and the mouth to talk. There is a figure of an actor, in the Metropolitan Museum of Art in New York, wearing a mask which is kind on one side and angry on the other, so that he could turn to the audience the appropriate face to suit his action. The audience must have been more concerned with the performance of the play than the players, or rather, they knew the play as a masterpiece, and were content to see it acted many times, and to judge between the performances.

133 The Choragic Monument of Lysicrates, Athens

Fig. 139 shows a scene from comedy. The two lower men are pretending to be Chiron, the wisest of all the centaurs. The man at the top is the slave Xanthias. The Greeks enjoyed broad fun as well as tragedy.

The architectural development of the Greek theatre can be traced in the following way: first there was a circular dancing-place surrounded by slopes on which the spectators could sit. When actors were added, a rough wooden stage was set up by the side of the dancing-place, or even a cart. The next step, as actors were added, would be to have a booth at the back of the stage, which could be used as a dressing-room, and a point of entry on to the stage. This type would have survived in the country places in its simplest form, and was probably rather more developed in the cities. It is said that the temporary structure of the theatre gave way when Æschylus was competing in 499 B.C. So we do not know what the theatres were like during the Classic period of the fifth century, when the masterpieces of tragedy were first performed. The theatres we know now were built in the fourth century, the one at Athens about 330 B.C. Then the grassy slopes were regularised and covered with marble seats. The dancing-place became the orchestra, the wooden stage the proscenium, and the booth at the back the scena. The priests and officials sat on the bottom row next the chorus, and at Athens there are sixty-seven seats, made like wooden arm-chairs, in marble.

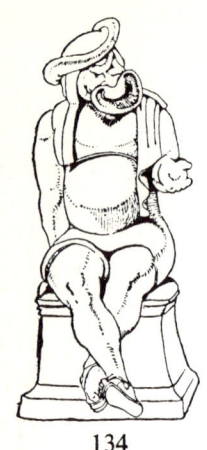

134
A comic actor seated on an altar. Moulded in terra-cotta

Instead of the theatre at Priene, we have given in Fig. 150 a photograph of the theatre at Epidaurus, designed by the younger Polycleitus in the fourth century. Pausanias said that it was most especially worth seeing: "for symmetry and beauty, what architect could vie with Polycleitus?"

The circle of the orchestra, with a diameter of about 65 ft., is the centre of the whole composition, and round this the seats are arranged tier after tier up the hill, broken only by the broader path (diazoma), about two-thirds up. The curve of the seats is flattened on either side, so that the auditorium is really slightly

5 (*right*) The Temple of Athena Niké at Athens (about 426 B.C.)

6 (*below*) The Athenian Treasury at Delphi (about 407 B.C.)

137 The Theatre and, below, the Temple of Apollo, looking south across the Valley of the Pleistos

DELPHI

THE GREEK THEATRE

horseshoe shaped in plan (141). There is a parados, or passage, on either side of the raised stage, or proscenium, in front of the scena. Vitruvius says the stage of the Greek theatre was raised not more than 12 ft., or less than 10 ft., and though this seems a dangerous height for the actors, anything lower would have looked sadly out of scale in an auditorium nearly 415 ft. in diameter. With the stage at 10 ft., only 1 ft. would have been cut off the legs of an actor standing at the back of the stage, when seen from the high priest's seat in the centre of the lowest tier of seats. Wooden shutters were filled in between the columns supporting the proscenium, and there were doors leading out on to the orchestra. Other doors lead from the scena on to the proscenium, and this was approached as well by stairs or ramps at each end. These side entrances played their part; the actor who entered from the left was supposed to have come from the harbour, while countrymen came from the right.

The architectural decoration of the front of the scena formed part of the scenery.

The acoustics of a Greek theatre are wonderfully good. Words spoken from the orchestra at Delphi or Epidaurus can be clearly heard in the highest row of seats.

A word as to later developments. The Roman theatre was on the same general lines as the Greek one, but when the peoples of Western Europe became Christians, the play suffered neglect because of its pagan associations. The Mystery, or Miracle, plays of the Middle Ages were more concerned with teaching people who could not read Bible history than presenting the drama of everyday life.

When we come to the Renaissance, naturally one of the things to be reborn was the theatre. The Elizabethan "Plaie-howse" had a pit shaped like the orchestra of a Greek theatre, and a stage like its proscenium, with a scena behind. The only difference is that the people are seated in galleries round the pit.

138 Mask of a negro
(*Notice holes in ears for fastening*)

THE TOWN AND ITS PUBLIC BUILDINGS

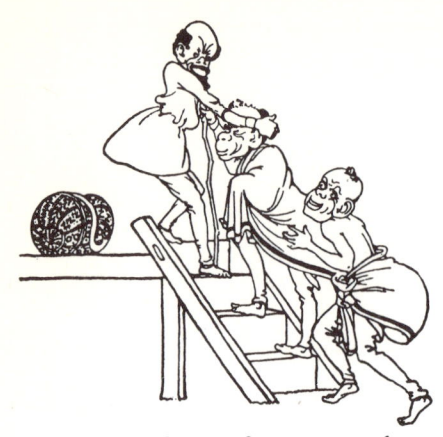

139 Comic performance: the two lower figures are the centaur Chiron
From a vase drawing

The same idea can be traced in the seventeenth-century theatre and the eighteenth-century circus.

Acropolis.—To go back to Priene. The Acropolis, as usual, was on the high land. There was at Priene a temple to Demeter, in the extreme north, at G, Fig. 129, and another to Athene at H, below it. The stadium is at the bottom of the picture.

The remainder of the town was cut up into islands by the broader east to west streets, and the narrow north to south ones. These islands average about 160 ft. by 120 ft., and were divided into four or eight sites for houses. It has been estimated that the population was about 4,000. The houses did not have gardens attached to them: there was no need, because the town was not large, and the country could be reached without going through dismal suburbs. We shall see later that the Greeks made the best of both worlds—they had town and country houses.

Walls and Fortifications.—We have said that Priene was walled for defence, and it is to the East that we must look for the beginnings of fortifications. Going back to Cnossos, we saw in Part I that the Minoans relied more on the wooden walls of their navy on the sea, than stone walls on the land. When, however, the scene moved to Mycenæ, we found at Tiryns some wonderful fortifications. Sculptures in the British Museum show an Assyrian walled city of 884–860 B.C., and Herodotus wrote of the walls of Babylon. Thucydides notes that one of the first things Themistocles did (478 B.C.) after the Persian defeat, was to renew and improve the walls of the city of Athens. Every man, woman, and child gave a hand, and the walls were of such a width that two wagons carrying stones could meet and pass on top of them. Peiræus, the port of Athens, was completed by

140 The ruined walls and towers of Ithome

THE TOWN AND ITS PUBLIC BUILDINGS

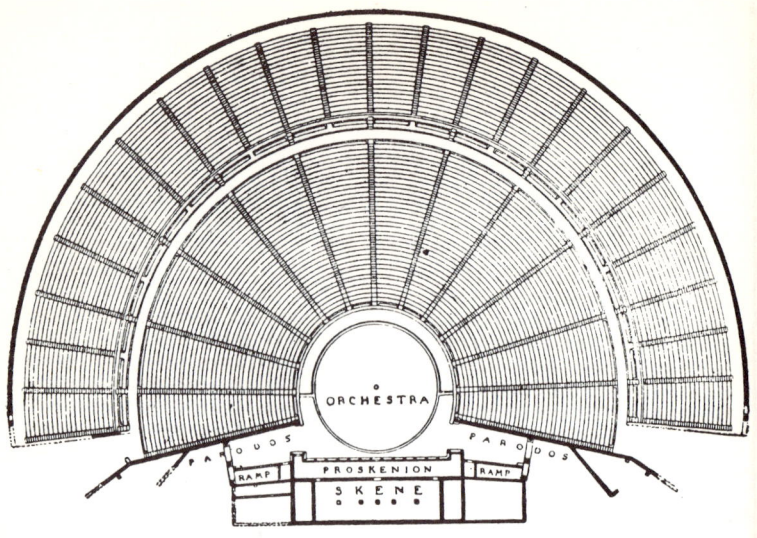

141   Plan of the Theatre at Epidaurus

Themistocles, because he foresaw that the Athenians must "make the sea their domain".

The walls of Messene, or Ithome, were celebrated in Pausanias' time. He wrote:

Messene is surrounded by a wall, the whole circuit of which is built of stone, and there are towers and battlements on it. I have not seen the walls of Babylon, or the Memnonian walls at Susa, in Persia, nor have I heard of them from people who have seen them; but Ambrosus in Phocis, Byzantium, and Rhodes are fortified in the best style, and yet the walls of Messene are stronger than theirs.

Homer, in the second book of the *Iliad*, refers to the town as "terraced Ithome". Ithome was the name of the mountain which became the Acropolis around which Messene was built. Fig. 140 is a sketch we made there of one of the towers and the ruined walls.

The masonry here is particularly fine, and admirably designed to suit its purpose. It was quite right that the surfaces of the Parthenon should be finished in the most exquisite way, but to have carried out the same idea for city walls would have been ridiculous. At Messene the blocks were rock faced, which gives the walls an appearance of even greater strength than they

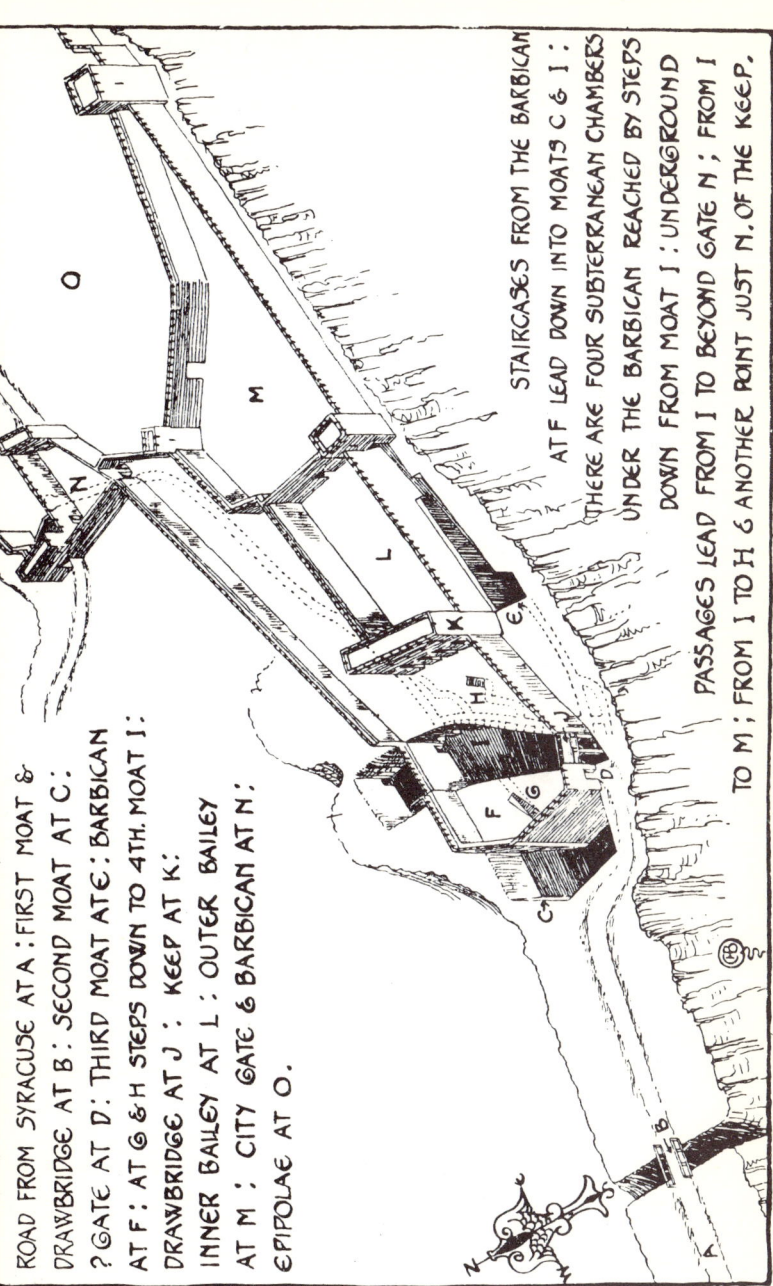

142 A reconstruction of the castle at Euryelus, Epipolae, Syracuse, Sicily

possess. Just below the tower in our sketch are the ruins of the gate on the Arcadian road. This had a circular court between the inner and outer gates, where travellers could be inspected before being allowed to enter the city. Pausanias says that here was a Hermes of Attic workmanship, and that "the use of square-shaped images of Hermes is Athenian". The arrow slits in the tower are of quite medieval appearance. The angles of the jambs in different slits are varied to suit the line of fire.

To return to fortifications, the castle at Euryelus (142) is of the greatest interest. Its position can be seen on Fig. 183. After the siege, which we describe on p. 240, the Syracusans realised that Epipolæ must be walled in, and this was done, with Euryelus as the spearhead. The walls are ruined now, but the plan can be traced as shown in Fig. 142. The moats are still there, cut in the solid rock, and so are all the underground passages.

Chapter XI

TOWN HOUSES AND EVERYDAY LIFE

WE can now pass on to a description of the houses in Priene, and Fig. 143 shows the plan of one. Perhaps the first thing to be noted is how the old Megaron type of plan, which we first saw at Tiryns (37), persists. In Fig. 143, 1 is the entrance, 2 the porter's lodge, 3 the court, 4 the porch, 5 the hall, 6 the bedchambers, and 7 the exedra, or outside sitting-place. Fig. 144 gives our idea of the appearance of the house seen from the exedra. The small rooms off the courtyard, which are not numbered on the plan, were possibly kitchen and offices, with an upper floor over for the women.

This was nearly the end of the Megaron type of plan in the south, because Fig. 145, of a third-century house at Delos, is much more like later Roman houses. Here 1 is the entrance, and the porter must have sat in the lobby; 2 is the court, with a colonnade all round it; 3 is the porch; 4 the hall or living-room; 5 may have been bedrooms; 6 the kitchen; and 7 stairs to an upper story. The courtyard had an impluvium, or shallow pool, to catch the rainwater from the roofs over, and conduct it to an underground reservoir. Latrines were provided, which were flushed by slops into stone drains. There were no hearths in the halls of the Delian houses, and any heating must have been done by braziers of charcoal. The walls were decorated with coloured plasters, the floors paved with mosaic. The court was lit at night by lamps set in niches in the walls.

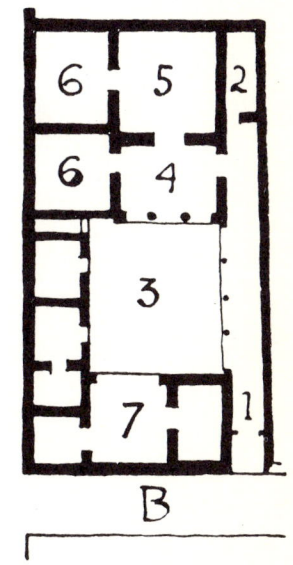

143   Plan of a house at Priene

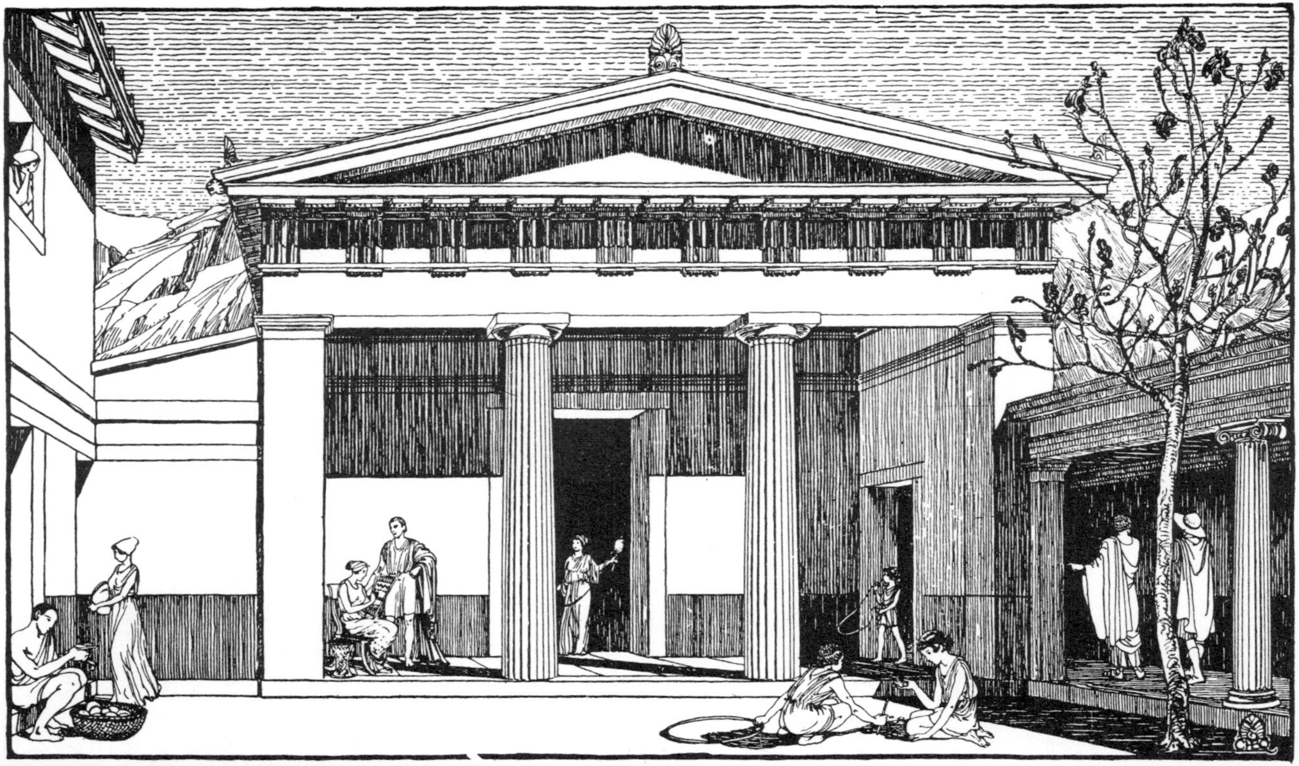

HOUSE PLANS. FURNITURE, POTTERY

At Delos the porch and hall have lost their identity as such, and become merged into the body of the house, which now resembles those the Romans were to build later at Pompeii; this became the typical house of the South. In the North, the Megaron, or hall, first introduced by the Achæan chieftains who descended on Greece, still survived, and it must have survived there for all the centuries until it appeared in England with the Anglo-Saxons.

Furniture.—So far as the furniture of Greek houses is concerned, there do not appear to have been any great developments in the fifth century. The interiors shown on the red-figure vases are much the same as those on the black-figure ones. The men still recline on couches when dining (169), and sleep on them at night. Of the other furniture in the Greek house, there were chests for storing clothes, but lyres and many other things were hung on nails driven into the walls. The tables were three-legged, and the stools of great variety. A new type of chair appears on the fifth-century red-figure vases: the klismos (146). We have reconstructed this from a side view of one of the fourth-century sepulchral monuments of Hegesa in the Athens Museum (151), and suggest that the seat was formed, like those of the couches, of interlacing thongs. Sometimes this chair is drawn on the vases so made that the sitter almost reclines in it.

Pottery.—It was in the Classical period of the fifth century that the potter's art reached its culmination. In the sixth century the figure was drawn in black on the red ground. In the fifth century the exact reverse became the fashion. The figures were lightly etched on to the red clay, and then a thick black line was drawn round them, and the whole background filled in with the black varnish. The detail was added to the figures in thin lines. The drawing is exquisite, and the convention employed expresses the desired action of the figures in a wonderful way. Greek vases have suffered much at the hands of their illustrators; many reproductions give the drawings a cast-iron quality which is entirely lacking in the originals. These should be studied on the actual vases; then it will be found that the old vase painters drew with far more freedom than is generally imagined. It should be noted how admirably the designs (e.g., 169) fill their circles, and how beautifully the blacks and whites are disposed. There is a

TOWN HOUSES AND EVERYDAY LIFE

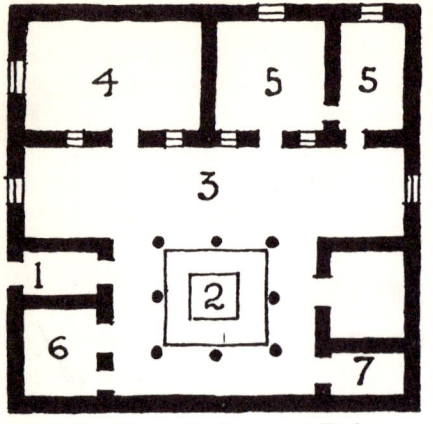

145 Plan of a house at Delos

fine collection of red-figure vases in the British Museum; two of these are shown in Figs. 174, 175.

The vases were not all in this red-figure treatment. There is in the Museum a drinking-cup (kylix) with a white ground on which Aphrodite is drawn riding on a goose. Other vases carried out in this white treatment were the lekythi (oil vessels) made for offerings at the tombs. The subjects on these generally had to do with death and mourning.

There is in the British Museum a Greek potter's wheel. This is of the same type as that used in India today—a plain, heavy, circular disc of terra-cotta, with a hole in the middle for it to be placed on the pivot on which it ran. It was spun by hand.

Commerce and Coinage.—Pottery enables us to remind our readers that the Greeks not only built temples, but laid the foundations of modern commerce. Pottery was a great industry at Athens. The Greeks could not grow all their foodstuffs, so they had to export wine, oil, and manufactured goods to pay for the food they imported. At first trade would have been carried on by barter.

Herodotus credits the Lydians with being the first people to use gold

146 The klismos
Reconstruction from Sepulchral Monument of Hegesa at Athens Museum

210

VASES, COINAGE, TERRA-COTTA

and silver coins, and to sell goods by retail. This came about because gold was found in Lydia. When Crœsus' messenger went to Delphi to consult the oracle there, he took with him a great store of golden ingots. These would have been stamped by Crœsus to guarantee their quality and weight, and they could have been used for trading. So gold became the medium for the exchange of goods, and widened the area over which business could be carried on.

Specimens of this Lydian ingot money can be seen at the British Museum. A small quantity of gold was smelted and poured into a mould, and then stamped with punches as a banker's mark. The Ionian Greeks, who were neighbours of the Lydians, soon saw the possibilities of money, and they adopted it, and from the Ionians its use spread over the Greek world. The coins in Fig. 176 are Greek examples of 550–330 B.C.; the originals are very beautiful, and they have a further claim on our attention in that all modern coinages have been modelled on Greek examples.

Terra-cottas.—Another industry carried on by the Greeks was modelling in terra-cotta. Like the vases, most of the terra-cottas have been found in tombs, or excavated at the shrines of divinities, but that can hardly have been their only use. They were buried with the dead, because they were part of their cherished possessions, which it was felt they would wish to have with them for use in the spirit world, or they were dedicated to a god at some shrine as an act of real sacrifice; before this they must have been used to beautify the chambers of a Greek house. Fig. 105 shows one of the small terra-cotta figures found at Tanagra in Bœotia. They are of great interest and charm, though the best of them are later than the Classical period.

Everyday Life.—Having set the scene by illustrating the Greek house and its furniture, we will now endeavour to show the life which was lived in it. Fortunately for us, Xenophon was moved to do the same thing when he wrote his *Œconomicus*, and we shall draw on this for our facts. Xenophon was an Athenian, who, born about 431 B.C., fell under the influence of Socrates when he was a young man. Another thing to be remembered is that he was one of the immortal 10,000 who took service with the Persians. Their leaders were seized and put to death. Xenophon put heart into the troops, and became one of their new generals, and the 10,000 fought their way back along the Tigris, past Nineveh, through the mountainous country of the Kurds, until, in the fifth month, their vanguard cried "the sea, the sea", and they had reached the Black Sea. Xenophon fought in other fights and returned to Athens. He was banished, as so many other Athenians were, and went to live near Olympia. Here he exchanged the sword for the pen, and wrote his books.

The *Œconomicus* opens with a discussion between Socrates, who is introduced as one of the characters, and Critobulus, on how to manage an estate—not only the practical details, but how to live happily.

After much preliminary Socratic argument about the conduct of life, and how one may do what is good and avoid what is harmful, Socrates tells how he has made inquiries to this end, and the conclusions at which he has arrived. Socrates had a very poor opinion of the handicrafts, because they weakened the body by compelling men to live indoors. It was therefore impossible for the carpenters, or the workers in brass or statuaries, or other persons of that kind, to reach the Socratic ideal. The city was not of primary importance, and Socrates would have agreed with Alexander that "a city depends on the fertility of the country surrounding it for its riches"; that in a city you might gain riches but not the character which can be held to make a man good. So to the country Socrates went to study its secrets. Then follows, in the *Œconomicus*, a panegyric of country life. Agriculture is extolled as the source of wealth and the means of enjoyment. Socrates tells us how the earth not only yields food and nourishes cattle but supplies the flowers to decorate the altars and statues; it makes men of men, because their bodies are exercised and strengthened to bear the cold of winter and heat of summer, and loving the land, they will fight for it. The countryman made the best soldier, and understood the management of horses. The earth taught men justice, because those who treated her best were recompensed with the most numerous benefits—it taught men kindliness, because on a farm you had to be prepared to lend a hand to your fellow-men. The farm was a jolly place even in winter, with plenty of fires and warm baths, and lovely in summer, when you could wander by streams or rest in the shade of woods.

So Socrates had come to the conclusion that agriculture was

AGRICULTURE

the mother and nurse of the other arts, and the best of all occupations by which men could gain a living—that when agriculture flourishes all the other occupations are vigorous, but when the land lies barren, men decay.

Critobulus then pointed out the difficulties with which the farmer may have to contend—how hail and frost may destroy his crops and disease his cattle. To which Socrates replied that all these things may be guarded against by good management; there are, to take one example, some men who will spend large sums in building houses which are quite useless, while others build much better houses for far less.

Socrates then proceeds to give Critobulus details of the life and work of another friend of his, Ischomachus by name, who seemed to him to deserve to be called "gentleman", which implies "beautiful" as well as "good". A point to be remembered about the Œconomicus is, that though the words you read are supposed to be the words of Ischomachus, the ideas are the ideas of Xenophon, the old soldier, explaining his scheme of life. His house had to be kept in order. He hated muddle and confusion, and his household had to understand the self-sacrifice which is implied in discipline. In much the same way he must have kept the 10,000 together on the great march, and saved them from falling a prey to their enemies by becoming a disorderly rabble. So Ischomachus now takes up the tale and tells us that his wife was not yet fifteen years old when they wed, and up till then had lived in leading strings, knowing "no more than how, when given wool, to turn out a cloak, and had seen only how the spinning is given out to the maids".

Ischomachus tells how, as soon as he found his wife "docile and sufficiently domesticated to carry on conversations", he offered sacrifice to the gods invoking their aid, and set about the task of educating her. First, he reminded his wife that their married life would be made successful, not by counting up which contributed the greater amount to the common stock at the beginning, but by their both being good managers. The man was to work outdoors, but the woman, like the queen bee, had to remain indoors and superintend the household. She received the incomings, and determined how much was to be saved, and how much spent. She was to "take care that the sum laid by for a year be not spent in a month". The wool was brought to

TOWN HOUSES AND EVERYDAY LIFE

147 Decking the bride
From a fifth-century toilet-box

her, and she saw that cloaks were made. The corn had to be kept in good condition for making food. Another duty of the wife was to see that any servants who were ill were well cared for, even if it seemed a thankless task. Ischomachus' wife, when told this, replied that it would be a delightful task if "they feel grateful". The wife's reward was "to feel confident that with advancing years the better partner you prove to me, and the better housewife to our children, the greater will be the honour paid to you in our home". In this paragraph Xenophon defines the position held by the women in the Greek scheme of life.

One feels a little sorry for this girl of fifteen, plunged so suddenly into such a responsible position. A child before her marriage, she put away childish things by dedicating her toys and playthings to Artemis on the day before the wedding, and then it was she took her bridal bath (147). On the wedding-day her bridegroom called for her at nightfall, and took her to her new home, where she was welcomed by her prospective father- and mother-in-law. Then a procession was formed, and the bridegroom led her by the hand to the hearth altar (148), while grain and fruits were showered on them, and on the following day the friends brought the wedding-presents.

There is an amusing passage where Ischomachus is impressing on his young wife the necessity of orderliness. "Yes, no serious man will smile when I claim that there is beauty in the order even of pots and pans set out in neat array, however much it may move the laughter of a wit." The old soldier is talking here, but, what is very extraordinary, Xenophon points out that regularly arranged vessels are not only beautiful in themselves but "the space that is between them pleases the eye". One would

HOUSEHOLD MANAGEMENT

148 Marriage ceremony
From a fifth-century toilet-box

hardly have expected an old soldier to be familiar with the problem which confronts an architect when designing a balustrade; to take one example, that the reverse shape of the space left between is as important as the profiles of the balusters themselves, or as the old Chinese proverb has it, "The soul of the wheel is the space between the spokes."

The young wife is next instructed how to dispose the furniture in the house. The most valuable couch-coverings and vessels were to be placed in the hall. The corn must always be kept dry and the wine cool. Vases must be in a good light. Ischomachus and his wife then collected their goods and chattels, and divided them up as follows: (1) whatever they used for offering sacrifices; (2) the festival dresses of the women; (3) the equipments for men, both festival and warfare; (4) the bed-coverings in the women's apartments; (5) bed-coverings in the men's apartments; (6) the shoes for the women; (7) the shoes for the men. The utensils were divided in this way: (1) for spinning; (2) preparing corn; (3) for cooking; (4) for the bath; (5) for kneading bread; (6) for the table. All these things were divided up into those for everyday use, and others only used on festive occasions. Places were found for everyday things, and the servants required to replace those not in use. The festal things were numbered and entered in a list, and placed in the care of the housekeeper.

The housekeeper was one of the female servants selected because she was moderate in eating and drinking, had a good memory, and was not a sluggard.

Ischomachus' wife may have felt a little jaded after so much hard work, because one day her husband "noticed that her face

TOWN HOUSES AND EVERYDAY LIFE

was made up: she had rubbed in white lead in order to look even whiter than she was, and alkanet juice to heighten the rosy colour of her cheeks, and she was wearing high-heeled shoes to increase her height". Ischomachus asks his wife if it would be honest for him to pretend to be richer than he was by showing her counterfeit money and necklaces of gilt wood, and then he points out to her that though tricks like the make-up may take in outsiders, they are sure to be found out by the people who live together: they may be seen while they are dressing in the morning; they got hot and perspire; a tear makes a channel on their cheek, or the bath gives the secret away. The wife promises to be good and asks "how she might make herself really beautiful, instead of merely seeming to be so". Ischomachus advised her not to sit about like a slave, but try, with the help of the gods, to behave as a mistress: she was to preside at the loom and be ready to teach those who knew less, and learn from those who knew more; she was to look after the bread-making and stand by the housekeeper when she was measuring out stores, and go round and see whether everything was in its place. She was told that it was excellent exercise to mix flour and knead dough; to shake and fold the cloaks and bedclothes, and that such exercise would give her a better appetite, improve her health, and add a natural colour to her cheeks.

149 The sunshade

Farming.—Ischomachus then tells Socrates how he spends his own day. Rising at such an hour that he could be sure of finding anybody at home whom he wished to see, he did his business in the town first, and then walked to his farm, his servant having taken his horse there beforehand.

After superintending the work of the farm, Ischomachus mounted his horse and went through the exercises needed in warfare, imitating them as closely as possible. As he states that

150 Epidaurus: the Theatre (fourth century B.C.)

151 (*left*) The monument to Hegesa, at Athens (end of fifth century B.C.)

152 (*right*) A relief from the Temple of Athena Niké at Athens (about 425 B.C.)

ISCHOMACHUS AND HIS WIFE

he did not avoid cross-roads, acclivities, ditches, or streams, it sounds like a good cross-country gallop. After these exercises the horse was allowed to have a roll, and was then taken home by a servant carrying anything that was needed from the farm. Ischomachus meanwhile walked home and, arrived there, cleaned himself with a strigil. The strigil was a very necessary implement of the toilet before the days of soap, the suds of which were easily rinsed away. The Greek used fuller's earth instead, so that half-way through his wash he was covered with a mud which needed to be scraped off. Ischomachus had luncheon on his return, because, before starting out, he probably only had a little bread and wine. Socrates sums up his philosophy and explains why our friend was a successful farmer. "You said, you know, that the greatest lesson to learn is how things ought to be done; and added that, if a man is ignorant what to do and how to do it, no good can come of his management", nor can he expect to have good workmen or good cattle. The best thing to fatten a horse with is the "master's eye". Ischomachus then tells Socrates how he deals with his slaves and bailiffs. He kept his eye on them, and some were just like puppies. These he punished when they were disobedient, but when they were good, rewarded them with food, and such men being rendered happy, worked well; but there were, and are still, others who thirst for praise much more than meat and drink. These were rewarded with better clothes and shoes than the others, for Ischomachus was of opinion that nothing makes a man more despondent than to find that good work does not obtain a higher reward than that which is indifferent. Socrates then asks Ischomachus to tell him about agriculture, and Ischomachus leads off by saying, "You shall now hear, then, Socrates, how friendly the character of this art is to mankind", and adds a very excellent point that whereas in some of the arts the students are nearly worn out before they can gain any results, in agriculture you are working in partnership with Mother Nature, who will always work miracles for you—you plant a tree, and, wonderful to relate, it actually grows. Again, in the other arts, because of the paucity of man-made knowledge, men are forced to petty secrecy for profit, but on the farm the work is done in the light of heaven, and so there can be no secrets, and the farmer has a generous disposition.

TOWN HOUSES AND EVERYDAY LIFE

153 Toy rabbit
Terra-cotta, British Museum

From the talk between Socrates and Ischomachus, we can gather many details of Greek farming. The first thing to know is the nature of the soil and what it will grow. Barley and wheat were the desirable crops. The fallow was prepared for sowing by ploughing in the spring—the grass turned up then "is long enough at that season to serve as manure, but, not having shed seed, it will not grow".

The land was turned up again in the summer as often as possible, so that the weeds withered, and the soil was baked in the sun. The seed was sown broadcast in the autumn, and it depended on the weather whether it was done early or late. Light land was lightly sown and heavier land given more seed. Sometimes the seed was ploughed in again on light land as soon as the blade appeared, because "it makes food for the soil and strengthens it like manure".

Men were put on to hoe the crops in the spring. The corn was cut with a sickle, the reapers standing back to the wind, so that the corn-stalks were not blown into their faces. If the stalk was short, it was cut low down; if it was long, in the middle, "in order that the threshers and winnowers may not spend needless trouble on what they don't want". The stubble was burnt. Oxen, mules, and horses were used for threshing by treading out the corn, the threshers turning it over and keeping it level on the circular threshing-floor. You started winnowing against the wind. The chaff and grain being thrown up, the wind carried the lighter chaff to one side. The grain being swept to the other side, the floor at the end had one heap of chaff and one of grain.

The planting of trees is described in the *Œconomicus*. Trenches were dug $2\frac{1}{2}$ ft. deep in dry soils, and $1\frac{1}{2}$ ft. by 2 ft. wide in damp ones. The vines were planted with good prepared soil put in under the cuttings. These were laid slanting, "like

154 Baby's rattle.
Moulded in terra-cotta

WORK AND PLAY

a gamma upside down", and trodden in firmly. Fig trees were planted in much the same way, but the olives in deeper trenches. The olive was very important to the Greek, because it provided him with the oil which takes the place of butter.

We can finish this section with one more quotation: "Agriculture is such a humane gentle art, that you have but to see her and listen to her, and she at once makes you understand her." And that is the end of the pleasant talks between Ischomachus and Socrates. The *Œconomicus* should be read in full in the translation we mention in our list of Recommended Books.

155 A terra-cotta toy

Socrates was condemned and died, 399 B.C., and left nothing written, but his disciples treasured his sayings and introduced him as a character in their books.

Games.—Xenophon's *Œconomicus* is rather like Hesiod's *Works and Days*, which we referred to in Part I—all work and very little play. The vase drawings, however, show that this was not so, and we have in this chapter collected several showing games. In the foreground of Fig. 144 one child has a hoop and the other is playing with knuckle-bones.

Women played knuckle-bones as well as the children (see p. 143). Aphrodite is shown playing the game with Pan, in a design engraved on a mirror-back at the British Museum. Women also employed their leisure in doing embroidery or tapestry. This seems to be the occupation of the lady under the portico in Fig. 144, drawn from a vase. Fig. 162 shows another playing a harp.

Boys indulged in cock- or quail-fighting.

Dress.—We dealt with dress in Parts I and II. Thucydides gives a few details, which can be added. He says that the Athenians were among the first to lay aside their arms. It was just before his time that the older men of the wealthier class gave up wearing tunics and doing up their hair in a knot and

TOWN HOUSES AND EVERYDAY LIFE

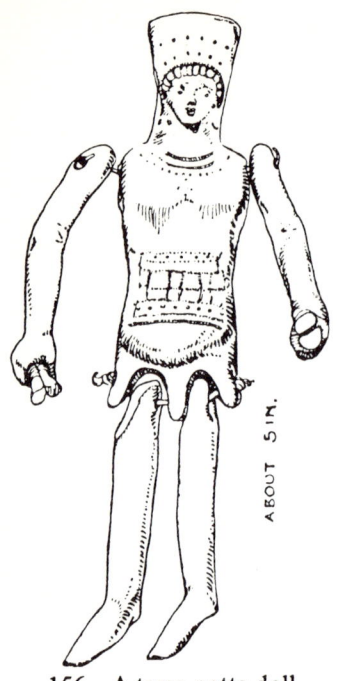

fastening it with a golden grasshopper. He says also that at first the athletes competing at Olympia wore girdles about their loins; then the Spartans, not many years before Thucydides, started the practice of stripping and anointing their bodies with oil when engaged in athletic exercises.

Talk.—If it has been a little difficult to find many amusements for women, there can be no doubt about the principal recreation of man; undoubtedly it was talk: not mere talkativeness, but good, hard, clever talk. In the *Œconomicus*, before they really began to talk, they had to clear the ground by discussion, so that they might know what they were going to talk about.

156 A terra-cotta doll (ABOUT 5 IN.)

In the opening of Plato's *Republic* the scene is laid in the house of Cephalus at the Peiræus. Socrates had been to the Peiræus with Glaucon that he might offer up his prayers to Bendis, the Thracian Artemis, and also because he wanted to see in what manner they would celebrate the festival, for it was a new thing. They were delighted with the procession of the inhabitants, but thought that of the Thracians equally, if not more, beautiful. When they had finished their prayers they turned for home, and at that instant Polemarchus, the son of Cephalus, saw them and sent his servant running after them to bid them wait for him. When Polemarchus came up to them with some of his friends, they threatened Socrates with coercion unless he and Glaucon stayed with them. They told him of the torch-race on horseback in honour of the goddess, which was to take place that evening: the horsemen would carry torches and pass them one to another during the race. They told Socrates not to be perverse, but to stay so that they could "have a good talk". He returned with Polemarchus to his home:

CONVERSATION

there, too, was Cephalus, the father of Polemarchus, whom I had not seen for a long time, and I thought him very much aged. He was seated on a cushioned chair, and had a garland on his head, for he had been sacrificing in the court; and there were some other chairs in the room arranged in a semicircle, upon which we sat down by him. He saluted me eagerly, and then he said: "You don't come to see me, Socrates, as often as you ought; if I were still able to

157
An unkind girl plays with a tortoise

go out and see you, I would not ask you to come to me. But at my age I can hardly get to the city, and therefore you should come oftener to the Peiræus. For let me tell you, that the more the pleasures of the body fade away, the greater to me is the pleasure and charm of conversation."

The whole of the *Republic* is cast in the form of conversation. It should be read to gain an idea of the quality of Greek conversation, and because it is one of the world's great books. It will explain the hold which the Classics have had on us since the Renaissance. If you are reading Bede or Froissart, your mind gropes its way in a world which is shadowy and obscure. In Plato, however, the thought and language shine as crystal clear as the Doric columns of the Parthenon in the Attic sunshine of the Acropolis. Herodotus said, "how brave a thing is freedom of speech!"

158 The swing
From a red-figure vase drawing

TOWN HOUSES AND EVERYDAY LIFE

159 The dancing lesson

and the *Republic* would not have been possible before the days of Classical Greece.

The Symposium. — The symposium, or banquet, was another opportunity for conversation. Xenophon describes one held at the house of Callias, at Athens, in 424 B.C. Nine guests, including Xenophon and Socrates, were invited, and all were men—the ladies of the household did not take part in these entertainments. They were proceeding with their dinner in silence, when a jester, Philippus by name, forced his way in, saying he thought it was more of a jest to come uninvited than invited. The host, noticing that his other guests were full of seriousness, allowed Philippus to be seated, and the uninvited one at once proceeded to try to earn his dinner by cracking jokes. These, however, were so badly received that in the end the joker threw his garment over his head and wept, and then the company did laugh.

We are not told what the guests ate, but at the end of the dinner the small three-legged tables standing in front of the couches were removed (86), libations were made, and the pæan, or hymn to Apollo, sung, like saying grace.

Then a Syracusan came in with a girl who played on the flute, another who danced and performed wonderful feats, and a boy who danced and played on the lyre. First, the girl played to them on the flute and the boy on his lyre, and then the dancing-girl gave her show. Twelve hoops were handed to her, and, dancing, she threw them up, whirling round, and caught them again in time to the music. Then another hoop was brought

160 The dance
From a red-figure vase drawing

A BANQUET

in with swords stuck into it, standing upright, and the dancing-girl leaped into it head foremost, and sprang out again in the same way, and she continued this feat with boldness and without injury. Then the boy danced, and this moved Socrates to tell the company that though he could not dance, he did do physical exercises. Then Philippus, who by this time had recovered his spirits, gave a ridiculous imitation of the boy dancing, and this time he was successful in amusing the guests—they laughed so much that wine had to be brought round.

161 A musician

By this time, however, Socrates had to remind them that music and dancing were only the preliminaries to the real business of the evening, which was to talk round the subject of what accomplishment or possession each of them most valued in himself. One found pride in his power of rendering other men honest, another in his knowledge of Homer, one in his riches, another his poverty, and so on. But all the parties were not so respectable as this. There are vase drawings of diners being very ill after the banquets. It may be that it was at such parties that kottabos was played. In this a stand was brought in which supported a vertical shaft, and this being set down in the room, a small bronze disc was balanced on the top of the shaft (168). The game was played by leaving a little wine in your two-handled drinking-cup, then holding the cup by one of its handles, you jerked or flipped out the wine so that it hit the disc and knocked it off its stand (169).

Travel by Land and Sea.—Having dealt with the life of men at home, we can now follow them in their travels abroad, and they were great travellers. Their eager, curious minds made them want to find out what other people were doing, and the

162 The harp
From a red-figure vase

TOWN HOUSES AND EVERYDAY LIFE

163 Hockey
From a relief in the Athens Museum

physical structure of their country was another cause. When the resources of the small Greek city-State were exhausted, like the bees they had to send out swarms to find their honey elsewhere. This must have been one of the causes of their frequent quarrels —one swarm might follow another, and find themselves not too welcome. When the Greek travelled by land he used the chariot or cart, both of which we have illustrated in Figs. 9 and 108, or the horse which we will consider here. Undoubtedly, the Greek was a great horseman with a good natural seat—the vase drawings and sculptures prove this. Fig. 170 shows the chlamys or cape worn by travellers. The only saddle was a rug strapped on to the back of the horse, and the Greeks rode without stirrups; perhaps this is the reason for the very formidable fifth- or fourth-century bit from the British Museum (171). Xenophon, in his treatise on horsemanship—which all horse-lovers should read—says that riders should have two bits, one smooth, the other with heavy rings and sharp points. Obviously Fig. 171 shows the severe type, and one can only hope that the Greek who used it had good hands. One interesting detail is that though the bit was

164 A boy with a fighting quail

LAND AND SEA TRAVEL

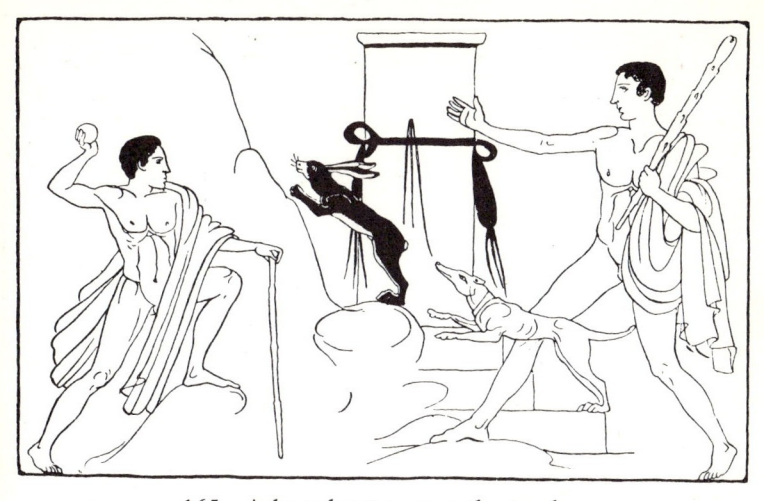

165   A hare hunt among the tombs
From a white lekythos

made of metal, it retains the form of the ivory cheek-pieces of the Homeric bit (Part I, p. 18).

Shipping.—The colonising habits of the Greeks developed their shipping, and the enormous mileage of their sea-coast gave them many harbours. The mountainous character of the interior often made the sea journey easier than one by land. Thucydides tells us that tradition accorded to Minos, King of Crete, the possession of the first fleet, and that with it he conquered the Cyclades, and cleared the sea of pirates; also that the ships of the Trojan expedition were not provided with decks, but were built after the early style, like pirate boats. Corinth was the first place where triremes were built (704 B.C.), but generally the pentecarbon and long boat were still used. Even at Salamis (480 B.C.) the Athenian vessels were still not decked throughout.

166   A shoemaker
From a red-figure vase

THE TRIREME

A double-banked launch, today, means a large ship's boat with two men to each oar, so with the trireme it may have had three men to each oar, or three oars (173). To us it is inconceivable that it meant three, or five, rows of rowers, superimposed one above the other, and it would be amusing to try setting out to scale a section showing how long their oars would have had to be to reach the water, and what would have happened to them when the boat rolled.

169 Men playing kottabos
From a red-figure vase

Death.—Now we come to the last journey of all, which the Greek has to take, to the land of Hades and dread Persephone, "where dwell the phantoms of men outworn". After death the body was laid out with an obol in its mouth for journey money, and a honey cake as an offering to the underworld gods, and an oil flask was placed at the head. At the funeral the body was placed on a bier and carried on the shoulders of friends, with hired mourners and flute players, to the place of burning. This freed the spirit from

170 Horseman wearing riding-cloak (chlamys)

the body: we saw, in Part I, how the spirit of Patroklos appeared to his friend Achilles, urging that he might be buried with all dispatch, and his body given its due of fire, so that he might pass the gate of Hades. The ashes were buried in an urn with some of the dead man's possessions for use in the spirit world, and after the burial there was a funeral feast.

In 430 the Spartans attacked Attica, and there was an outbreak of plague in Athens caused by the crowding in of the countrymen. The mortality was so great that the funeral customs were violated. The bodies were burned, and some people stole the funeral piles of others, or put their own dead where another corpse was already burning.

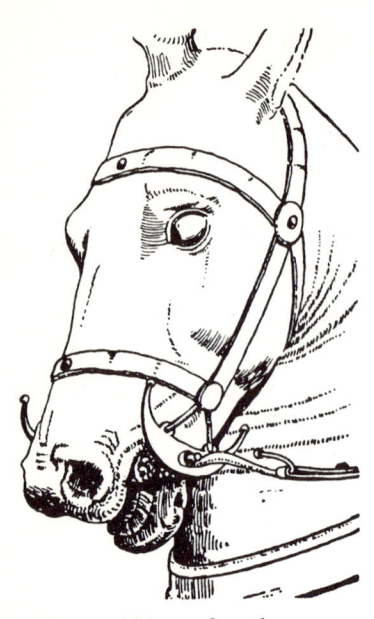

171   A fifth- or fourth-century Greek bit

Pausanias tells us that "outside of the city, in the townships and on the roads, the Athenians have sanctuaries of the gods and graves of heroes and men—and tombstones stand on their graves". The main Athenian cemetery was outside the Dipylon Gate to the north-west of the city, in the Cerameicus or ancient Potters' Quarter; it was excavated before the Second World War by German archæologists, who discovered and restored many interesting monuments. Slaves who had been faithful to their masters in war shared the honour of a public burial.

In the second book, or chapter, of his *History*, Thucydides gives the funeral oration delivered by Pericles in the winter of 431 B.C. over the bodies of the Athenians who had fallen in the beginning of the Peloponnesian War. Three days before the funeral the bones of the dead were laid out in a tent, and the mourners brought their own offerings. On the third day the bones were placed in cypress wood chests, one for each tribe,

FUNERAL RITES

172 A Greek trireme

and a single empty litter, decked with a pall, was carried along for those whose bodies were missing. All were free to join in the procession, and the female relatives came and made lamentation at the sepulchre outside the walls.

Pericles spoke from a lofty stage. He first reminded them of their ancestors who had given them freedom and empire, and then of the greatness of Athens, to show how great a sacrifice the dead had made.

The sacrifice which they collectively made was individually repaid to them; for they received again each one for himself a praise which grows not old, and the noblest of all sepulchres—I speak not of that in which their remains are laid, but of that in which their glory survives, and is proclaimed always and on every fitting occasion both in word and deed. For the whole earth is the sepulchre of famous men.

Sometimes the tombstones were just plain slabs of marble, terminating in a piece of pleasant ornament, and with an inscription. The inscriptions are models of brevity. Here is one from a tombstone preserved in the Metropolitan Museum of Art, New York: "Amphichares, the dead youth's father, mourning a good son, erected this stone to Chairedemos. Phaidimos made it." Other monuments give portraits of the

TOWN HOUSES AND EVERYDAY LIFE

173 How the trireme was rowed

deceased: Fig. 151 is a very beautiful one. An interesting point is that Greek, Roman, and Renaissance funeral monuments always show the people as they were in life, and as if they left the world behind them with regret. The Christian monuments of the Middle Ages always show the people as dead, and as if they left the world behind them without regret.

A typical monument from Athens, now in the British Museum, shows a man on horseback with a boy running behind. The inscription reads: "After many pleasant sports with my companions, I who sprang from earth am earth once more. I am Aristocles, of Peiræus, son of Menon."

Chapter XII

SEA FIGHTS AND LAND BATTLES

In this chapter we come to the tragic part of our tale. Not quite fifty years had elapsed since the Persians were overthrown at Salamis, and in this time the Greeks had raised the fabric of a civilisation which ever since has been regarded as Classical. And then all their superb creative faculties were diverted from peace to war, and they were moved to destroy themselves. We cannot do better than follow Thucydides, whose second book opens with the outbreak of the Peloponnesian War in 431. The youth of the day, however, had never seen war, and gladly took up their arms.

Three hundred Thebans, seeing that war was inevitable, made a surprise attack on Plataea (an ally of Athens) by night, and gained the city by a stratagem. The Plataeans, discovering how few Thebans there were in the streets, made their way to suitable points by breaking a way through the party walls of the houses. Barricades of wagons were made to confine the attackers, and then, at dawn, the Plataeans issued from their houses and fell on the Thebans. The women and slaves on the house-tops screamed and yelled, and threw down stones and tiles, and heavy rain added to the misery.

Thucydides says that the Greeks generally were not shocked by the war. Their sympathies were on the side of the Spartans, whom they regarded as the liberators of Hellas.

Meanwhile, the Spartans invaded Attica, "when the corn was in full ear", and ravaged the country, hoping to draw the Athenians from their city. Pericles, the Athenian leader, would not allow them to give battle to the Spartans, but sent a fleet of 100 ships to ravage the Peloponnesian coast.

All the Athenians were moved into the city, bringing even the woodwork of their houses. Their cattle were taken to Euboea and the adjacent islands. This was miserable for the Athenians, who had "always been accustomed to reside in the country".

Again, in 430, acting on Pericles' advice, the Athenians allowed the Spartans to ravage Attica, but sent their fleet of

SEA FIGHTS AND LAND BATTLES

100 ships against the coasts of Sparta. There were 4,000 hoplites (foot-soldiers) on board and 300 cavalry, and for the first time these were carried in horse transports made out of old ships.

The Athenians became enraged with Pericles, and he called an assembly. Here he pointed out that if they would only keep to the sea, of which they were the masters, all would be well. Pericles died two and a half years after the beginning of the war, and Athens, though nominally a democracy, had been ruled by him. He had come to the front about 469, and was chiefly responsible for the rebuilding and beautification of Athens.

In 429 the Spartans, instead of invading Attica again, went against Platæa. Thucydides gives an interesting account of their siege of this town. First they cut down all the fruit trees and built a stockade round the town, and then raised a mound confined at the base by timber framing. Opposite the mound, on their city wall, the Platæans built up a timber tower, covered with hides. The idea in each case was to gain a vantage-point from which the archers could see and shoot at their enemies. The Platæans then drove an underground gallery from the town to beneath the mound, and then as fast as the Spartans heaped earth on top they dug it away from the bottom. With the earth from the mound the Platæans built a crescent-shaped rampart inside their wall, opposite the mound, in case the wall was breached. The Spartans brought engines against the city, but the Platæans threw nooses over these and dragged them up, or suspended great beams by chains from the walls, over the battering-rams, and then dropped them down and broke off the heads of the rams. The Spartans tried to fire the city with sulphur and pitch on wood. Then they built a wall round the city with a ditch on each side, out of which the clay for the bricks came. Then they settled down to starve out the besieged. There were only 400 Platæans, 80 Athenians, and 110 women to make bread in the city.

In this second book we get a good description of naval warfare. The Spartans were no match at first for the Athenians at sea. In one sea fight they acted rather like frightened sheep, and drew up their ships in a large circle, prows outside. Inside the circle were light boats, and five ships to stop the gap if the circle were broken. The Athenians, like sea-wolves, sailed round and round, and the Spartans fell into confusion. Another Athenian

PAINTED VASES

174 (*left*) A sacrifice, on a vase of the fourth century B.C.

175 (*right*) Theseus killing the Minotaur, on a vase of the fifth century B.C.

176 *top row* Peparethus, *c.* 500 B.C. (British Museum); Athens, *c.* 450 B.C. (E. S. G. Robinson); *centre* Syracuse, *c.* 411 B.C. (Ashmolean Museum); *bottom row* Aetna, *c.* 470 B.C. (Brussels); Syracuse, *c.* 479 B.C. (British Museum)

SILVER COINS

SIEGE OF PLATÆA

trick was to pretend to retreat, and keeping just ahead of the pursuer, sail round a stationary ship, ram the pursuer amidships, and sink it; a feat which filled the Spartans with consternation.

This marked an advance, because we are told that in a sea fight between Corinth and Corcyra, "the standards were raised on both sides, and the two fleets met and fought. The decks of both were crowded with heavy infantry, with archers and with javelin-men ... it had almost the appearance of a battle by land."

BOOK III (428).—The Spartans again invaded Attica. During the winter the unfortunate Platæans began to suffer hunger. They were still confined within the Spartan wall. This was built on two encircling lines about 16 ft. apart, and the space between was divided up into rooms for the guard, with battlements over. At intervals there were higher towers, with a passage through them at the battlement level.

Food began to be scarce in the city, so the Platæans determined to make a sortie. First, they had to decide the height of the Spartan wall, and this they did by counting the bricks of which it was built, and they had to count time and again and then strike an average. Then ladders were made of the same height, and on a stormy night, when the Spartans had retreated to the towers for shelter, the Platæans stole forth and scaled the wall; they were assisted in this by those who were left in the city, who made a sortie on the opposite side.

In the end, the remainder of the Platæans had to surrender to the Spartans, who killed all the men and sold the women as slaves. They then razed the city to the ground, and, using the timber of the roofs and doors, built, near the Sanctuary of Hera, an inn of 200 ft. square on two floors.

In 427 the Spartans again invaded Attica. The Athenians about this time captured the island of Minoa, near the coast at Megara, "by the help of engines from the sea". We now hear of Cleon, and the plague reappeared in Athens. In 426 earthquakes alarmed the Spartans who did not invade Attica. The Athenians purified the island of Delos by taking away all the dead who had been buried there, and decreeing that in future no one should die, or give birth to a child, on the island. We find in the Homeric hymn that Delos was sacred to the Greeks, because Apollo, the son of Leto, was born there. It is in the hymn of Apollo that Homer refers to himself as "a blind man is

SEA FIGHTS AND LAND BATTLES

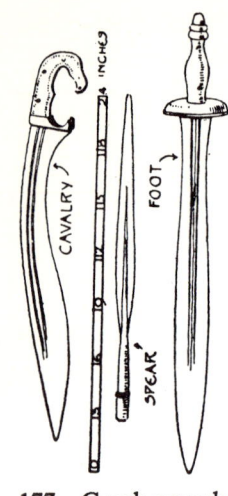

he, and he dwells in rocky Chios; his songs will ever have the mastery, ay, in all time to come". After the purification the Athenians revived the Delian Games, and for the first time introduced horse-races.

In this book there is a description which explains the Greek method of fighting. The usual practice was to form up in two lines, face to face, and seek to defeat your opponent by sheer weight and fighting power. The right wing of each line, however, was inclined to give way, because the shield was carried on the left arm, leaving the right side exposed. In a battle between the Spartans and Athenians, the left wing of the Spartans "out-flanked the right wing of their opponents and threatened to surround them". The Athenian commander had foreseen this, and stationed about 400 troops in a sunken road overgrown with bushes, and these, coming out of their ambush at the critical moment, fell upon the Spartans from the rear, and routed them. There does not appear to have been very much in the way of strategy, nor were archers used.

177 Greek swords and spear

Fig. 177 shows the arms the Greeks used. The foot sword was suitable for cutting or thrusting, and was carried in a sheath on the left side.

The cavalry sword (machaira) was recommended by Xenophon for use by horsemen, because its weight made it suitable for a downstroke.

The spear continued to be used for thrusting, and smaller ones were thrown. All these weapons were made of iron, except the spearshafts and the wood or ivory plating to the sword-handles.

The Corinthian helmet is shown in Fig. 178. It was just a well-shaped pot, with a long nasal guard and cheek-pieces, which left holes for the eyes. As it had to be big enough to go over the head, and was lined with leather, the eyes must have been well behind the eye-holes and the helmet difficult to see out of, and the ears were covered up, which made it doubly dangerous. It

TACTICS AND ARMOUR

was often worn pushed back on the head, and Athene and Britannia on our coins wear their Corinthian helmets in this way.

The Attic helmet (179) followed, and was a better piece of armour. The soldier could both see and hear better. The bronze example which is here drawn was discovered during the First World War, in a grave of about 500 B.C., by the British Salonika force. The Attic and Corinthian were the two general helmet forms, and crests and plumes were worn with both.

The cuirass, which at first was two bronze plates moulded to the body and secured with straps at the sides, was superseded, in the fifth century, by one where bronze plates were mounted on to leather, as shown in Fig. 178. This type fastened in the front, and had epaulettes over the shoulders.

Greaves for the legs continued to be modelled out of bronze, and made to fit over and keep on the leg by the spring of the metal.

Shields were oval, circular, or of the Bœotian shape, shown in Fig. 178; leather seems to have been mounted on to a wooden frame with metal platings. The shield was carried by passing the left arm under a central cross-bar, and by the left hand holding a loop on the shield's edge.

In BOOK IV (425) the area of hostilities widens and takes in Sicily. The Syracusans had taken possession of Messina, which was the key to Sicily, commanding the Straits of Messina; the Charybdis through which Odysseus sailed.

The Spartans invaded Attica for the fifth time, so the Athenians seized and fortified Pylos on the west coast of the

178 Arms and armour

SEA FIGHTS AND LAND BATTLES

Peloponnesus. Not being provided with iron tools or hods, they used their hands, and carried the mortar on their backs. Pylos being strongly fortified by Nature, the Athenians were able to build a wall on the land side at A, Fig. 180, and towards the sea, where required, in six days, and then they sailed away, leaving a garrison with five ships. The Spartans returned from Attica after only fifteen days when they heard of this and recalled sixty ships from Corcyra, and these, to escape the notice of the Athenians, were carried over the Leucadian Isthmus. Dispatches were sent in this way: a long strip of paper was rolled diagonally along a circular staff, and the message was written in lines on the paper along the length of the staff. When unrolled it was, of course, quite unintelligible, until it was rerolled by the recipient on a similar staff. This was called a skytale dispatch.

179 An Attic helmet (500 B.C.) discovered in a grave at Salonika

The intention of the Spartans was to attack the Athenians in Pylos from both land and sea, and they contemplated closing the entrance to the harbour at B, where there was only a passage for two ships, and at C for eight or nine, by anchoring ships prows outwards. The Spartans as well garrisoned Sphacteria with 420 hoplites (infantry) with their attendant helots. The Athenians drew three of their ships up on to land, and stationed some of their men on the mainland side, and others at D. The Spartans attacked at A and D. The attack failed, and the Spartans sent for timber to make engines.

Fifty Athenian ships now arrived, and as the Spartans had neglected to close the mouths of the harbour, they sailed in and engaged the Spartan ships. Some of these they tied to their own ships, and the Spartans dashed into the water and tried to pull them back. In the end they were defeated, and the Athenians, gaining possession of the sea, cut off the Spartans on Sphacteria from their friends on the mainland.

PYLOS AND SPHACTERIA

This was the end of the first round, and the Spartans were so dispirited that they sent ambassadors to Athens to suggest that peace should be made and the war ended. Cleon, who was now more powerful, persuaded the Athenians to propose impossible terms, and the negotiations broke off.

Meanwhile the Spartans, cut off in Sphacteria, were helped in a variety of ways from the mainland. In some cases men swam across the harbour from the mainland, drawing after them skins filled with "pounded linseed and poppy seeds mixed with honey".

It became obvious to the Athenians that the island must be taken before the winter, when they would be unable to send reinforcements. Cleon boasted that if he were in charge of the operations he could easily capture the island, and then became alarmed and tried to draw back when he was taken at his word. However, he had to go. Arrived at Sphacteria, a force of 800 men was landed, and the crews of the ships, excepting the thalamites (see p. 226), and the battle went against the Spartans, whose felt cuirasses were not proof against arrows, and in which the heads of the javelins broke off and clung when thrown at them. Cleon, unfortunately, was able to keep his promise, and within twenty days returned to Athens with 292 Spartan prisoners. "Nothing which happened in the war caused greater astonishment in Hellas." There was no chance now of peace.

The Athenians next attacked, and so the miserable business of the war continued. During the summer of 424 the Athenians sent an expedition against Cythera, the large island to the south of the Peloponnesus, and, capturing it, left a garrison there. The Spartans planned an expedition to Chalcidice to draw the Athenians away from Sparta.

There was another expedition against Bœotia, allies of Sparta. The Athenians encamped and fortified Delium, which was a temple of Apollo. They dug a trench around this, and threw up a rampart, and crowned this with a double palisade, and cutting down the vines threw these between, with stones and bricks from

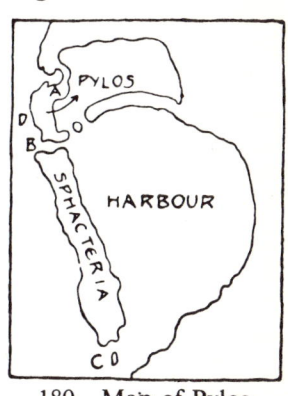

180 Map of Pylos

SEA FIGHTS AND LAND BATTLES

181 The flame-thrower, described by Thucydides

the houses near by, and they erected wooden towers. The Bœotians attacked the Athenians, and used an engine made in the following manner: they sawed a great beam or tree-trunk down the middle, and then hollowed it out and joined it together, so that it formed a pipe, one end of which was plated with iron. From this a great cauldron was suspended by chains, and an iron pipe was fitted between this end of the beam and the cauldron. At the other end a large bellows was fitted, which forced a blast of air through the pipe into the cauldron, which contained burning coals, sulphur, and pitch, and so directed the flames against the wooden rampart, which was destroyed, so that the garrison fled and the fort was taken. We have attempted a reconstruction of this in Fig. 181.

In the spring of 423 the Athenians, who were alarmed at the success of Brasidas, the Spartan general, agreed to a truce of a year. Thucydides gives the terms of the peace, which seemed fair and reasonable, and included a clause, "to make arrangements about the termination of the war". The truce was more or less kept. Brasidas made an attempt on Potidæa, which failed. We read here of the Greek method of keeping their sentinels awake: a bell was passed all round the walls, from man to man, and Brasidas tried fixing his scaling-ladders just after it had passed.

DELIUM. MELOS

BOOK V.—In 422 the year of truce expired, but hostilities were not resumed until after the Pythian Games; this shows that Greek athletics were a part of Greek religion. Cleon took an expedition to the Chalcidicean cities, where the Athenians were defeated, and both Cleon and Brasidas killed.

In 421 Athens and Sparta signed a peace for fifty years, but in 420 Alcibiades appeared as leader of a war party in Athens.

During the summer the Olympic Games were held, and the Spartans were excluded because they had not observed the Olympic Truce (p. 156). There was almost a riot because Lichas, a young Spartan, entered his chariot in the race in the name of the Bœotian State, and was victorious. When this was discovered he was disqualified.

182 Hermes

The rest of this book is taken up with a recital of petty quarrels and battles between the various Greek States. In one battle the Spartans marched slowly, with even steps, to the music of many flute players in their ranks, while their opponents, the Argives, advanced eagerly and impetuously.

In 416 the Athenians made an expedition against Melos, who was friendly with Sparta. The wretched Melians pointed out the iniquity of the attack, but their city was taken, and all the men killed and the women and children sold as slaves.

Notwithstanding all this, the Spartans did not renounce the peace with Athens as yet, but the Melian massacre marks the point at which Thucydides' history enters its tragic phase.

In BOOK VI (415) the Athenians conceive the idea of the Sicilian expedition. As Thucydides says, they had no real idea of the size of the island, which a merchant vessel in his day took eight days to sail round, or the magnitude of the task of its capture.

Then an extraordinary thing happened. Everywhere in Athens, before the doors of the temples and houses, there stood square pillars surmounted by the head of Hermes; these were called Hermæ (182), and one night nearly all these had the faces mutilated. The Athenians were greatly shocked at the impious outrage, and took it as a bad omen and the work of men who were trying to overthrow the State. The enemies of Alcibiades said that he and some of his drunken friends had done it, but he was allowed to sail with the expedition in the middle of the summer to muster at Corcyra.

The fleet for the expedition was built up at great expense. Just before it left the Peiræus, prayers were offered by the whole fleet and the spectators on the shore, and then the ships raced with one another as far as Ægina. When the fleet left Corcyra for Sicily, it consisted of 134 triremes and two Rhodian 50-oared galleys (pentecontors). There were 5,100 hoplites, 480 bowmen, 700 slingers, and 120 light-armed troops, with one horse transport with 30 horsemen and horses. This was a badly arranged force, because the Syracusans were strong in cavalry. There were 30 transports for food supplies with bakers, stonemasons, carpenters, and tools for wall building. One hundred other boats were pressed into service, as well as many merchant ships and lesser craft, who followed for the purposes of trade. Nicias was the leader.

As they sailed along the south coast of Italy, none of the Italian cities would let them within their cities; Tarentum and Locri even refused them water and anchorage, and at Rhegium (Reggio) they had to camp outside the city walls. The Segestæans, who had promised their aid, were found not to have the money they had boasted about. Nicias proposed that, after demonstrating the might of Athens by sailing along the coasts of Sicily, they should return; but Alcibiades was still for war. The Athenians, however, sent for Alcibiades, who was one of the generals in charge of the expedition, to return to Athens to stand his trial on the charge of having mutilated the Hermæ. On his way back he slipped away, and went to the Peloponnesus instead, and took service with the Spartans.

By this time the Athenians had settled down at Catana, on the east coast of Sicily, and thither the Syracusans were drawn by a stratagem. Meanwhile the Athenians boarded their ships and sailed to Syracuse, and having arrived there, landed opposite the Olympieum, or Temple of the Olympian Zeus, and made a camp there,

> on one side walls and houses and trees and a swamp furnished a barrier; on the other side a line of cliffs. They also cut down the trees near at hand, and bringing them down to the sea, built a stockade

THE SICILIAN EXPEDITION

by the ships; and on the shore at Dascon, where the place was most accessible to the enemy, they quickly erected a bulwark of stones—picked up in the fields—and of timbers, and pulled down the bridge over the Anapus (183).

The Syracusans, who had been drawn away by a false rumour to Catana, hurried back to find the Athenians encamped, and they camped on the other side of the Elorine Road. In the battle that followed the next day, the Athenians under Nicias won, but were unable to follow up their success because of the Syracusan cavalry, so they sailed back to Catana after, as it was still winter and they wished to send to Athens for horsemen. At Naxos, to the north of Catana, they constructed dockyards and built stockades round their camp. The Syracusans meanwhile built a new wall round Temenites, fortified and garrisoned Megara, and raised a fort at the Olympieum and stockades at all landing-places, and then sent envoys for help to Sparta and Corinth. Alcibiades urged the Spartans to support the Syracusans and take Decelea, in Attica, which not only controlled the silver-mines at Laurium but the overland route by which provisions were imported into Attica. This was the weakness of Athens, that she could not feed herself. The Spartans appointed Gylippus to lead an expedition to Syracuse, and renewed the war with Athens.

Hostilities opened in Sicily in the spring of 414 by skirmishes, and in the summer 250 horsemen arrived from Athens. The Athenians sailed by night and put in at Leon, the ships going back to Thapsus, a little to the north. "The land force advanced at once at a run to Epipolæ, and got up by way of Euryelus." The Syracusans again were surprised, and advancing to the attack were defeated by the Athenians and retired into the city. The Athenians then built a fort at Labdalum. They then advanced to Syce, and built a circular fort in the middle of the plateau of the high ground of Epipolæ, a distinct menace to the Syracusans, who tried to stop the building, but were again routed. The next day the double wall of circumvallation was started from the circular fort, Syce, northwards to Trogilus, but not completed. The Syracusans retaliated by building a counter-wall to the south of Syce and at right angles to the Athenian wall, and their army protected the workmen, but did not risk a battle with the Athenians, who allowed the work to proceed:

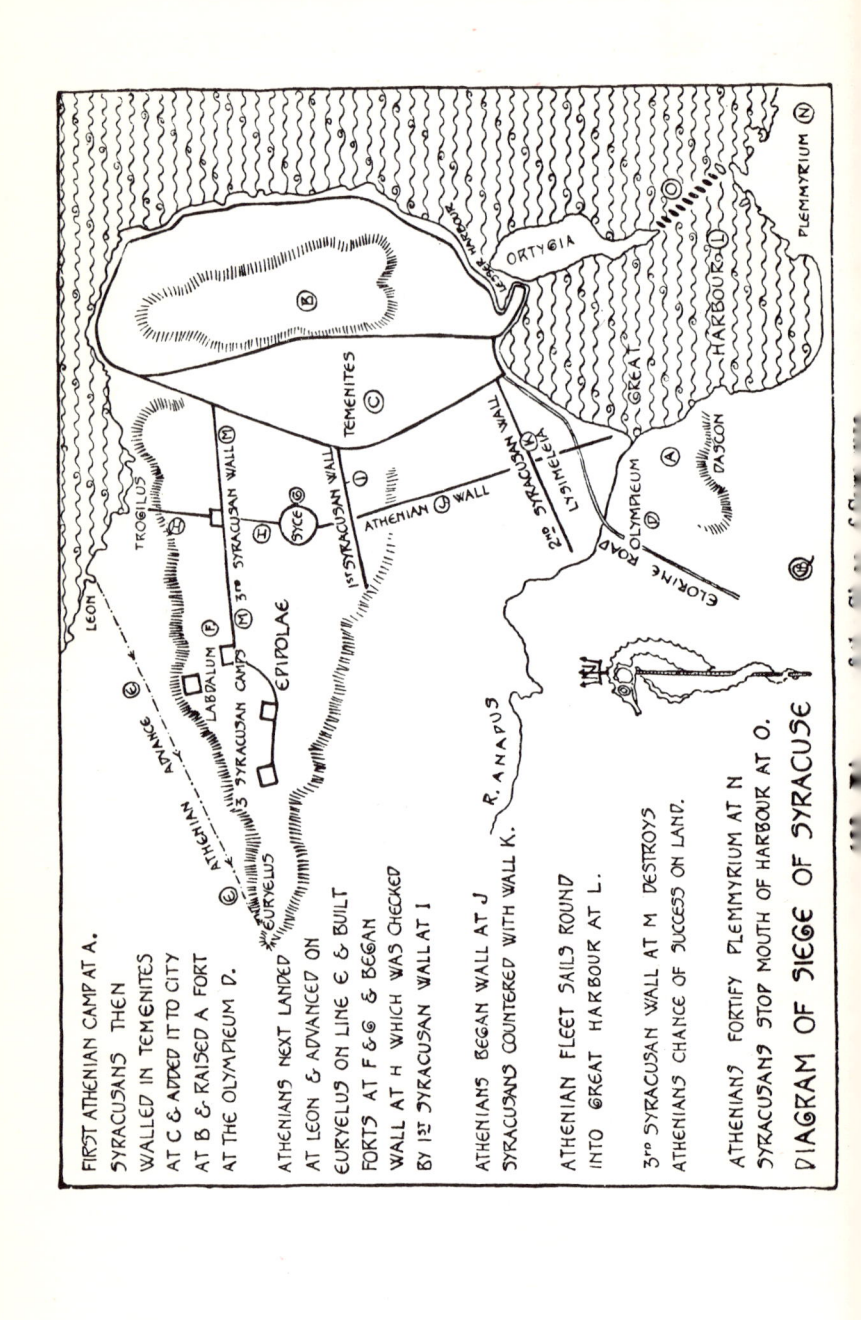

FIRST ATHENIAN CAMP AT A.
SYRACUSANS THEN
WALLED IN TEMENITES
AT C & ADDED IT TO CITY
AT B & RAISED A FORT
AT THE OLYMPIEUM D.

ATHENIANS NEXT LANDED
AT LEON & ADVANCED ON
EURYELUS ON LINE E & BUILT
FORTS AT F & G & BEGAN
WALL AT H WHICH WAS CHECKED
BY 1ST SYRACUSAN WALL I

ATHENIANS BEGAN WALL AT J
SYRACUSANS COUNTERED WITH WALL K.

ATHENIAN FLEET SAILS ROUND
INTO GREAT HARBOUR AT L.

3RD SYRACUSAN WALL AT M DESTROYS
ATHENIANS CHANCE OF SUCCESS ON LAND.

ATHENIANS FORTIFY PLEMMYRIUM AT N
SYRACUSANS STOP MOUTH OF HARBOUR AT O.

DIAGRAM OF SIEGE OF SYRACUSE

SIEGE OF SYRACUSE

"the Athenian ships had not yet sailed round from Thapsus into the Great Harbour, but the Syracusans were still masters of the parts about the sea, and the Athenians brought their supplies from Thapsus by land".

The Athenians then destroyed the underground water-pipes to the city; then attacked the counter-wall and pulled it down, and began their own wall down to the sea. The Syracusans then started their second counter-wall, or stockade, through the middle of the marsh, Lysimeleia. This stockade was taken by the Athenians, whose fleet now sailed round into the Great Harbour. The Athenians lost Lamachus in this battle, leaving Nicias in sole command, and the Syracusans were successful in a counter-attack and destroyed part of the wall by the round fort at Syce. The Athenians now proceeded with their double wall down to the sea from Syce, and the Syracusans began to despair. Remember the closeness of all this fighting, when only the length of a bow-shot took one out of danger.

BOOK VII.—It was at this time that the Spartans, under Gylippus, and the Corinthians arrived, and landed at Himera. The Athenian wall had nearly reached the Great Harbour, but the northern portion between Syce and Trogilus was only half-built. Gylippus' first success was to take the fort at Labdalum, and having got rid of this on their flank, the Syracusans started their third wall; they captured as well the Athenian trireme which kept watch at the harbour mouth. Nicias now fortified Plemmyrium, and built three forts there, in which most of the stores were deposited, and the large boats and ships of war were moved there. These were not drawn on shore, so that they became waterlogged.

The Athenians were already beginning to give "attention more to naval warfare, seeing that matters on land were less hopeful for themselves, now that Gylippus had come".

The Syracusans posted a third part of their cavalry at a hamlet near the Olympieum, where they came between the Athenians on the wall and their troops at Plemmyrium, and they continued their third counter-wall until it nearly reached the line of the Athenian wall. The Athenians had to give battle, and were defeated; the Syracusans' wall passed their own, and away went the hopes of the Athenians, and so the summer ended.

SEA FIGHTS AND LAND BATTLES

The following winter the Spartans sent for help, and so did Nicias to Athens. He reported the bad state of affairs with the Athenians, and the fact that he was suffering from kidney disease. The Athenians promised to send Demosthenes and Eurymedon to help him with reinforcements. One feels sorry for Nicias, who had been against the expedition from the first, and who was now racked with disease; his lieutenant, Alcibiades, had proved a traitor, and yet he still struggled on. The Athenians at home were feeling the pinch of poverty and were exhausted by plague, yet they set their teeth and made their last spurt.

March 413 B.C. The Spartans invaded Attica and fortified Decelea, about 14 miles north of Athens, and proceeded to raid the most fertile parts of the country, and, as well, they dispatched reinforcements to Sicily, and Gylippus returned to Syracuse and urged the Syracusans to try their luck in fighting at sea. He led out his whole land force under cover of night against the forts of Plemmyrium, and at the same time thirty-five Syracusan triremes from the Great Harbour and forty-five from the Lesser Harbour moved out to sea. The Athenians defeated the Syracusans at sea, but Gylippus captured the three forts on Plemmyrium with all the goods stored there, including the sails and other tackle of forty triremes, as well as three triremes that had been drawn up on shore. This meant that the pincers were closing on the Athenians. They were now cut off on the north by the third wall and to the south by the camps on Plemmyrium. The Syracusans had thus command of both sides of the entrance to the Great Harbour, and from now on the Athenian convoys could only gain an entrance by fighting.

The Syracusans had formed a "stockade, which had been planted in the sea in front of their ships to serve in place of an enclosed harbour". The Athenians attacked this with a ship of 10,000 talents burden (250 tons), with wooden towers and bulwarks, and tore up the palisade.

The Syracusans, meanwhile, hearing of the approach of the Athenian reinforcements under Demosthenes and Eurymedon, wished to make another trial of their fleet before these arrived. They "shortened the prows of their ships, and had made them stouter by attaching to them thick catheads and stretching underneath stay-beams extending from thence to the ships' sides for the length of 9 ft. both inside and outside the vessels".

ATHENIAN DEFEAT

Catheads projected on each side of the prow, and the anchors were hung to them.

The Syracusans realised that in the confined space of the harbour a prow-to-prow attack would be more effective than the favourite Athenian method of deploying and ramming from the sides.

The Syracusan land force was brought out against the Athenian wall opposite the city. The Syracusans at the Olympieum advanced against the wall from the other side, and then eighty ships sailed out against the seventy-five of the Athenian fleet, but nothing more than skirmishing was done on land or sea. The Athenians' ships were protected by palisades driven into the sea, with merchant ships anchored in front. These had leaden dolphins suspended from beams, apparently to be dropped on any pursuing ship.

The next day the Syracusans again put to sea, and then pretended to go home to dinner, which the Athenians really did, only to find that the Syracusans had put to sea again, so that the Athenians, in following, were in great confusion.

The prow-to-prow attacks of the Syracusans were successful, "but far greater damage was done by the Syracusans who rowed around in light boats, darted under the oar-banks of the hostile ships, and running up alongside, hurled javelins from their boats among the sailors" (through the port-holes). The Syracusans won the fight.

At this juncture, however, Demosthenes and Eurymedon arrived with the reinforcements from Athens—73 ships, 5,000 hoplites, and additional javelin-men, slingers and bowmen, and abundant supplies. It was an amazing but tragic last effort after all the years of war. The Athenians, on their arrival, first ravaged the land by the River Anapus; they then attacked the third Syracusan wall, but were beaten off. Then a night attack, the only one of the war, was made upon Epipolæ by way of Euryelus, on the same line as the first attempt, and the first of the Syracusan camps was captured. After this the Athenians lost touch with one another in the dark, and were badly defeated. Demosthenes wanted to go back to Athens, but Nicias would not do so. Later he agreed, but the moon was eclipsed on 27th August 413 B.C., and then Nicias "who was somewhat too much given to divination and the like, refused even to discuss further

SEA FIGHTS AND LAND BATTLES

the question of their removal until they should have waited thrice nine days, as the soothsayers prescribed".

This information, coming to the ears of the Syracusans, encouraged them. They made a demonstration against the Athenian walls, and the next day seventy-six of their ships sailed out, and another attack was made on the walls. Eurymedon was killed in a sea fight, and the Syracusans captured eighteen Athenian ships. It is interesting to note that they employed a fire-ship; they "turned loose an old merchant ship, which they had filled with faggots and pine-wood".

The Syracusans were very anxious that the Athenians should not escape to Catana, or any other part of Sicily where they could ravage the land, so their next step was to close the entrance to the harbour, "which was about half a mile wide, with triremes ranged broadside, and with large and small boats, mooring them at anchor" and chaining them together. The Athenians, realising their danger, abandoned the upper part of their walls, keeping only the end by the harbour, "cutting off by means of a cross-wall the smallest possible space close to the ships, that would suffice for the stores and for the sick, to put a garrison in this". They then manned 110 ships, putting many bowmen and javelin-men on board, and provided them with grappling-irons, to ensure a hand-to-hand fight.

The Syracusans countered by stretching hides over the prows and a considerable portion of the upper works of the ships, so that the grappling-irons could not get hold. The Athenian fleet was unable to break the barrier, so the battle between nearly 200 ships raged all over the harbour, and in the end the Athenians were beaten. Their ships, overladen with soldiers, lost mobility. It must have been an agonising spectacle for the remainder of the Athenian army on the shore. The Athenians had about sixty ships left, the Syracusans less than fifty. Demosthenes urged that they should try to force the passage at daybreak, but the sailors refused. The Athenians burned some few of their ships, but the remainder fell into the hands of the Syracusans. Then began the tragic retreat. The Athenians formed up in a hollow oblong, enclosing the baggage bearers, and crossed the ford of the Anapus and marched south, the wounded and sick, despite their agonised entreaties, being left behind. The Athenians being continually attacked by the Syracusans, their

END OF AN ERA

forces became divided, and on the sixth day 6,000, under Demosthenes, surrendered, and the miserable remainder of 1,000, under Nicias, on the eighth day. Before the surrender the Athenians numbered 40,000. Nicias and Demosthenes were put to death. The captives were sent to the stone quarries at Syracuse, where

> they had to do everything in the same place; moreover, the dead were heaped together upon one another, some having died from wounds, or because of the change in temperature, or like causes, so that there was a stench that was intolerable. At the same time they were oppressed by both hunger and thirst, the Syracusans having for eight months given them each only a half-pint of water and a pint of food a day.

There were not less than 7,000.

This event proved to be the greatest of all that had happened in the course of this war, and, as it seems to me, of all Hellenic events of which we have record—for the victors most splendid, for the vanquished most disastrous. For the vanquished, beaten utterly at every point, and having suffered no slight ill in any respect—having met, as the saying goes, with utter destruction—land force and fleet and everything perished, and few out of many came back home. Such was the course of events in Sicily.

There was no need to trace here what happened between 413 and 404 B.C., when Athens surrendered. The Long Walls were thrown down, and the "strong house of Erechtheus" lay open to the attack of its enemies; but it was a needless precaution—the walls could have remained. The turbulent spirits had died on the field of battle, or in the quarries of Syracuse, and those who were left were old and tired. Something else died, too, in the hecatombs of young men who were sacrificed to Ares, the god of war, and that something was the genius of a whole people. So Athens and Greece, when the Empire ended, began to stand in the position of a university, or a shrine for the Near East; here the Macedonian and the Roman came, and all the other peoples from the Old and the New Worlds have followed, to wander about from place to place and see if they could discover for themselves the Glory that was Greece.

INDEX

The numerals in **heavy** type denote the figure numbers of the illustrations.

Abacus (arch.), 112; **63, 64**
  (mathem.), 138
Achæans, 12, 23, 24, 29, 34, 101, 108, 110
Achilles, 5, 14, 19, 24, 25, 26, 27, 46, 78
Acragas, Temple at, 115; **57**
Acropolis (Athens), 22, 63, 119, 133, 145, 165; **1, 115, 116, 119, 121, 122, 124**
  (Priene), 202
Acte Canal, 102
Actors, 196–202; **131, 132, 134, 138, 139**
Æa, *see* Colchis
Ææan Isle, 45
Ægean Sea, 97
Ægeus, 172, 179
Ægina, Temple at, 116; **65**
Ægis, 20, 22, 78
Æolia, 87, 88, 89, 100
Æschylus, 196, 200
Æetes, 3, 8, 9
Agamemnon, 14, 24, 25, 27, 36, 46, 59, 87
  Tomb of (so-called), 60–2, 121; **35**
Agarista, 101
Agora (market-place), 122, 190
Agraulus, 175
Agriculture, 77, 79, 145, 149, 212, 216 et seq.; **46, 51**
Aias (Ajax), 22, 31
Aineias (Æneas), 19
Alcibiades, 239, 240
Alcinous, 39, 40, 41, 42, 47
Alexandria, 190
Alexandros (Paris), 15, 16, 17, 24
Alpheus, River, 157
Altars, 175, 186, 190; **127**
Amentum (javelin), 37, 159
Amphipolis, 103
Amphora, 77
Amycus, 6, 160
Anapus, River, 245, 246
Ancæus, 4
Andromache, 22, 29, 32, 39
"Angle of repose" (arch.), 102
Antæ (arch.), 64, 123; **72**
Antefix, 113; **64**
Anticlus, 37
Antinous (wooer of Penelope), 34, 50, 53, 54, 74
Antithalamus, 123, **72**
Apaturia, 88
Aphrodite, 17, 19, 20, 28, 79, 108

Apollo, 4, 14, 15, 20, 22, 28, 29, 78, 108, 182, 233
  Close of, 186; **127**
  Temple of, 114, 186; **127, 137**
Apollonius Rhodius, 3
Architecture, 60–9, Chaps. VI, IX; **1, 33–9, 47, 48, 56–8, 63–5, 70, 71, 73, 117, 118, 125, 126, 135–7, 150**
Architrave, 112, 118, 167; **64**
Areopagus, 166, 180
Ares, 7, 20, 21, 28, 79, 108, 247
Arete, 41
Argo, Argonauts, 3, 4–10, 12, 191
Argonautica (Apollonius Rhodius), 3, 9
Argos (city), Argolis, Argives, 15, 16, 60, 90, 195, 239
  Hut, 77, 110
Argos (Odysseus' dog), 49, 65
Aristocles, 230
Aristophanes, 197
Aristotle, 196
Armour, arms, 16, 21, 27, 72, 234; **6, 8, 13, 54, 177–9**
Army Organisation, 91
Arnæus (beggar), 49, 126
Artemis, 28, 78, 79, 220
  Temple of (Ephesus), 117; **58, 67**
Artemis Aphæa, Temple of, 116
Artemis Brauronia, Precinct of, 173
Artemisium, 103, 104
Asclepius (Asklepios), Asclepiadæ, 18, 191
Askos (oil flask), 79
Asphodel, 46; **22**
Assyria, 10, 89, 91, 202
Athena, Athene, 4, 8, 14, 17, 19, 20, 22, 28, 29, 34, 47, 78, 79, 111, 172, 174, 176, 178, 235
Athena Niké, 166, 171; **121, 135, 152**
Athena Promachos, 172; **121**
Athene, statues of, 172, 178–9; **121**
Athens, Athenians, 15, 22, 63, 88, 98, 100, 103, 104, 108, 112, 156, 165 et seq., 231–47; **1, 115–19, 121, 122, 124–6**
Athenian pottery, **78, 79**
Athenian Treasury (Delphi), 119, 183; **127, 136**
Athos, Mount, 100, 102, 103
Atreus, 36
  Treasury of, 62
Attic helmet, 235; **179**

INDEX

Attica, 165, 196, 231, 232–5
Auger, 38, 81
Aurelius, Marcus, 66
Axe, 38, 52, 74, 81

Babylon, 93, 190, 202
Balios (horse), 76
Ball games, 42, 76, 144; **19**
Bas-reliefs, 119; **53, 55, 59, 103, 104, 151, 152**
Bath, 36
Bebrycians, 6
Bed, bedroom, bedstead, 68
"Beehive" tombs, 62
Beulé Gate, **121**
Bird-dance, 197; **132**
Birds, The (Aristophanes), 197
Bit, horse's, 224; **171**
Black-figure vase, 130, 133; **79**
Black puddings, 49, 126
Blast-furnace, 153; **107**
Blegen, Professor, 35
Boar hunt, **31**
Boatbuilding, 74; **27**
Boats, Bridge of, 102
Bœotia, 88, 104, 127, 145, 237
　House, 121; **69**
　Shield, 72, 235; **8, 178**
Bosphorus, 95
Bow (weapon), 17, 18, 53, 73; **7, 29**
Boxing, 6, 31, 50, 155, 159; **4**
Branchidæ, Oracle at, 62
　Figures from, 135; **92**
Bride, 101, 214; **147, 148**
Briseis, 14, 24, 27
Bronze, 27, 72, 73, 81, 235
　Age, 127
　statuette, **82**
Brooch, 72, 98, 99
Builder's tools, 81, 151

Callias, 101, 222
Callimachus, 198
Calypso, 34, 37, 38, 47
Cambyses, 92, 93, 94, 149
Canal of Acte, 102
　of Suez, 94
Cantharos, **77**
Cape of Good Hope, 95
Cape Sepias, 104
Capital, Ionic, 118; **67**
Cappadocia, 90
Capture of Miletus (Phrynichus), 196
Caria, 87, 88, 93
Carpenter, 81; **101**
Cart, 155; **108**
Carthage, Carthaginians, 93, 96, 97, 117
Caryatidæ, 119
Castalian spring, 183, 184

Castle at Euryelus, 206; **142**
Castor and Pollux, Temple of, 115
Caucasus, 7
Cauldron, 31, 68; **77**
Cavalry, 232
Cella, 110, 118, 176; **124**
Cemetery, 228
Centaur, 4, 179, 191, 200
Chair, 135, 209; **88–93, 146**
Chariot, Charioteer, 19, 36, 65, 73, 74, 123, 133, 154, 188, 224; **9, 54 106**
　Racing, 31
Charybdis, 47, 235
Chersiphron, 119
Chest (receptacle), 209; **12**
Chios, 92, 137
Chiron, 191, 200
Chiton, 72, 131; **80, 81**
Chlamys, **170**
Choragic Monument of Lysicrates, 198; **133**
Chorus, 196
Church, Christian, 114
Cianian Land, 6
Circe, 45, 46
City-States, 10, 88, 156, 224
Cladeus, River, 157
Cleomenes, 98, 101
Cleon, 233, 237
Cloaks, outer, 81; **170**
Close of Apollo, 186; **127**
Clothes, *see* Dress
Cnidians, Lesche of the, 186; **127**
Cnossos, 10, 63, 121, 128, 172, 182, 202
　Palace of (plan), 12; **5**
Cock-fighting, 160, 219; **53, 111**
Coins, 91, 153, 210; **176**
Colchis, 4, 5, 6, 7
Colonnade, 64, 65, 176
Column, 112, 114, 115, 118, 167, 176; **63**
Comedy, 196, 200; **138, 139**
Commerce, 91, 96, 128, 129, 148, 151, 210; **102**
Concord, Temple of, 115; **57**
Constantinople, 188
Cooking, 126
Corcyra, 47, 88, 233, 240
Corinth, Corinthians, 15, 89, 225, 226 233, 243
Corinthian helmet, 234; **8, 178**
Corinthian Order (arch.), 198; **133**
Corn, 59, 80
Cornice, 113, 118; **64**
Corselet, 16, 72; **6**
Corsica, 93
Cosmetics, 216
Cot, Baby's, **87**
Couch, 106, 134, 209; **86**

250

INDEX

Counting, 103, 138
Country life, 77 et seq., 212 et seq.
Court of Justice, 166
Courtyard of house at Priene, **144**
Cratinus, 197
Cremation, 26, 30, 32, 227, 228
Crest (helmet), 93, 178; **60**
Crete, Cretan, 10, 88, 128
Critobulus, 213
Crœsus, 89, 92, 118, 154, 211
Cronos, 14, 20, 28, 78
Cuirass, 27, 72, 235; **178**
Cyclades, 88, 97, 98, 119
Cyclopean Wall, 61
Cyclops, 34, 43
Cyprus, 105
Cyrene, 96, 151; **102**
Cyrus, 89, 91–3, 118

Danaans, 22
Dance, Dancing, 41, 42, 143, 196, 222; **20, 131, 132, 159, 160**
Dareius, 94, 95–102
Decelea, 241, 244
Delos, 233
 House at, 207, 209; **145**
Delphi, 89, 111, 182; **127**
 Oracle of, 89, 90, 93, 104, 106, 183–6, 211
 Theatre, **137**
 Treasury, 119, 183; **136**
Demeter, 8, 78, 79, 105, 108, 147
 Temple to, 201; **129**
Demetrius, 117
Demodocus (minstrel), 41
Demosthenes (orator), 122
Demosthenes (general), 244, 245, 247
Dendra, 72
Device on shield, **61**
Diana, 79, 117
 Temple of, at Ephesus, 117; **58, 67**
Diaphantes, 139
Dinocrates, 190
Diomedes, 19, 21, 24
Dionysia, 196
Dionysus, 79, 105, 108, 130, 147, 195; **98**
Dipylon ware (pottery), 129
Dipylon Gate, 228
Discus, Discobolus, 37, 158
Distaff, 70, 71
Distyle in antis (arch.), 64, 186
Doctor, 18, 93, 191;, **130**
Dodona figure, **8**
Dorian, 87, 88, 89, 100, 108
 Dress for women, 99, 131; **80**
Doric Order (arch.), 112–17, 167, 175, 186; **63–6, 116, 124**
Dörpfeld, W., 63, 169
Drain-pipe, 68; **43**
Drama, 32, 99, 195

Draughts (game), 76; **32**
Dress, 72, 81, 131–4, 219; **80–6, 103, 157–65, 169, 170**
Dystus, house at, 123, 125; **72**

Echinus, 112; **63, 64**
Echo, 141, 143
Education, 137–40
Egypt, 10, 88, 93, 94, 128, 139
 Egyptian sailors, 105
Elgin, Lord, 178
Elgin Marbles, 178
Elorine Road, the, 241
Entablature, 113, 167, 176; **64**
Ephesus, 88, 89, 117
 Temple of Artemis at, 117; **58, 67**
Epidaurus, 195
 Theatre at, 200; **141, 150**
Epinetron, 70; **23**
Epipolæ, 206, 241, 245; **142**
Erectheum, Erectheus, 119, 166, 173–5; **117, 121, 122**
Eretria, 100
Eros, 8, 79
Eubœa, 98, 100, 105, 123
Euclid, 139
Eumæus, 47, 48, 55
Euripides, 32, 197
Euripus, 104
Euryclea, 51, 52, 56, 68
Eurydamas, 50
Euryelus, 206, 241, 245; **142**
Eurymedon, 244, 245, 246
Evans, Sir Arthur, 10, 12
Everyday life, 211 et seq.
Exedra, 124, 207; **72**

Farming, 77, 79, 145–8, 212; **46, 51**
Feeding-bottle, Athenian, **78**
Felloe (wheel), 20, 75
Fig, 77, 90, 219
Fighting, methods of, 18, 73, 100, 234
Fish and fishing, 76, 97, 190
Flame-thrower, 238; **181**
Flute, 140, 143, 222; **94, 103, 104**
Food, 148
Fortifications, 202, 206; **142**
Fountain, 126, 190; **73**
Frieze, 113, 176, 179, 180; **64**
Funeral, 26, 30, 32, 96, 101, 155, 227
Furnace for smelting, 153; **107**
Furies, 166
Furniture, 25, 134–6, 209, 215; **88–93, 146**

Galen, 194
Galley (ship), 225, 226, 240; **52**
 slaves, 226
Games, 6, 31, 42, 50, 76, 91, 93, 143, 155, 219, 234, 239; **4, 15, 16, 19, 32, 110, 153–8, 163, 169**

251

INDEX

Gate, Lion, 60, 61, 128; **34, 48**
Geography, Greek ideas of, 94
Geometric ware, 129
Geometry, 93, 139
Girgenti, *see* Acragas
Glaucus, 91, 101
Gnomon, 93, 139
Goat, 49
 dance, 196; **131**
Gods and Goddesses, Chap. II, 78, 91, 108, 110; **17, 85, 182**
Golden Age, 59, 87
Golden Fleece, 4, 8, 9
Gorgon, 21; **10**
Grapes, 80, 81, 147; **96**
Grave Circle at Mycenæ, **33**
Great Altar at Delphi, 183, 186; **127**
Greaves, 16, 27, 72, 235; **6, 178**
Gregory, Pope, on sacrificial meals, 15
Gylippus, 241, 243, 244
Gymnasium, 145, 186, 195

Hades (god), 78, 79, 108, 147
 (underworld), 29, 30, 46, 227
Hair-dressing, 133; **82, 123**
Harness, horse, 18, 75, 224; **171**
Harp, 140
Harpies, 6
 Chairs from Tomb of, **88–90**
 Tomb of the, 160; **114**
Harvest, 80
Hat, 134; **85**
Hearth, 126, 207
Heating, 207
Hector, 16, 22, 25, 29, 31
Hegesa, Monument of, 210; **151**
Helen, 15, 24, 31, 36, 57, 59, 71, 94
Helios, 47, 179
Hellespont, 10, 99, 102
Helmet, 16, 21, 27, 72, 93, 234; **6, 8, 13, 32, 60, 178, 179**
Hephæstos, 14, 26, 27, 28, 79, 108, 175, 178
 Temple of, 115
Heptastyle pseudo-peripteral, 115
Hera, 8, 14, 17, 20, 28, 78, 79, 108
 Temple of, 111, 112, 118
Heracles (Hercules), 46, 100, 173, 179
 Temple of, 115
Hermæ, mutilation of the, 239; **182**
Hermes, 28, 31, 34, 45, 79, 108, 111, 140, 147, 188, 206, 239; **17, 85, 182**
Herodotus, Chap. V, 88–107, 137, 139, 148, 154, 158, 189, 210, 221
Herse, 175
Hesiod, 78, 79, 88, 110, 145
Hestia, 78, 79, 108
Hide, boxing-gloves of raw, 6
Himation (mantle), 132; **82**
Himera, Temple at, Lion's head from, 117; **66**

Hippocleides, 101, 102, 143
Hippocrates, 191
 Hippocratic Oath, 191
Hockey, **163**
Homer, 3, Chaps. II, III, 59, 64, 175
Homeric Hymns, 130, 140, 141, 147, 182, 233
Honey, 24, 30, 80
Hoplites (infantry), 232, 236
Horse, 18, 20, 65, 75, 154, 224; **9, 108, 171**
 Sacrifice of, 103
Horseman, 159, 216, 224; **170**
Hospital, 191
House, 119–24, Chap. XI; **68–72, 143–5**
Housekeeping, 39, 70, 213–16
House of the Giants, 116
Hunt, Huntsman, 160; **31, 112, 113, 165**
Hut, **70**
Hydria (pitcher), **73, 77**

Icarus, 196
Ictinus, 175, 176
Iliad (Homer), Chap. II, 59, 60, 191
Imperial Hippodrome, 188
Industry, 151
Infantry, 73, 232, 236
Inlaying, 91
Ionia, Ionian, 87, 88, 89, 95, 98, 105
 Dress for women, 131, 132, **81**
Ionic Order (arch.), 114, 117–19, 170, 171, 173; **67**
Iphidamas, 82
Iron, 51, 73, 151, 153, 234; **107**
Ischomachus, 140, 213
Itea, 186; **127**
Ithaca, 15, 34, 37, 64, 87
Ithome, 204; **140**

Jason, 3, 4, 8, 9
Javelin, 37
 Throwing the, 159
Jumping, 158; **16**
Justice, Court of, 166

Kamares vase, 128; **74**
Karian women, 18
Keftiu (Minoans), 10
Key, 53, 68; **28**
Kings, funeral of, 96, 101
Kithara, 141; **120**
Klismos, 209; **146**
Knuckle-bones, 143, 219
Korakou, house at, 122; **71**
Kottabos (game), 223; **168, 169**
Krater (wine and water mixer), 154; **77**
Kylix (cup), 130, 210; **77**

Laërtes, 34, 48, 52, 57, 58, 77
Lamp from Cyprus, **41**
Lapithæ, 4, 179

252

INDEX

Latrines, 207
Leather, 72, 90
  curing, 81
Lekythi (oil jars), 210; **77**
Lemnos, 23, 97
Lesche of the Cnidians, 186; **127**
Leto, 28, 233
Leucadian Isthmus, 236
Libya, 94, 96
Lighthouses, 84
Lighting, **41**
Lion frieze at Xanthos, 55
Lion Gate at Mycenæ, 60, 61, 128; **34, 48**
Lion's head from Himera, 117; **66**
Lock, 53, 62, 68; **28**
Loom, 71; **25**
Lotus eaters, 42
Ludovisi Throne, bas-reliefs from, **103, 104**
Lydia, Lydian, 89, 90, 112, 154, 210
Lyre, 140; **95**
Lysicrates, Choragic Monument, 198; **133**

Macedonia, 10
Macedonian Age, 190
Machaira (sword), 234; **177**
Magasa, house at, 121; **68**
Maidens of the Erectheum, 174, 175; **122**
Maionian women, 18
Mantles, 72, 132
Marathon, 100, 102, 157
Marble, 119, 170, 177
Mardonius, 99, 102, 105, 106
Markets, 190
Marmora, Sea of, 5
Marriage, 82, 101, 214; **147, 148**
Masks, 61, 198; **134, 138, 139**
Meat, 125, 190
Medea, 8, 9
Medes, 91
Medicine, 93, 191
Medusa, 21, 178; **10**
Megara, 233, 241
Megaron, 65, 126, 176, 207, 209; **37, 39**
Melanthius, 49, 53, 55
Melos, house at, 121; **70**
  Massacre at, 53, 239
Menelaos, 15, 16, 17, 34, 36, 37, 94
Messene (Ithome), 204; **140**
Metope (arch.), 167, 179
Miletus, 88, 99, 117, 126, 139, 190
Miltiades, 100, 122
Minoa (island), 233
Minoan, 10, 61, 202
  House, **68**
  Vase, 128; **75**
Minos, 11, 225

Minotaur, 11, 172; **175**
Minstrel, 41, 76, 140–3, 170, 222; **94, 95, 120, 161, 162**
Minyan ware, 128
Mortars, 81
Mosaic, 207
Mount Athos, 100, 102, 103
Mule, 79
Mummers, 196
Museum, British, 119, 129, 141, 178
Music, 41, 76, 140–3, 170, 222; **94, 95, 120, 161, 162**
Mutule, 113; **64**
Mycenæ, Mycenæan, 4, 13, 36, 60, 87, 128
  Arms, 72, 73; **40**
  Drain-pipes, 68; **43**
  Figures, **44**
  Grave Circle, 33
  Lamp, Bronze, **41**
  Lion Gate at, 60, 61, 128; **34, 48**
  Pottery, 128; **45**
  "Tomb of Agamemnon", 60–2; **35**
  Treasury of Atreus, 62
  Vase, **76**
Myrmidons, 14, 25, 78

Naos Hecatompedoscella (arch.), 176
Nausicaa, 39, 70, 76, 144, 170
Navy, Persian, 103, 105
Naxos, 97, 241
Neatherd, 56, 57
Nestor, 18, 24, 34, 35, 73
Nestor's Cup, 24; **50**
New Stone Age, 121, 127, 128
Nicias, 240, 243, 247
Niké Apteros, 167, 171; **121, 135, 152**
Nomads, 96
Normans, 12
Norsemen, 10, 12

Odysseus, 14, Chap. III, 65, 68, 126, 155, 158, 170; **21**
  Bow of, 7, **29**
  Raft of, 38, 81; **18**
Odyssey (Homer), 3, Chap. III, 59, 60
Œconomicus (Xenophon), 139, 175, 211 et seq.
Œcus (living-room), 123; **72**
Ogygia, 47
Oil, 70
  Anointing with, 220
Oil flask, **79**
Oinochoë (wine jug), **77**
Olives, 70, 219
  Gathering the, 145; **14**
  Sacred Tree, 174
Olympia, 88, 157, 211
  Temple of Hera, 111, 112
Olympic Games, **101**, 156, 157, 239

INDEX

Olympieum (Syracuse), 114, 240, 241, 243, 245
Olympus, 14, 21, 24, 108
  Pass of, 104
Oracle, 89, 90, 93, 94, 104, 106, 183-6
Orchomenus, house at, 121, 128; **69**
Orpheus, 4, 5

Pæstum, 116
  Temple at, 115; **56**
Pan, 141
  Pipe, 143
Panathenaic Festival, 180
Pandaros, 17, 73
Pandrosos, Sanctuary of, 174, 175; **122**
Pankration, 160; **110**
Paper, 137
Papyrus, 137
Paris (Alexandros), 15, 16, 17, 24
Parnassus, 182, 186
Parthenon, 63, 77, 111, 113, 123, 166, 175-82; **118, 121, 124-6**
  Frieze from, 179-81
Patriotism, local, 156
Patroklos, 24, 25, 26, 30, 46, 75, 76, 155, 158, 228; **13**
Patterns, 127, 129; **74-6**
Paul, Saint, 117
Pausanias, 105, 106, 112, 113, 166, 169 171, 188, 200, 204, 228
Pedasos (horse), 76
Pediment, 113, 116
Peisistratus (companion of Telemachus), 36
Pelion, Mount, 179
Peloponnesian War, 59, 167, 182, 228, 231 et seq.
Penelope, 34, 49-58, 66, 68, 76, 84, 124; **25**
Pentathlon, 156, 157, 158-60
Penteconter, 92, 148, 240; **99**
Pentelic marble, 170, 177
Pericles, 22, 88, 229, 231
Peristyle, Peristylium, 123, 176; **72, 125**
Persephone, 46, 78, 79, 105, 148, 227
Perses, 78, 79
Perseus, 21
Persia, Persians, 10, 87, 89, 91, 94-106, 133, 157, 183, 211
  Navy, 103, 105
Petasos (hat), 134; **85**
Pets, **157**
Phæacians, 39, 41, 47, 155
Phaistos, 128
Phasis, River, 7
Pheidias, 157, 172, 175, 178
Phidippides, 100
Phocæa, 88, 92, 148, 155
Phocis, 89, 127
Phœbus Apollo, *see* Apollo
Phœnicians, 98, 102, 105

Phrynichus, 99, 196
Picture Gallery (Acropolis), 167, 170
Pilgrims, 183, 184
Pillars, 121
  of Hercules, 95
Pipes (musical), 143; **44**
Piræus, 100, 189, 202, 220
Pitcher, **73, 77**
Plaster, coloured, 207
Platæa, 90, 100, 105, 231-3
  Tripod of, 186; **127**
Plato, 140, 182, 220
Pleistos Valley, **137**
Plemmyrium, 243, 244
Plough, ploughing, 79, 145, 218; **46, 51**
Pnyx, 166
Polybus, 42
Polycleitus (sculptor), 200
Polydamas (Trojan), 29
Polydeuces (Argonaut), 6, 160
Polygnotus (painter), 170, 186
Polymarchus, 220
Polyphemus, 4, 6, 34, 44, 81
Porch, portica, 110, 122
Porch of the Maidens, 174; **122**
Poseidon, 25, 28, 34, 35, 44, 46, 47, 78, 79, 108, 174, 179
  Temple of, 116; **56**
Potidæa, 238
Pottery, 127-31, 210; **44, 45, 74-9**
Praxiteles, 111, 188
Priam, 16, 17, 22, 31
Priene, 126, 190; **129**
  House at, 207; **143, 144**
Priests, 186
Procession, **1**
Prometheus, 7
Prometheus Bound (Æschylus), 197
Pronaos, 110, 123, 176; **124**
Propylæ, 63, 166, 167; **1, 116, 119, 121**
Proscenium, 201
Proteus, 37, 94
Prytaneum, 88, 195
Psycter (wine-cooler), **77**
Pylos, Pylian, 18, 35, 37, 70, 82, 182, 235; **180**
Pyre, 26, 30, 32, 227, 228
Pythagoras, 139, 141
Pythian Games, 183, 186, 239
Python, Pythoness, 90, 183, 184

Quail-fighting, 219; **164**

Raft of Odysseus, 38, 81; **18**
Red-figure vase, 210
Religion, 78, 91, 108, 239
Republic (Plato), 220
Rhea, 6, 78
Rhodes, 204
Rome, Roman, 89

INDEX

Rowing, 226
Running, 155

Sacred Fire, 195
  Ground, 111
  Olive Tree, 174
  Way (Delphi), 183, 186; **127**
Sacrifice, 4, 5, 15, 16, 30, 41, 68, 101, 110, 111, 156, 169, 170, 184, 190; **1, 3**
Sailing, 84; **11, 18, 52**
St. Chad, 194
St. Mark's Venice, Greek Horses at, 188; **128**
Salamis, 87, 88, 89, 98, 105, 225
Samos, 37, 88, 149
Sandal, 81
Satyr, 147, 179, 196; **17, 97**
Scales (weighing), 151; **102**
Scalping, 95
Schliemann, H., 13, 60, 61, 63, 64, 128
Sculpture, 156, 178–81; **48, 55, 66, 103, 104, 106**
Scythia, Scythians, 94, 95–6, 101
Sea fights, Chap. XII; **52**
Sea travel, 23, 35, 52, 82, 92, 148–50, 225, 227; **11, 27, 99, 100, 102, 172, 173**
Shield, 16, 22, 72, 235; **6, 8, 13, 32, 61, 178**
Ship, 23, 35, 74, 82, 92, 102, 103, 104, 148–50, 225–7, 243, 244; **11, 27, 52, 99, 100, 102, 172, 173**
Shoes, shoemaker, 133; **166**
Sicily, 88, 173, 235, 239
Sidon, 31
Sieges, 231 et seq.
Silchester, 189
Silphion, 151; **102**
Siphnos, Siphnian, 119, 186
Sirens, 47
Slaves, slavery, 23, 97, 137, 145, 190, 217, 226, 228
Smelting, 153; **107**
Smith, 151
Smyrna, 88
Soap, 105
Socrates, 211–19
Soldier, *see* Warrior
Sophocles, 197
Sowing, 79
Sparta, Spartan, 15, 35, 47, 65, 75, 90, 92, 98, 100, 104, 108, 149, 156, 183, 220, 231–9, 243
Spear, 16, 73, 234; **6, 32, 40, 177, 178**
Spear-stands, 68
Sphacteria, 236, 237
Sphinx, Naxian, 188
Spinning, 70, 125; **23, 24**
Spinsters, 123, 125

Sport, 155–60, 219; **110–13, 164, 165**
Stadium, 157
Stamnos (jar), **77**
Statues, 172, 176, 206
Statuette, Bronze, **82**
Steel, 91
Steelyard (scale), 151
Stoa, 186, 195; **127**
Stool, 209; **91, 93**
Straits of Gibraltar, 95
Strymon, River, 103
Stylobate, 116, 118, 176, 181
Stylus, 137
Suez Canal, 94
Sundial, 93
Sun-hat, **105**
Sunshade, **149**
Swineherd, 48, 57, 64, 72, 77
Swing, **158**
Sword, 16, 73, 234; **40, 177**
Sybil, Rock of the, **127**
Syracuse, 33, 114, 115, 117, 173, 206, 235, 240–7; **142**
  Siege of, 241; **183**

Table, 68, 106, 209, 222; **12, 86**
Tablets, writing, 137
Tallies, 101
Tanagra figures, 211; **105**
Tantalus, 46
Taslet, 18
Teiresias, 46
Telemachus, 34, 35, 36, 37, 47, 48–58, 65, 70, 75, 82; **25**
Telemon, 31
Temenos, 167, 183, 186
Temple, 108 et seq.; **62, 65–7**
  at Acragas, 115; **57**
  Ægina, 116
  Delphi, 114, 127, 137
  Ephesus, 117; **58, 67**
  Himera, 117; **66**
  Pæstum, 115, 116; **56**
  Selinus, 115
  of Apollo, 114; **127, 137**
    Artemis, 117; **58, 67**
    Artemis Aphæa, 116
    Asclepius, 191, 194
    Athena Niké, 166, 171; **121, 152**
    Athene (Priene), 202; **130**
    Castor and Pollux, 115
    Concord, 115; **57**
    Demeter, 202; **130**
    Hephæstos, 115
    Hera, 111, 112, 113
    Hera Laconia, 115
    Niké Apteros, 167, 171; **121, 152**
    Poseidon, 116; **56**
    Theseus, 112
    Zeus Olympius, 115, 157

INDEX

Terra-cotta, 77, 113, 211
  toys, **155, 156**
Tetrastyle amphiprostyle, 171
Thalamites, 226
Thalamus, 123; **72**
Thales, 139
Thapsus, 243
Theatre, 195–201; **137, 141, 150**
Thebes, Thebans, 231
Themistocles, 100, 158, 202
Theogony (Hesiod), 78
Theoris, 226
Thermopylæ, 104
Theseus, 11, 12, 165, 172, 179; **175,**
  Temple of, 112
Thespis, 196
Thessaly, 10, 87, 104, 127
Thetis, 14, 26, 27
Thrace, 97
Thranites, 226
Threshing, 218
Thrinacia, Isle of, 47
Thucydides, 3, 73, 165, 179, 202, 231, 238
Timber construction, 79, 81
  felling, 81
Tin Islands, 94
Tiryns, 13, 15, 60, 63, 165, 202; **36–8**
  Gallery in Wall at, **47**
  Megaron at, 65–8, 110, 126; **37, 39**
Tisander, 101
"Tomb of Agamemnon" (Mycenæ), 60–2, 121; **35**
Tool, 81
Torch race, 220
Tortoise, **157**
Town, the, Chap. X
Town houses, Chap XI; **143–5**
Town planning, 189
Toys, **153–6**
Trade, *see* Commerce
Tragedy, 195
Travel, 154, 223 et seq.
Treasure chamber, 35
Treasury of Athens, 119, 183; **127, 136**
  of Atreus (Mycenæ), 62
  of Siphnos, 119
Tree planting, 218
Trial of the Axes (*Odyssey*), 53
Triclinia, 123; **72**
Trident, 175
Triglyph, 112, 167, 179; **64**
Tripod, 31
  of Platæa, 186; **127**
Trireme, 225, 226, 240, 244; **172, 173**
Trogilus, 241
Trojan War, Chap. II, 94, 191, 225
Trojan Women (Euripides), 32
Troy, Trojan, 13, Chap. II, 59, 94, 173
Trumpet, **83, 84**

Tumbler, 76; **167**
Tunic, 72, 99, 155
Turk, 133, 178
Tychios, 22

Urn, 31, 32

Vaphio Cup, 12; **49**
Vase, 60, 127, 128, 210, 215; **74–6, 77, 174–5**
Vermilion, 149
Victory, 178
Vintage, 77, 80, 81, 147, 218; **96**
Vitruvius, 110, 114, 117, 119, 123, 125, 190, 201
Volute, 171

Wall, 202, 207
  at Ithome, **140**
  Paintings, 68
Walled city, 202, 204; **140**
War galley, 225, 226, 240; **52**
Warrior, Chap. II; **6, 8, 13, 54, 83, 84**
Washing, 26, 70
  feet of Odysseus, **26**
Water, 126, 127, 190; **73**
Wax tablets, 137
Weapons, *see* Arms
Weaving, 34, 35, 71, 125; **25**
Wedding, 214; **147, 148**
Weights, lead, for jumpers, 76; **16**
Wife, 82, 213, 214; **147, 148**
Wine, 80, 101, 147, 148, 223; **96**
Women, position of, 82, 213, 214
Wooden Horse, 42, 173
Wooers (*Odyssey*), 34, 35, 49–58, 68, 74; **29, 30**
Works and Days (Hesiod), 78, 79
Wrestling, 31, 155, 159; **15**
Writing, 98, 137

Xanthias (slave), 200
Xanthos (horse), 76
Xanthos (river god), 28
Xanthos (town)
  frieze from, 119; **53, 55, 59**
Xenophon, 3, 139, 145, 159, 211, 222, 224
Xerxes, 102

Yoke, 75, 76

Zancle (Messina), 99
Zeus, 14, 17, 21, 22, 28, 37, 58, 78, 79, 108, 147
Zeus Olympius, Temple of, 115, 157
Zygites, 226